Goodness Gracious, Miss Agnes

COVER: *A Twenty-one Day Battle,* by Joy Petty

Goodness Gracious, Miss Agnes

Patchwork of Country Living

By Lera Knox

Illustrated by Joy Petty

Edited by Margaret Knox Morgan
and Carol Knox Ball

Newfound Press
THE UNIVERSITY OF TENNESSEE LIBRARIES, KNOXVILLE

For all other uses, contact:

Newfound Press
University of Tennessee Libraries
1015 Volunteer Boulevard
Knoxville, TN 37996-1000
www.newfoundpress.utk.edu

Library of Congress Control Number: 2007934866

ISBN-13: 978-0-9797292-0-1
ISBN-10: 0-9797292-0-3

Knox, Lera, 1896-
    Goodness gracious, Miss Agnes : patchwork of country living /
by Lera Knox ; illustrated by Joy Petty ; edited by Margaret Knox Morgan
and Carol Knox Ball.
        xiii, 380 p. : ill ; 23 cm.
        1. Knox, Lera, 1896- 2. Women journalists—Tennessee, Middle—
History—20th century—Biography.   3. Farmers' spouses—Tennessee,
Middle—History—20th century—Biography.   I. Petty, Joy.   II. Morgan,
Margaret Knox.   III. Ball, Carol Knox.   IV. Title.
        PN4874.K624 A3 2005

Book design by Martha Rudolph

Dedicated to the Grandchildren
Carol, Nancy, Susy, John Jr.

Contents

Illustrations

Cast of Characters

"Me"	Lera Margaret Ussery Knox	b. 7 Jun 1896; d. 3 Feb 1975
Dad	Alex Lee Knox	b. 5 Jan 1889; d. 24 Dec 1967
Margaret	Margaret Ussery Knox Morgan	b. 14 Feb 1919
Jack	John Carroll Knox, Sr.	b. 16 Jun 1921; d. 19 Dec 2000
Mama	Elnora Jones Ussery Vaughan	b. 9 Mar 1872/1873; d. 1964
Papa	William Wallace Ussery	b. 14 Feb 1867; d. 20 Mar 1906
Sister Elsie	Mary Elsie Ussery Burt	b. Jul 8, 1899
Brother Clarence	Clarence Ussery	b. Abt. 1901
Dr. Rutha	Rutha Magillbury Hall	
Jasper Hall, worked on Tennessee Capitol	Jasper Hall	
Daughters of Rutha and Jasper	Mary Ann, Sarah, & Anna Katherine Hall	
Great Grandpa Jones	Ernest Jones	
Great Grandma Jones	Mary Ann Hall Jones	
Grandpa Jones	John A. Jones	
Grandma Jones	Mary Ann Jones	
Aunt Ada	Ada Jones	
Aunt Daisy	Daisy Jones	
Aunt Mamie	Mamie Jones	
Uncle Bubber	Bubber Jones	b. Abt. 1888
Uncle Great Bear	Uncle Jones	
Jolly Uncle	Noona Jones	
Primped-up Uncle	Herman Jones	
Grandma Ussery	Matilda Edith Wright Ussery	b. 29 Oct 1838; d. 15 Jun 1906
Grandpa Ussery	Rev. William Thomas Ussery	b. 29 Mar 1836; d. 4 May 1920
Uncle Gillie	Gilbert Gideon Ussery	b. 8 Aug 1864; d. 10 Feb 1898
Aunt Beulah	Mattie Beulah Ussery	b. 24 Aug 1873
Aunt Agnes	Edith Agnes Ussery Nichols	b. 7 Mar 1870
Uncle George	George Nichols	
Aunt Molly	Mary Lutitia "Molly" Ussery Barker	b. 1861
Cousin Alfred	Alfred Barker	b. Feb 1880
Cousin Edi Mai'	Edi Mai' Barker	
Uncle Fayette, ex-slave	Fayette Thornton	b. June, 1861; d. 1936

Knoxdale Farm, circa 1930
Columbia, Tennessee

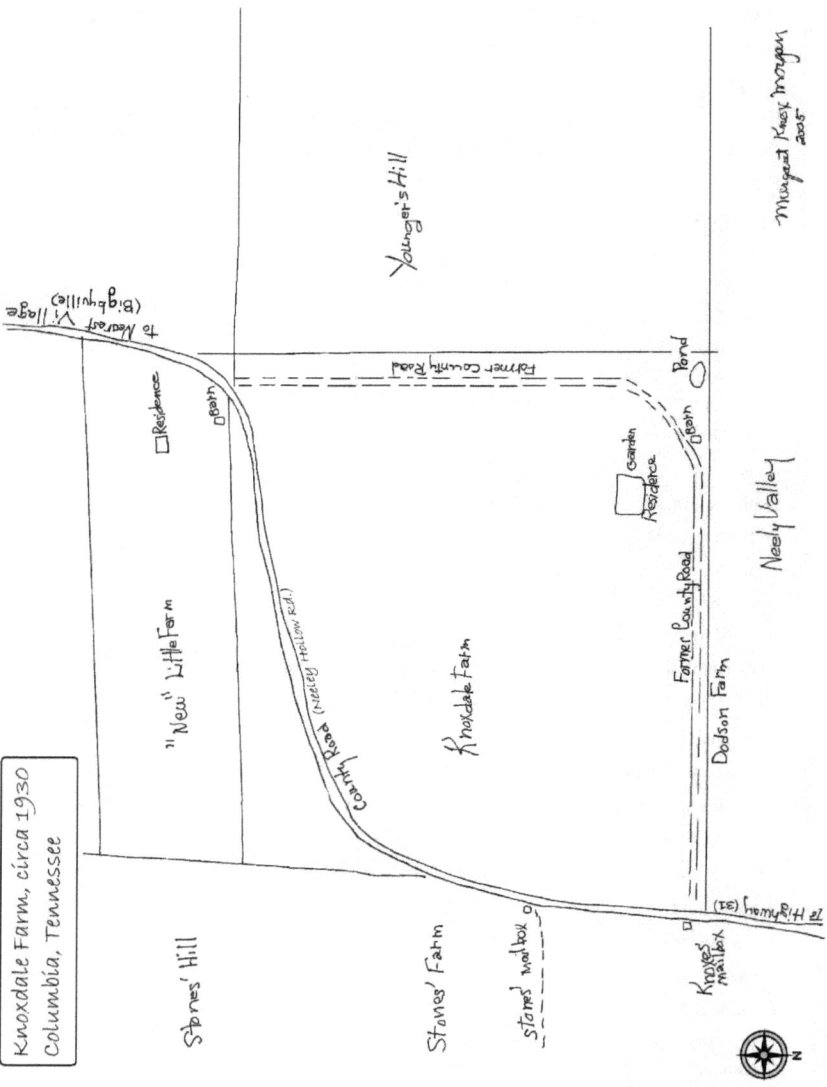

Stones' Hill

"New" Little Farm

to Nearest Village (Bigbyville)

Residence

Barn

County Road (Neeley Hollow Rd.)

Younger's Hill

Palmer County Road

Pond

Garden
Residence

Barn

Knoxdale Farm

Former County Road

Dodson Farm

Neely Valley

Margaret Knox Morgan
2005

Stones' Farm

Stones' mailbox

Knox's mailbox

to Highway 31 (TE)

N

Preface

Lera Knox was born Lera Margaret Ussery on June 7, 1896, in Columbia, Tennessee. She grew up in the Victorian South, learned to teach, and became a farm wife and a mother during the Great Depression. She early established her skill with words, earning a life-long press-pass that took her "backstage" to events great and small. She was a popular columnist for the Nashville (TN) *Banner* and the Columbia (TN) *Daily Herald & Democrat* from 1933 through 1965, and her work could be found in many other fashionable publications of the period.

This is her account of a Tennessee family in the first half of the century that we, her daughter, Margaret, and Carol, the oldest daughter of Jack, have put together from family collections of her columns and book drafts.

Lera later went on to travel extensively, from interviewing Mrs. Roosevelt, to watching Elizabeth II go to and from her Coronation, to being recognized by a Paris fashion designer and by fellow Tennesseans in Hamlet's Castle. All of these experiences she chronicled in her columns.

We hope you enjoy this look back to a gentler, if not easier, time.

Carol Knox Ball and
Margaret Knox Morgan

Acknowledgments

This book would not have been possible without the guidance, support, and friendship of Barbara Dewey and Erica Clark. We extend our warmest thanks to the University of Tennessee Libraries, especially the staff of the Digital Library Center.

Margaret Knox Morgan
and Carol Knox Ball

Patchwork

Life's moments might become a quilt at that,
If one would piece them, fitting as they will
While kettles boil, when neighbors sit and chat,
Of reading by the fire on evenings chill.

Oh, blessed simple things that make life sweet—
Those daisies growing golden in the sun,
A baby's gurgle playing with his feet,
Or someone's eager step when day is done.

The flash of wings outside an open door,
Life's colored moments, prismlike they seem,
If one could piece them—comforts, laid in store
For bleaker days … to warm us while we dream!

By Edna Jones Martin
From *Good Housekeeping*
September, 1938

INTRODUCTION

Some of My Family Roots

Rutha Magillbury and her pioneer relatives came down the river on a flatboat, through the woods, Indian paths, and game trails, from North Carolina or Virginia, to what is now Nashville, Tennessee. At that time it was known as the Great Salt Lick on the Cumberland River. Rutha remembered growing up on the banks of that river, playing with the other children, exploring the caves and streams, and learning Indian lore and pioneer methods. She was an orphan. Her parents had been killed by Indians. She was left to be brought up by a Mr. and Mrs. Williams, her aunt and uncle. Rutha remembered how the pioneers settled and built old Fort Nashburry, their first stopping place on the Cumberland.

She remembered when Fort Nashburry was attacked by the Indians. The men in the settlement had gone out to cut wood, work the corn, and build cabins. Someone called out, "The Indians are coming!" Everyone was frightened. What did the pioneer women, left alone in the fort, do? Mrs. James Robinson, wife of the leader of the settlement and later Tennessee governor, did an unheard of, unmentionable thing. She opened the gates of the fort. People thought the Indians would rush in, but, no, the dogs rushed out! That stopped the Indians and saved Fort Nashburry at that time.

Where the children went, the dogs went, so the children felt safe and protected from the Indians and wild animals.

One youth Rutha played with was Jasper Hall. Later Jasper worked on building the new capitol on the cedar knoll above the Cumberland. In time they were married.

After their marriage they moved westward, to what is now White Bluff in Dickson County. There they built a log house. It was later covered with siding and modernized. Rutha Magillbury Hall planted a garden. Down the middle of the garden was a path, bordered on each side with herbs that were used for medicines. Rutha acquired some medical books, and what she had learned from the books, the Indians, and the early settlers, she put together. She was called Dr. Rutha Magillbury Hall. She traveled the length and breadth of the land on horseback to minister to the sick. She was not just a "granny woman;" she knew she was a doctor because she had studied her doctor books.

After the Halls moved from Nashville, if a member of one of the old Nashville families became ill, Dr. Hall went to stay with the family until the sickness was over. She was there at the birthing of every baby of pioneer Nashville. She rode on horseback or the family would send a carriage. Rutha did not trust those new fangled trains. If there was going to be a baby in a family, for instance, the family would send a carriage from Nashville to White Bluff, 30 or more miles, to pick up Dr. Hall, and she would live with the family during that time.

The Hall family grew their own food, and killed their own game from the woods. But the garden provided medicines for the area that was later Middle Tennessee. The Halls had three daughters, Anna Katherine, Sarah, and Mary Ann, who married Ernest Jones. Each daughter had ten children, and Mary Ann had a stillborn baby. That meant that Dr. Rutha presided over the birth of 31 grandchildren and was the only doctor ever to enter those households. When the oldest grandson of Mary Ann and Ernest Jones was almost grown, and a blacksmith, he was kicked in the groin. This injury became an abscess. Dr. Hall stayed with him and applied poultices, day and night, until he was healed.

During the spring and summer Dr. Hall gathered herbs in the woods and along the creeks and roadsides, or wherever she could find them, looked them up in her medical books, dried them, then stored them in the attic of the cabin. Nora, or Elnora, who would become my mother, was one of the older grandchildren who helped Dr. Hall in the garden, and walked the garden path with her, gathering and learning the herbs and medical plants.

Nora also learned sewing, cooking, and other household duties while visiting this grandmother, whom she idolized.

In the Jasper Halls' home a black couple tended the kitchen and garden. Early in the Civil War, Yankee soldiers came over the hill when the woman was working in the garden. Jasper Hall was indignant at their behavior. He kicked over two beehives. That rapidly cleared the area of soldiers.

On another day Rutha was cooking lye soap in a kettle when soldiers came. She wouldn't leave, but she threatened the soldiers with the boiling soap. That also cleared the area of troops.

At another time the Yankees came and demanded money. All the money in the house was Confederate bills, about $300. While Rutha and Jasper were talking with the soldiers the black woman put the money into her bosom, ran out to the barn, and hid it under an old setting hen.

Lera Knox

CHAPTER 1

My Quilting Frame

I had two grandmothers, Grandma Jones and Grandma Ussery, and two grandfathers with the same last names. Much that I am and hope to be—or not to be—I owe to those four and varied grandparents. Their inheritable characteristics and their early influences stretched my patchwork personality four ways for a lifetime. They were the sides and ends of my "quilting frame."

Grandma Jones and Grandpa, as I remember them, were a respectable and respected couple of rural landowners. They tried to make a good living; set a good table; rear a good family; and make a good impression on the neighbors. They seemed to believe these objectives constituted the whole duty of man and woman.

My mother, one of the Joneses, was much like her parents, and she expected me to be the same, just as my father hoped I'd be like the Usserys. But to the despair of each parent, I always seemed to take after the "other side of the house."

Grandma Was a Lady

Grandma Jones was a lady; there could be little doubt of that. She looked like one, she talked and walked like one, and she frequently reminded us that she had been born one. On her Family Tree there seemed to be no women at all—just Ladies.

Grandma wore her hair high and her hem low. And many times during my tomboyish teens and my "younger generation" years she modestly repeated to me the story of how Grandpa had said he didn't know she had ankles until he'd married her. I remember thinking what a shock it must have been to Grandpa to realize later that his half-dozen daughters and a like number of granddaughters all had knees. He never seemed to notice, however, or to show signs of shock.

Then, too, I had some doubts about that ankle notion, for, you see, Grandpa was a sort of horse trader, and generally he didn't deal sight unseen. He must have known that Grandma had a sound and substantial support under the ruffle she always wore on the hem of her skirt.

Grandma's everyday dress was of calico or percale. It was invariably a pattern of black, white, and gray all mixed up together in leaves, flowers, dots, and scrolls. It was made to hang in one long full line from yoke to ruffle—a wrapper, she called it; but when Grandpa wanted to provoke her, he twinkled and spoke of it as "that old Mother Hubbard."

She wore her wrapper belted tightly at the waistline with a full-gathered apron of black-and-white checked gingham. She never looked right at home without her "specs" and her apron, but she never permitted "Company" to see her in either.

&

Apronology

Grandma always bought her apron-checks in the fall and in the spring; and never bought more nor less than ten yards at a time; trading eggs at the General Store for the material. Ten yards in those days cost fifty-cents—ten dozen eggs.

If I happened to be visiting Grandma Jones at apron-making time, she would let me help her stitch the seams and turn the hems. She taught me how to cut out the aprons, too; one full width of the gingham the length of her skirt made the front; another length split down the middle made the sides. They were stitched to the front piece with French-felled seams. Then we would hollow-out the top of the front piece just a little, not more than an inch; gather the apron to the belt with neat bastings; stitch; turn; baste and stitch again. Next came the pockets and the hem. They were easier, but they too had to be basted. Grandma was that kind of a person; everything had to be just so and basted that way.

If I happened to be at Grandma's when she was laying in her semi-annual apron supply, she almost always bought me some apron checks too. Blue and white, always blue and white! Pink? Never! Pink would fade. Yet, it seemed that all my life I had wanted a pink apron. Even a faded pink would have been more desirable than that same old durable, dirt-hiding, practical blue and white.

Grandma cut out my small blue and white aprons by a newspaper pattern borrowed from a neighbor who had a little girl about my size. Then she helped me make them. They were different from hers; they were the all-over kind. They had collars—one half-moon-shaped piece under each ear; they had long, droll-looking sleeves; and they were *serviceable*. I hate that word even yet.

I was permitted to stitch the seams and turn the hems in my aprons, but the sleeves, cuffs, collars, and buttonholes were Grandma's part of the apron-making. I did, however, finally learn to pull the four-eyed white "salt" buttons off their bright blue cards and sew them through and through, up and down the back to the spots Grandma had marked with chalk or pins.

My aprons rarely had pockets, though I needed pockets much. But Grandma declared that pockets on children's clothes were not practical; they would only catch dirt or tear off.

Aprons were institutions in the household of Grandma Jones, so much so that I learned to read their signs much as Grandpa Jones read the weather signs in the sky or almanac. A fresh apron meant somebody coming or a pleasant task ahead. A second-day apron meant drudgery resumed.

Grandma's Sunday dress was black. It was usually made waist-and-skirt fashion; its sleeves were long; its collar high;

its skirt had plenty of width and plenty of length—even a slight train; and it had that inevitable ruffle or flounce around the bottom.

She always wore with that black Sunday dress never fewer than three petticoats in addition to her knee-length chemise (pronounced in our family "shimmy," always in a whisper). One petticoat in winter was flannel, and it usually had hand-embroidered buttonhole scallops—laid off with a spool—all around the five-yard ruffle. The next petticoat was a stiffly-starched, white, thick muslin, or "Hope" domestic. It, too, had a ruffle; one of Hamburg or Swiss embroidery; and tucks to the knees. The third and top petticoat was of rustly, stiff, black taffeta or "spun glass" in more pecunious days. That skirt had a ruffle on a ruffle; a smaller one on the bottom of a wide one and a dust ruffle under both.

With those three petticoats and their five ruffles, in addition to the flounce on her dress, Grandma swept the floors, swept the street, swept the board sidewalk, and swept the church aisle—but never the steps. With a deft left hand she gracefully lifted skirt, petticoats, ruffles and all from the rear when she went down the steps. With her right thumb and two fingers she dexterously lifted all skirts and ruffles up stairs. They never seemed too much nor too bothersome, not even on ironing day. And they were distinctly ladylike.

Never Too Much Nor Too Bothersome

With her everyday dress and apron the petticoats were only two: one of flannel and one of gingham in winter, and both of stiffly starched domestic or chambray or cambric in summer. If for any reason Grandma took off her apron she hurriedly put on a third petticoat.

When Grandma went to church, to town, or to call, she always wore her bonnet. It was a black lace-cloth-and-braid-covered wire-and-crinoline affair. In shape it looked much like a cross between a round pillbox and a sad flapjack. It had wide black ribbon strings that tied fetchingly under her chin and a black veil that reached to her waist. When "thrown back" it covered her shoulders like a shawl.

That veil, I noticed, varied in thickness with the season of the year and her stage of mourning. When winter came, or if a third cousin died, Grandma changed to her heavier or "first mourning" veil. But always, no matter what the weather or her mood, Grandma, when dressed up, wore a black veil.

From the knobby little mourning pins, which skewered her veil to her crinoline crown, down to the shirt-tail hem of her swishing dust-ruffle, Grandma was a study in neatness, primness, and aristocratic slenderness. Even with that pair or trio of full petticoats she had the appearance of being slim. She was neat at home, but particularly neat when ready to go somewhere.

℀

Black Bonnet and a Turkey Wing

Grandma Jones was one of those "very nice" housekeepers—crampingly nice, I thought. She put cleanliness so close to Godliness that Grandpa always stayed around the back of the house; and unless the weather was very rough, he rarely went inside except to eat and sleep. On the back porch, hanging on a nail over the washstand, was an old turkey-wing which was used regularly to brush Grandpa before he went into the kitchen to eat, or into his little back bedroom to sleep.

Grandpa Jones was a miller, a blacksmith, and a farmer, as well as a trader and store-porch sitter. From Monday noon until Saturday afternoon, he had cornmeal dust on the tops of his ears, axle grease on his knuckles, corn silks in his trouser cuffs and candy in his pockets—red and white striped sticks in his right coat pocket, peppermint pillows, gumdrops, and chocolate cream "mountains" in the left. Sometimes there was an extra: a little blue-and-green striped sack of cheese and crackers, licorice, or "Long Johnny" (paraffin) chewing wax in the mixed-candy pocket.

Grandpa was away from the house much of the daytime, but for half an hour or so before and after meals he could be found on the back porch sitting in his little stubbed-off ladder-back hickory chair leaning against the whitewashed weatherboards, dozing, or using his goose-quill toothpick.

When he wasn't asleep, he was looking out across his fields. His brows were bushy and dusty with cornmeal; his eyes were blue, and for all their slight squint they seemed to see through you and far away. His thin, smooth-shaven lips, over an ever-moving patch of chin whiskers, seemed always smiling. He had little to say; but what he did say seemed important.

What kept Grandpa's whiskers jiggling up and down was a mystery to me. I knew he didn't eat the candy he carried in his pockets. I knew he didn't use chewing wax or plug tobacco. Then one day I saw him take a yellow grain of corn from his lower right vest pocket. That was the secret; Grandpa chewed corn.

There was something about Grandpa Jones—something else, I mean, besides the candy and cheese-and-crackers—that caused us children and Fido and Bugler to meet him at the gate, or even down the road, and follow him around the back way to sit at his feet on the porch while he dozed or chewed or rested.

I remember that as we three children sat on the floor around his chair, and as the dogs took turns curling up on the plaited corn shuck doormat—placed suggestively for muddy shoes—Grandpa's coat pockets hung down on each side much as did his saddlebags when he rode "the old mare," as he called Old Fan.

His coat always seemed too large and his vest too small. Only the top vest-button was ever fastened, until that popped off; then the second from the top. The third button, however, was as far down as his plump abdomen permitted him to fasten, but that generally lasted out the life of the vest. If it didn't, much to Grandma's exasperation, Grandpa used a nail.

A vest was an all-day-long and year-round necessity to Grandpa. He took it off only when he went to bed. He wore his dusty old black hat too, all the time except when in bed or at the table, or on Sundays in the parlor.

His trousers were evidently always too long when they arrived from the mail-order house; but several extra turn-overs of the cuffs, and a gradually-acquired accumulation of horizontal wrinkles between the turnovers and the knee bulges took up the slack.

I don't know how we knew it, for Grandpa never complained; or perhaps we only suspected that when he came home his feet were tired. Anyway, before we settled down on the floor around him, before we even reached for the candy that he would hand us a piece at a time from his convenient saddlebag pockets, we snatched the little oblong foot-tub from its nail by the washbench, trotted with it out to the rainbarrel under the eaves of the smokehouse (that water was so stained by the chestnut-board-shingles that it was only used for colored clothes and baths), reached for the gourd dipper, and half-filled the tub with rainwater. Then we fished out the wiggle tails, got a chunk of brown lye soap from the smokehouse, and carried tub and soap back to the porch.

And Candy in his Pockets

There we put Grandpa's feet to soak in the cool sudsy water. One of us usually had remained on the porch to unlace and remove his shoes, while the other two got soap and water ready. Much to Grandma's chagrin, he rarely wore socks. Soaking Grandpa's feet was a noon and night ritual, one rarely neglected on weekdays in the summer.

But on Sundays all arrangements and operations were different. On Saturday afternoons, of course, Grandpa had his weekly shave at Harry Peck's Barber Shop, at the "Bluff," as White Bluff's village-center was known. Grandpa's one gripe was that Peck always stole a few more hairs from around the edges of his thin and scraggly goatee. On Saturday nights Grandpa had his bath—in the wooden washtub in the smoke-house.

On Sunday mornings he put on his Suit, boiled shirt, and celluloid collar. After church and after dinner he sat stiffly—and I suspected miserably—in the parlor. We didn't join him there, for in those days everybody knew that the parlor was no place for young'uns, much less dogs. It belonged, then, to grownups and to Company.

ॐ

Parlor Prison

On warm, summer weekday afternoons, however, we children served our terms in the parlor. At such times under the influence of our very clean Grandma we took our baths (in the smokehouse), brushed and re-pigtailed our hair, and put on clean clothes so we could lie down on the parlor carpet and take our prescribed naps.

That parlor was always prim, darkened, cool, and smelly. It had, like other proper parlors of its day, a peculiar fragrance that could never be analyzed, duplicated, or forgotten.

For half an hour or so each afternoon we were supposed to be sleeping. But when we were inside and the door was closed, nobody could tell how tightly shut our eyes were.

We hardly dared touch the furnishings and decorations, but we did do a lot of looking in that dusky room. I can trace, even yet, the pattern of leaves and scrolls on that precious wall-to-wall ingrain carpet, the colors of which must be protected from fading by constantly closed window blinds.

I know by heart the intricate designs of cutout wood-carving on red plush above the organ keys. I remember too, the intermingled roses, Greek banding, and polka dots of the Nottingham lace curtains; the similarly almost-indescribable pattern of blue, pink, gray, and silver wallpaper, with its eighteen-inch border; and all the frills, drapes, and festoons of the pink or pale blue crepe paper lambrequin, which hung from the mantel piece by permission of brass head tacks.

The winter lambrequin, usually of red felt chain-stitched in yellow scrolls and daisies, obligingly caught dust and flying ashes when the winter time log fire was stirred.

Grandma Couldn't Stand Meddlers

Many's the half hour or more I've lain on the straw-cushioned carpet—which, by the way, was preferable to the scratchy horsehair sofa—and have held that conch-shell doorstop to my ear "listening to the sea roar." The shell wasn't needed when the door was closed, so we used it for entertainment.

I longed to pull a "tidied" roseback chair up to the mantel piece and uncurl a few of those fancy frilled and varicolored lamplighters, or slip my fingers through the fluffiness of the Pampas grass bouquet in its mirror-like vase; but I feared that the chair might topple, or that the fluffy stuff might come to pieces and leave on the hearth below the tell-tale signs of my meddling. Grandma couldn't stand meddlers.

Another object that I dared not go near was the highly decorated memory jug in the corner. It was made from a large bottle plastered all over with home-made putty, studded with trinkets such as keys; small bits of chain; doll arms and faces; marbles; corkscrews; tin tags from Brown's Mule; R&R and Red Apple tobacco plugs, and other such treasure, then gilded all over. That jug was a handsome and interesting ornament, very attractive to a child or adult with curiosity, but it was strictly taboo. One reason for our fear of it was that it contained half a dozen dried cattail stalks from down at the pond; and cattails, we were told, would make our eyes go out if we happened to be near them when they began to shed.

I did, however, as did my brother and sister, dare to take the stereoscope with its stack of twin-faced pictures from the

Meeting Niagara Falls

lower part of the parlor table; and we marveled at the depths and colors of these pictures as the two made one before our eyes. It was through the stereoscope in Grandma's parlor that we first met Niagara Falls, and Grand Canyon, and Garden of the Gods.

We studied carefully and examined one by one all the articles on the parlor what-not. There were the little man made of Zephyr wool and wiggledy wire on the top shelf; the stone shaped like a potato; the little pink and white cup and saucer; the ruby-glass mug, souvenir of Tennessee's Centennial; the little blue glass slipper which I thought must have been the one lost by Cinderella; and the little white china hen sitting patiently on her powderbox nest. On the bottom shelf, of course, was the family's collection of Sunday School cards, rich with "Motto Texts" and bright with colored pictures of priest and prophets in long robes and other sorts of funny clothes. The Sunday School cards were interesting, but not so much so as the stereoscope pictures. The what-not itself was made of spools strung on clothesline wire and was stained dark brown, probably with walnut hulls. It was a masterpiece to us.

In other wakeful hours and half hours I stared at the pictures on the parlor walls. The one with a man and sheep in bright green pastures, the one of the village house with snow on roof and road and fenceposts, and the one of the pretty girl with golden curls down on her shoulders, one curl hanging over her forehead—I always wanted to brush that curl back.

There was also on the wall a flock of worsted mottoes, headed by that universal plea, "God Bless Our Home." This particular card, I remember, was cross-stitched in red, orange, and brown, with a border of green. Of course, there was the sampler that Grandma had made when she was twelve years old. It had her name, age, year, a house, two alphabets, and a row of beautiful arithmetic on it, all in embroidery and cross-stitch.

There was the gilded frame that held the marvelous wreath of miniature flowers made from the vari-colored locks of the Jones family hair. There was, also, a somber "In Memoriam" with two white doves at the top, two white hands clasped at the bottom, and a white trail winding about over the black background, going to Heaven or the Bad Place, I thought.

The objects that made those parlor imprisonment terms endurable—I mean besides the patterns, what-not, conch shell, hair flowers, and stereoscope—were the books, four of them. They were *The Holy Bible*, *The Family Album*, *Uncle Tom's Cabin*, and later, *The Circuit Rider's Wife*.

The first two books were kept on top of the parlor table, one on either side of the parlor lamp (with its globe-like shade and bowl covered with American Beauty roses). The other two lay on a crocheted doily on the bottom shelf of the table, and as Grandma said, gathered dust from Friday to Friday.

That was special dusting day in Grandma's parlor, and books to her were merely dust-catchers. Nevertheless, she kept those four books on the parlor table because "Company" expected to see books in a parlor. Grandma undoubtedly knew something of what was in the *Bible* and the *Album*, although I never saw her turning the pages of either. I am sure she had no idea, however, of the contents of the other two books. She kept them because they had been given to members of the family and because they looked well on the crocheted doily.

I have chuckled to myself many times in years since over the thought of Grandma, of all people, keeping a copy of *Uncle Tom's Cabin* on the bottom shelf of her parlor table. The idea of Grandma harboring the cause of the fight for the "Cause!" How shocked she would have been had she suspected that the peaceable-looking red-backed book, resting there in her cherished sanctum, had anything to do with the raids of the Yankees that she talked about so much – "the scoundrels!" How they rode into the yard and shot her frying-size chickens, and then, insult of all insult, forced their horses' heads into her very door and made her cook her chickens for them, and made her use the last dust of hoarded cornmeal to make hoecakes for them!

During those wakeful afternoon-nap periods I read the Twenty-third Psalm many times. That was easy. I had memorized it well in Sunday School. I stumbled through the story of Creation and through the genealogy of Jesus in a brave attempt to start at the beginning and read through the whole Bible, or at least the New Testament.

I became thoroughly familiar with the pictures in the *Album*, with the gentlemen seated and the ladies standing. In *Uncle Tom's Cabin* I traveled with Eliza as far as the river, but could go no farther. I was like Grandma; I didn't know what it was all about, but I do remember thinking Little Eva a sissy and Uncle Tom not to be compared with Uncle Luke, Grandma's yardman and gardener. I never did know what became of the circuit rider, or his wife, but observations in the household of my Methodist grandparents made me suspect that they wound up at somebody's house for dinner.

There were two other books at Grandma Jones's house; two that were more interesting even than the Album. One was Aunt Ada's Scrapbook. Aunt Ada was different from the other Joneses. In addition to doing Battenberg and crochet work, she collected poetry. The poetry pages of *Hearth and Home* and *Comfort* magazines were her treasures.

The other important book in the Jones household was the mail order catalogue. This book, like the scrapbook, never gathered dust; but neither was it kept in the parlor. The current copy held a place of honor on the Damask-covered sewing machine in Grandma's sitting room. The discarded copies went their way into a place of less honor in a little house at the far end of the garden.

The Other Side of the House

Whereas my mother's mother had four books, a scrapbook, and a Sears catalogue, my father's father had four rooms of books and a little office full besides. In fact, the Ussery side of the house seemed bounded on four sides and top and bottom by books—books which were actually read—also by newspapers, magazines, and a craving for literary culture. Grandma Ussery had been a teacher; Grandpa was a teacher and preacher; and all the aunts, at one time or another, taught.

The "Front Room" at the Ussery house had glass-doored bookcases for the best-looking books. The company bedroom had shelves for the good but plain books. Grandma's room, which was naturally the family room but was never so called, caught the most frequently read books. In a little back room upstairs over the kitchen, where the sun shone in and frankly showed the dust, were stacked the "retired" books. Four rooms had books. Yet no room was called the "library." The Usserys were just book-loving plain people.

But the most precious books of all, the oldest, best-loved, and most dog-eared, were strewn and stacked, from floor to top shelf—and the floor was covered and top shelf was stacked to the ceiling—in Grandpa Ussery's little "sanctum-sanctorum," as he called the little office built high on a sort of shelf over the cellar in the backyard.

In his little office Grandpa was privileged to live as he pleased. There with his books, the ones that nobody else seemed to love except him and me, we spent hundreds of happy hours, and hundreds were too few.

To put on an old dress, one that Mama didn't mind my ruining, and to get into that office with Grandpa Ussery on a rainy day was more to me than Heaven is likely to be unless Heaven exceeds most human expectations. The star-decked crowns and pearly gates that Grandpa preached about on Sundays had small appeal to me compared with his dusty old books and yellowed old papers, with him as a kindred soul for company.

But four rooms and an office full of books were not enough for Grandpa. He was, I suppose, what might have been called a "book drunkard." Never by word but frequently by behavior had he showed his conviction that reading maketh a full man. An essay or a published sermon, such as he found in *The Ram's Horn* or the *Christian Herald*, his two favorite magazines, meant more to Grandpa than meat and bread or a slice of cake. A good book was more to him than several square meals. Not that he had an aversion to food—not Grandpa; it was just that, compared to books, food mattered so little that he'd forget it. Food, that is, except hoecakes.

He'd be helping me at night with my long division, and we'd sit up late, until after everybody else had gone to bed. Grandma Ussery would call us "night owls." After we'd finished the lessons, Grandpa Ussery would suggest, or rather hint, that his whiskers needed combing; so I'd climb to the arm of his chair and start drawing the comb through his long white beard. It reached down as far as his second coat button and spread out fan-wise over his lapels.

Grandpa Ussery was amusingly proud of his whiskers. I'd comb and brush for a while, then I'd braid them into tight, funny, little pigtails, intending that they should be all curly next morning. Grandpa said he knew a man with curly whiskers, and that he'd always wanted his to be like that. He would promise to leave the pigtails plaited tight until next morning, but I believed he never did.

If I got my fingers too close to his mouth during the combing and plaiting processes, he would snap at them, "just like a frog snapping at flies" he would say; then he would laugh heartily. When he snapped that way at me, I would almost jump off the arm of his chair, and Grandpa would shake with laughter.

Grandpa Wanted Curly Whiskers

Whiskers done and braided, I'd examine carefully the top of his head to discover if I could possibly count a few more hairs on his bald spot than had been there the night before, or even the week before. Then I would notice particularly to see if the few hairs that were there were any longer than they had been when last measured. I always tried to give an optimistic report, because I knew he couldn't see them anyway and those few extra hairs seemed to mean so much to Grandpa.

After examination and report of the state of baldness came treatment: I would get down off the arm of his chair and drag a "straight" chair up to the mantelpiece. From beside the clock I would take the little blue bottle of yellow Vaseline and carefully climb down again. His scalp was thoroughly massaged with my childish fingertips as Grandpa would doze and lightly snore there in the firelight.

Sometimes while I brushed the fringe of hair above his ears and that along the back of his neck, he would hum and gently chant my favorite of all his songs:

"Wher-rre, ne-ow, are the Hebrew Child-ren?

Where now are the Hebrew Children?

Wher-r-re, ne-ow, are the He-e--brew Children?

Safe at la-a-st in the Promised Land!"

It was a sad song, I knew, telling about the fiery furnace and all that; but I'd always giggle when Grandpa called their names:

"Shadrach, Meshack, and Abednego.
Shad-rack! Me-shack! And A-bed-ne-go-oh!"

❧

Hoecakes

That word "Abednego" (sounding like to-bed-we-go) would always remind us that it was getting late; so Grandpa would sit up straight and say, "Tot, let's go out to the kitchen and see if we can stir up a little snack."

I knew what he meant. I also knew what we'd find, and where we'd find them. Out to the kitchen we'd go and out to the chilly back porch.

In the kitchen we'd get two forks, two glasses, and a stack of hoecakes, as cold and as stiff as shovels. From the high shelf on the back porch Grandpa would take a pitcher of cold sweet milk, so cold that on winter nights it would have ice flakes in it. Then we'd tiptoe back to the fire in Grandma's room where Grandma in her white nightcap pretended to be asleep, but knew all the time what we were up to. It was a real adventure, that tiptoeing out to the kitchen and back porch; and no less fun the last time than the first.

We'd pour our glasses of milk and set them on the hearth to warm while we skewered the hoecakes on the forks and held them close to the fire to toast. Often I'd doze, day dream, or forget what I was doing until I'd notice that my cake was getting too black, or too much smoked, or had dropped into the ashes. When I did, Grandpa would always swap forks with me and take the smoked or burnt cake for himself, saying, "Why, Tot, that's just the way I like 'em."

To compensate for this kindness I'd remember just then that Grandpa liked a pinch of salt in his sweet milk; so while he crumbled the once-fried and over-toasted cornmeal-dough cake into his glass of milk, I'd tiptoe out to the dark kitchen, feel around on the table until I found the salt cellar, tiptoe back and slip it down beside his glass of milk. No word was spoken during this incident, nor until we had each scraped the last milk-soaked crumbs from the bottoms of our glasses.

But back to Grandpa and his books—which he valued even more than hoecakes: many's the time I've known him to rush off on the early morning train to Nashville for a business trip and return at dusk on "Cap'n Kidd's Accommodation" with no business attended to, no lunch under his Prince Albert coat, but with half a dozen or so ragged-looking second-hand books tucked apologetically under his arm.

A Book Drunkard

As I grew older and found for myself Nashville's dustiest second-hand book stores, I knew how Grandpa had spent those days and why he forgot his lunch.

My Grandma Ussery could hardly endure this kind of biblio-delinquency, even as much as she herself loved books. She liked, however, new, clean books, ones with the pages uncut, the latest, the most up-to-date. Up-to-date was exactly the phrase for that Grandma. Her favorite reading would have been page one of tomorrow's newspaper; her favorite book, the one that wasn't "out" yet.

On most matters of mind she had advanced ideas, but the latest styles in clothes didn't interest her one bit. Odd, but I cannot remember any particular dress or other piece of cloth-ing that Grandma Ussery wore except the lavender crocheted shawl around her shoulders. I remember her face well, her smoothly arranged white hair parted in the middle and coiled under a tucking comb in the back. I remember the way she wore her spectacles pushed high on her forehead when she stopped in the midst of her reading to talk. Of course, she often "lost" them there; and I was always delighted to find them on her forehead after she had searched the mantel, windowsill, workbasket, and bedside table.

As a housekeeper, Grandma Ussery seemed to reason that dust on her furniture wouldn't hurt anybody as long as it wasn't stirred up. Dust, to her, was merely good earth temporarily out of place. I never could understand the difference in the attitudes of Grandma Jones and Grandma Ussery toward the same kind of dust.

Grandma Ussery figured that if she swept under the beds once a week she got seven times as much lint for her labor as if she swept every day. Also, this weekly sweeping made a better showing than a daily one. When she worked she liked to make a showing. This comfortable philosophy about cleaning saved her back, her broom, her turkey-tail feather duster, and gave her more time to keep up with what was new.

However, if someone else was doing the cleaning—and usually someone else was, for Grandma was often temporarily "indisposed"—if someone else was doing the dusting and sweeping, Grandma's attitude underwent a change. She wanted every swipe of dust removed from the furniture and the surface polished; every thread swept off the ingrain carpet; and every cobweb removed from the ceiling, especially in the room where she was sometimes up and sometimes down, but always reading, or talking and crocheting.

⤬

I Sat on Salmon Cans

It was when Grandma was crocheting, I think, that I liked her best for then she was usually talking, and talking to me. Her pet economy and favorite pastime was saving the cotton string that came around the grocer's packages and crocheting it into washrags and dishcloths. These crocheted "rags" were about the most practical articles in the Ussery household. I never knew an Ussery to wear an apron.

Grandma Ussery gave me the red-and-white strings, while she collected for herself the white and the blue-and-white. I always suspected that the reason she did most of her trading with Grocer Cameron was because he had the smoothest wrapping twine of all the merchants in town, and because he used it most lavishly.

I Sat on Salmon Cans

She made a little stool of seven salmon cans. The cans were encased first in old black stocking legs, then whipped together in shape of a daisy—one in the middle and six all around like petals—then topped off with cotton batting and covered with a piece of the carpeting that had been left from fitting the bay window in the "Front Room."

After I got settled down on the little stool at her feet, Grandma would hand me my small crochet needle and ball of red-and-white twisted twine, and as our needles hooked in and out, she talked to me about what was proper and what was not, what she did when she was a little girl and what she didn't.

It was as we crocheted that Grandma corrected my grammar and reprimanded my slang. She told me I mustn't say "awful" unless I really meant "full of awe." I had no idea what "awe" meant, but it seemed too ugly a word for anything to be full of. Nor could anything be "terribly nice" or "pretty bad." She explained that if anything was "nice," it wouldn't be "terrible"; and if it was bad, it wouldn't be "pretty."

As for slang, I didn't quite know what that was, but I got the impression that it was something to be classed with nicknames. Grandma hated nicknames, and she hated slang. Full and complete sincerity, to her, was the chiefest of virtues. In her estimation, Truth was pure white, and "stories" were entirely black, no shades between. There could be no such thing as a "white lie" or even a pale gray one.

Grandma Ussery was an inveterate talker. She had an uncanny gift for remembering the contours of family skeletons among neighbors and acquaintances. When she mentioned the existence of those skeletons, however, it was not to jangle their "bones" in a malicious or gossipy manner, but to use them in explaining why certain members of that family in later years did so and so or such.

Grandma treated news and gossip analytically. She had a nose for one, an ear for the other, and a surprising capacity for both.

When able to be up and about the kitchen, Grandma Ussery made delicious cookies (or tea cakes) and the best of hoecakes. Her biscuits were unforgettable, the flaky, melting kind. I used to think it was because she beat her dough with a slim cedar rolling pin and because she rolled it on a red marble "biscuit board."

On the other hand, Mama used a fat white rolling pin and a common looking wooden board despite all my efforts to convert her to cedar and marble. Mama's biscuits were never beaten; but in Grandma's kitchen everyday-biscuits got from 200 to 300 licks; Sunday and company-biscuits got a full 500, or were beaten until the dough blistered. I used to stand by the beater and count carefully or watch closely for the first blister.

I suspect now, in the light of my own years of daily biscuit making, that it must have been the amount of shortening rather than the color of the rolling pin or board, or even the number of beats to the batch that made Grandma's biscuits different. I might have been more tactful too, not to mention Grandma's biscuits so many times to Mama. I didn't know then about mothers-in-law.

It was Grandma Ussery who gave me my first book, a small green and gold volume called *Line Upon Line*. Years ago I lost that book or wore it out, but I remember passages from it.

The stories were of Biblical characters and were plainly and interestingly told. The people were clearly described. Each chapter ended in a poem which I didn't read—the poetry had too many hard words, and some of the sentences seemed to read almost backwards in order to make the rhymes come out right—but I read and enjoyed the chapters and re-read them, again and again. It was from that book that I got most of the Biblical impressions I have today.

Perhaps the reason my father's mother made such a lasting impression on me was because she was the first grandparent I lost. She died in my eleventh year, shortly after Papa's death. But more likely the reason I was so fond of her was that she seemed rather a different sort of person, one never fully understood nor appreciated by the grownups around her. It was given to me, a child under ten, to see qualities in her that other members of the family and even her closest friends never saw.

Many's the spanking I've taken for "running away to Grandma's," and if my childhood were here again and I could have the privilege of sitting on the little salmon-can stool at her feet, I'd gladly take many more. Grandma was one of those rare persons who knows how to treat a child like a human being and not like a "young 'un in the way," to be seen and not heard, and not even seen too much. I was treated like Company when I went to Grandma Ussery's. So those were the four people who made up my original "quilting frame," who stretched me between heredity and environment and left their influences stamped upon me. The prim, ladylike, modest, stern, and very clean Grandma Jones; the quiet, dusty, candy-carrying, and ever-smiling Grandpa Jones; the absent-minded, book-loving, long-whiskered Grandpa Ussery; and the ambitious, culture-loving, sincere, and sympathetic Grandma Ussery.

Their names and faces are forgotten now by all except the family and the oldest citizens of their respective neighborhoods. The dust of two lies under the rambling honeysuckle of a country graveyard; that of the other two under a polished stone in a city cemetery. But the "pull" of each one is in me every day. It is in my children, too, and will go on and grow on out the branches of the family tree. Even when they are forgotten, they will not be gone. They and their influences are largely responsible for the point of view from which I write this book.

The Family Tree Grows On

CHAPTER 2

Dark Angel in a White Apron

Aunt Ann

I think I must have known "Aunt" Ann from the time I was born. She hushed my first wail, and many another. She gave me my first bath, and many another. Much of my early childhood seemed surrounded by her stiffly starched and neatly ironed white apron.

Whether my survival was due to, or despite, her ministrations of sugar tits, catnip tea, fat-meat suckers, horehound syrup, and asafetida bags, I don't know. But I do know they were faithful ministrations.

I must have been a puny baby, very puny indeed, I have heard them say so many times. Mama was a frail, ladylike little slip of a girl who supposed—until shortly before I came—that babies grew on rosebushes.

At birth I weighed four and one-half pounds; at nine months, nine pounds; and even at a year old, they said I could have slept in papa's shoebox. Of course I didn't, for by that time he had bought me a cradle of latest design and wide rockers. He had added to that a fancy lace-trimmed, wicker baby-buggy—big enough for twins two years old, Grandma Ussery said.

And in his workshop out in the backyard he had made me a trundle-bed—a low flat bed on rollers, which took up all the space under Mama's big, high-headed, golden oak family bed in daytime and was rolled out beside the big bed for me to sleep in at night.

But with all those—cradle, trundle-bed, and buggy—I spent most of my first fifteen months on a pillow. Much of the time that pillow was in Aunt Ann's arms.

Even with all that Aunt Ann did—and Mama and Papa and both Grandmas and Dr. Biddle and Rose, the hired girl—it took the combined concern and dozens of remedies, suggestions, and prescriptions from other relatives and friends and neighbors—and not a little praying and conjuring, said Aunt Ann—to pull me through. Let the credit or blame fall where it may.

㊦

A Feather-Bed Lap

My earliest memories of Aunt Ann are of her feather-bed lap and her two-pillow bosom. Loneliness began when I grew too big for her to rock me to sleep.

A Feather-Bed Lap And A Two-Pillow Bosom

I remember well looking up at her round black face, glistening with sweat beads that became trickles. Aunt Ann's face seemed as dark and shiny, also as round, as the buckeye she carried in her pocket to ward off "rheumatiz." Her face was always framed with a halo of white flour sack.

Somewhere I have seen a picture that was like my child-mind's portrait of Aunt Ann's face. It was a landscape silhouette with a black sun outstanding in a white sky. Aunt Ann's face was that sun; her white head-rag was the sky.

Wherever she went and whatever else she wore, her principal garment, according to my recollection, was always a stiffly starched and distinctly creased white apron—three deep creases up and down and three creases crosswise. Of course, Aunt Ann had a "checkeredy" apron that she put on over the white one when frying fish or splattery doughnuts, or when leaning against the tub on washdays. But when she "appeared," she was two-thirds enveloped in a fresh white apron with a deep hem at the bottom, two large square pockets on the front, and a butterfly bow of wide and well-starched "strings" at the back.

As a child takes a below-the-belt view of life, I classified women largely by the aprons they wore or didn't wear; but even so, I began to suspect that the apron-test was not always to be relied upon. There was one woman in the neighborhood who wore a lace-frilled organdy apron with heart-shaped pockets and a small blue ribbon bow on each pocket. But for all its fanciness that apron never seemed as ladylike as Grandma Jones's checked gingham, nor as attractive as Aunt Ann's starched, bleached domestic.

During the Aunt Ann era of my childhood, Monday seemed the most important day of all the week. Monday was Ladies' Aid Day. That meant Mama must always go, for Mama was secretary. Being secretary meant that she must spend hours on Monday morning writing up the minutes and hours Monday afternoon waiting to read them. That gave me a full day at Aunt Ann's house.

Aunt Ann did our washing on Monday and ironing on Tuesday for a dollar a week. She came early on Monday morning to get the clothes, and, as it was "Aid Day," to get me. As soon as I had finished breakfast, she dressed me in a starched-up dress to go home with her.

Her house was a short block away beside the railroad, but on our side of the tracks. Aunt Ann wouldn't have lived on the other side. She had a husband, Albert (I don't know why I never called him "Uncle"; he was always just Albert); a daughter, Louise; and a grandson, Burton. In addition there was a boarder, a man named Jim who worked at the mill and slept in a little back room off Aunt Ann's kitchen.

Aunt Ann's house was a most desirable place to visit. I don't know why. It just was. A plain little weatherboarded cabin, it was innocent of paint, grayed with soot and cinders, with a door that always stood open. Inside was a tiny entrance hall with half-closed door on the right, the parlor; and a wide-open door on the left—Aunt Ann's room. Back of this room was the dining room and back of that the kitchen, always dingy but always fragrant. Once its ceiled walls had been painted sky blue, but a kitchen next door to a railroad couldn't stay sky blue for long; so Aunt Ann seemed reconciled.

The dining room had only the big cloth-covered table, some chairs, and the "safe." The bedroom had a dresser, a wardrobe for everyday clothes, a table for the lamp, two rocking chairs with fancy "tidies," and two beds covered with white counterpanes which were changed every Saturday. One bed, I understood, was for Aunt Ann and Albert; one for Louise and Burton. There was, of course, a red lambrequin around the mantelpiece.

This lambrequin, together with the turkey-red embroidered cherubs on the pillow shams, and the scrap of red flannel pinned to the short wick in the clear-glass oil-lamp bowl, always caught my eye. At Aunt Ann's windows were two pairs of many-times-washed and many-times-mended lace curtains. Not Nottinghams! The dream of Aunt Ann's life was to own a pair of real Nottingham lace curtains.

But it was Aunt Ann's hall and, most of all, her parlor that were the show places of the house. The hall held the big hall-tree with its brass umbrella stand on each side. Albert had bought that hall-tree at a sale and had paid five dollars for it, Aunt Ann said; so that piece of furniture was really important.

It had brass hooks for hats and coats and a streaked and freckled mirror set too high for use, but on the lower part, on the box-like shelf between the two umbrella stands, reposed the chief object of art of the entire household, a polished tray holding a pitcher and six glasses of the most peculiar bright and mingledy colors. I asked Aunt Ann many questions about that water set, as she called it, but she answered with such a big word I never could remember what she said by the time I got back as far as the dining room. I learned later from an antique dealer that glassware of that kind is known as "Iridescent."

A Honey-colored Room

Aunt Ann's parlor, which I always peeked at through the half-opened door, was a sight to be remembered. It seemed to have a honey-colored glow over all, caused, no doubt by the close-drawn honey-colored window shades.

In one corner was the "company" bed, plump and covered with a lace spread over pink cambric. The pillow shams, too, were lace over pink. And both the shams and the spread had patterns of huge peafowls, with flowing tails, right in the middle of each. Sometimes Aunt Ann's company bed wore a yellow petticoat and yellow pillow slips under the smooth lace spread and shams. Then the parlor was honey-colored indeed.

Of course, Aunt Ann's parlor had a sofa, one with sky-blue velvet "muffins" and gold buttons across the back. On this was kept the family's Sunday clothes. It also had a carpet of red and green and a parlor lamp on a parlor table. But it had something else. Across the room from the bed stood a white-framed picture on three tall white legs, an easel, she called it. That picture, I was told many times, was Louise. But just as many times I doubted. Louise was a fat and roundish woman when I knew her. The girl in the picture was slim.

Aunt Ann's parlor mantelpiece always wore a crepe paper lambrequin ruffled all around and fastened with brasshead tacks, just as our parlor lambrequin at home was attached. In fact, the tacks all came out of the same box. At spring cleaning time Mama always gave Aunt Ann what tacks were left over after our own lambrequins were changed.

Sometimes Aunt Ann's lambrequin was pale blue, sometimes pink, at other times light green or bright yellow. One time, I remember, it was flowered with large red roses. Some seasons it was gathered and draped in the middle. Other times it hung in box pleats all around. But I've heard Aunt Ann say that in whatever way she arranged it, it always took a whole bolt of crepe paper (10 feet) to make a parlor lam 'kin look right.

The parlor was frilly; the bedroom was neat; the dining room was dark and cool. But we spent most of our Mondays in the kitchen. Even before I left home on those Monday mornings I knew exactly what we would have for dinner—chicken and dumplings! Always chicken and dumplings on Monday. I don't know why, unless it was because Monday came after Sunday, and Sunday meant chicken and dressing. At any rate, while sheets, towels, and counterpanes rolled and bubbled in their suds in a copper-bottomed wash-boiler on the front of the stove, the chicken and dumplings rumbled in their black iron pot on the back of the stove, and I sat in the high chair inhaling and watching as Aunt Ann would rub and wring, rub and wring, and drop the clothes over into the boiler.

Monday

Aunt Ann placed her tubs midway between the kitchen stove and the window, and usually she put my highchair by the window. Even when I was a big girl, as I thought, I sat in the highchair at Aunt Ann's house because from there I could see out the window and, as she said, being up there kept me out of drafts on the floor and kept my dress clean.

If the weather was warm, I could play on a clean rug on the floor. If it was very warm, I could stay in the sun on the back porch. For a playmate I had my rag doll, Susie Jane, in her red calico dress. Sometimes I had a crayon pencil that Albert gave me to color paper dolls. Louise had given me a pair of little blunt-pointed scissors that I could use in cutting ladies from an old mail-order catalogue.

Thus, the Monday mornings passed. When the noon whistle blew down at the mill Aunt Ann left her tubs and began to "hustle up" dinner. She moved my highchair to the damask-covered table in the dining room "h'isted" me into it, and began to dish up chicken and dumplings with a saucer and to fill her green-flowered soup tureen and the deep and flared soup bowls.

She set a bowl before me on the shelf of my highchair, tied a napkin under my chin, and gave me a spoon. Then, by force of habit, I suppose, because the table looked so bare, she would go to the "safe" and bring out that marvel to me, that glass and silver "salt-pepper-and-vinegar thing"—caster, I believe they now call it. To me it was something to want very much, but she set it right in the middle of the table where I couldn't possibly reach it.

"No, no, Honey," Aunt Ann would say. "Dumplings don't need salt. Pepper's not good for chil'ren. We don't use vinegar on nothin' 'ceptin' turnip sallet."

So I ate dumplings, good though they were, still wanting to sprinkle them with salt, pepper, and vinegar, just to get my hands on that beautiful caster.

Next, Aunt Ann brought out of the "safe" that tall glass-stemmed cake stand with its five-layer, chocolate-covered marble cake, left over from Saturday's baking for Sunday's dinner. The cake was good—Aunt Ann's cakes always were. But still I couldn't forget how much I wanted to get my hands on that caster. I think I still want one.

Aunt Ann, Albert, Louise, Jim, and Burton, after he was old enough, ate their dumplings in the kitchen. I'd much rather have stayed in the kitchen with them, but Aunt Ann wouldn't "hear to white folks eatin' in colored folks' kitchens." So I ate, lonely as royalty in the big dim dining room.

I didn't see much of Albert except as he came through the dining room during those Monday dinners. Usually he was carrying a small sack of red and yellow all-day suckers for Burton and me. I scarcely saw Jim at all. He always came and went through the back door and was in the house only long enough to eat his two bowls of dumplings. But I remember Louise as being much like Aunt Ann, except a lighter brown in color; and Burton as being a very satisfactory playmate.

It Was July

One day when I was about four years old something truly unusual happened. I was permitted to go over to Mrs. Well's next door to home to stay for a long time. It really was unusual for me or anyone else I knew to set foot in Mr. Well's yard because the Wells had a biting dog. But on this day the dog was in the cellar, and Papa handed me over the high back fence to Mr. Wells, and I stayed and stayed. Mrs. Wells showed me lots of things in her house and told me about her little girl, Minnie, who died with meningitis. Minnie and meningitis! The similarity of those two names is what I remember best about the entire visit. At last I was passed back over the high fence again and went into our house.

In Mama's room everything was dark and Mama was in bed. That in itself frightened me. Aunt Ann was there and Grandma; and they told me I must be very quiet. My trundle bed was pulled out in the middle of the floor—that had never happened before in daytime as I remembered—and Aunt Ann called me to the side of the little bed, drew the covers back, and told me to look at my little sister. All I could see was a little round red head, a squirmed-up face, and two little-bitty fists—and they called that a sister!

They Called That A Sister

I don't remember feeling very favorably impressed. I do remember being furious that they had put the thing in my bed. I remember wanting to know why Mama was in bed. They told me she had to stay in bed to keep the baby warm. But that explanation didn't satisfy me for the baby was in my trundle-bed and Mama was in her big bed—and it was July.

❧

For a Rosebush Has Briers

One day, three years later, I came home from a visit to Grandma's to find the room dark again and Mama in bed. Aunt Ann soon came into the room with a grape basket. She turned back the towel to show me another round, red head, a little brother, she said that was. She said Dr. Biddle had found him in a rose-bush and had given him to her to give to us. I didn't believe a word of that because I knew how many briars the rosebush had, and that baby wasn't scratched at all. From that time on I was skeptical about a lot of things.

But when Elsie, the sister, and Clarence, the brother, and Burton, Aunt Ann's grandson, and I were all large enough to turn loose in Aunt Ann's back-yard to play by ourselves on Ladies' Aid Day, we had fun. We made mountain ranges in the ashbank, tunnels under the garden fence, rivers below the hydrant, and a surprising amount of "geography" all over the place.

We also conceived what to us was superb mischief and adventure. The railroad had a part in that. Burton said he had heard that if you rubbed soap on the railroad rails the train couldn't go. We didn't believe a cake of soap could stop a train; so the four of us, three against one, argued long and earnestly. At last we decided to try it. Burton sneaked into the kitchen, stole a sliver of yellow soap from Aunt Ann's washboard, and came back to the yard with it deep in his pocket.

We had the soap, but who would grease the rails? All of us had been forbidden to open the gate in the high board fence between the backyard and the railroad tracks. There was much discussion about that. Finally it was decided that Burton, being the black boy, would have to do the work—white folks didn't soap railroad rails, we told him. He finally gave in, but he wouldn't open the gate. None of us would be so bold as that.

We found a place, however, where he could crawl under the fence. That hadn't been forbidden.

He soaped the rails well as we watched and directed him, each through a knothole or a crack between the boards, and then he rushed back and crawled under to our side of the fence again. Jesse James never felt more wicked than we. Then we all took our stands again, each at a knothole or a crack, to watch Mr. Engine get caught in our trap. We watched and waited patiently; it seemed hours, and the sun beaming down on our backs was hot.

While we waited, Burton got another idea. He said he had heard that if you would cross two pins and lay them on the railroad tracks, when the train went by you would have a pair of scissors. We decided to try that too. Again Burton must obtain the pins, just as he had the soap. It was his house, we told him, and his Grandma, and certainly with three against one, the white vote carried.

He found two pins on the bedroom dresser but only two. That would make one pair of scissors—but whose would they be? I thought I ought to have them because I was the oldest, and a girl. Elsie thought she ought to have them because she was the youngest, and a girl. Boys didn't use scissors. Burton reminded us that, after all, they were his Grandma's pins. Clarence, for once, didn't join the argument. He was still watching for the engine to get stuck on the yellow soap.

The ownership of the scissors-to-be was still unsettled when Burton scrambled under the fence again and under our direction carefully crossed the pins on the hot black rail. Again we took our places at our respective knotholes to wait for what seemed hours. In fact, the Ladies' Aid meeting was over, and Mama had called for us, but still no train had come.

We lost the pins and argument, and we never did know whether an engine could pull on a yellow soap skid.

A Trap for Mr. Engine

The Aid Was Endangered

When I first learned that Aunt Ann was going to move, I was shocked beyond believing. I thought we couldn't, simply couldn't get along without her. The first blow was that I would never have another clean, stiffly-starched, and carefully ironed dress.

Then I realized there'd be no more five-layer chocolate marble cakes on Saturdays and Sundays and no more chicken and dumplings on Mondays. And the Ladies' Aid! I was sure that Aunt Ann's moving would break up the Ladies' Aid. There would be nowhere else for us to stay while Mama was secretarying. It didn't occur to me that Grandma and Grandpa Ussery lived across the street from us on Mondays as well as other days, and that we could just as well stay there—except for the fact that Grandma didn't approve the Aid.

She did move, however, and the Society and the rest of the world went on. She moved all the way across town to the farthest edge. She continued, though, to do our Monday washing and Tuesday ironing and to come back and help with the Saturday cleaning and baking for a dollar a week until her rheumatiz got her down. And she continued to be my "Aunt" Ann even after that.

CHAPTER 3

Mama and Papa

Mama and Papa Had a Sunrise Wedding

A Sunrise Wedding

We children were always grateful to our grandparents for giving us Mama and Papa and some interesting aunts and uncles.

Mama and Papa had a sunrise wedding in the family parlor, June 3, 1894. As it was the time of lilies, the family garden supplied blooms for the parlor decorations and for the bride's bouquet. The Jones family farm furnished evergreens: I've heard Mama say many times that she remembered standing under a huge bell made of rhododendrons, which her brothers brought in from the bluffs along the Harpeth River.

The early morning hour was chosen because of the train schedule. The wedding journey was to be a boat trip from Johnsonville, Tennessee, up the Tennessee River to Florence, Alabama. The train passed through White Bluff at 8 a.m. There had to be time for the bride to change from her white flowered silk to her gray travel dress, and time for the wedding breakfast.

Mama said all she could ever remember about that breakfast was the cold, sliced turkey.

She did recall very well her first wifely duty. She and Papa were sitting on the boat deck that afternoon, enjoying the scenery, and as happy as honeymooners could be, when the bridegroom suddenly grabbed his knee, leaped from his chair, and yelled.

A spark from the smokestack had burned through his pants and into the skin. Mama ventured to borrow a needle with gray thread to sew up the trousers of her new husband's black Prince Albert suit.

In packing for the journey Mama had carefully packed her comb and brush, her curling irons, her face powder, and all such articles as a bride might need, in a small box and had left it on her trunk, ready to be put in at the last moment. But when the last moment came, the trunk was closed and the box forgotten.

Next morning Papa had to find the housekeeper of the boat and borrow comb, brush, curling irons, and face powder before his bride could come to breakfast.

After three days and two nights on the riverboat, they arrived in Florence, spent the night at a hotel there, and then took the train for Columbia, Tennessee, where Papa had a new house almost finished—just across the street from his family home. They arrived late in the evening and were rushed immediately into a huge reception.

Mama said what she remembered best about that reception was that she had been traveling four days without curling irons, and that they had cold sliced turkey.

❧

When Papa Came Home

Papa was tall, quiet, and mustached. He was foreman of a bridge-building crew for a railroad company and was home only on week-ends. As I remember Papa, he must have had a keen sense of humor under a solemn exterior. Other people laughed at the few words he spoke and frequently quoted him; but I don't remember ever seeing him even smile, much less break into a laugh.

He was not so bookish as other members of his family, but rather liked to tinker, or "invent," as he called it, in a cluttered little shop joining the woodshed in our backyard.

He used to perch me on a small box on one corner of his work bench while he puttered about, and by asking questions and getting one-syllable answers, I learned the names and uses of drill, auger, vice, and various hammers and other tools. From those days in Papa's shop, I resolved to be a mechanic, tinkerer, inventor, and whatever Papa was. To be able to operate a drill press or lathe would have made me almost as happy as to own a pink silk dress and parasol.

From the time Papa came home on Saturday afternoon until supper time, he belonged somewhat to us. We followed him around telling him everything that had happened throughout the week. But after supper, we were allotted our bananas and candy and sent to bed. Then it was Mama's time to tell him of the week's happenings.

Papa never punished one of us children, and I've heard him boast to Mama that he never had to speak to one of us twice. But there was a reason—his bicycle bell!

One particularly strenuous week when Papa was home with the grippe and Mama was very nervous, and the weather was too bad for us to play anywhere else except behind the stove, family tension was running high.

Papa went out to his shop, returned, saying nothing, but bearing a discarded bicycle bell. He fastened the bell on the underside of the arm of his big porch rocker (brought inside for the winter) and took his seat.

All went well until one of us children got too noisy, too slack in obedience, or otherwise out of line. Then Papa instantly clicked that bell, and fixed on the reprobate a glaring blue-eyed stare. Result: instant obedience. That's the only discipline Papa ever gave us.

I don't know why Mama never rang the bell during trying weekdays. She struggled along, scolding, threatening, spanking, sometimes by hand, sometimes by peach-tree switch or hairbrush, but the bell was reserved for Papa's private use.

Our family life during the entire week was always slanted toward Papa's homecoming on Saturday night. Mama dressed a hen, baked a chocolate cake, a lemon pie, an egg custard, (and let us lick or scrape the pans, spoons, and mixing bowls). She also boiled a pot of rice and baked a pan of macaroni and cheese. Those were Papa's favorite foods. Then she bathed us and dressed us in our next-to-bests and had us all ready for his homecoming before she started to bedeck herself. The house itself was already clean, and we dared not "mess up" anything.

We would hang on the front gate until we could recognize his long legs ambling down the hill from toward the railroad depot. Then we broke out like wild young horses galloping and racing down the rattley old board sidewalk to meet him.

It was not merely that Papa was coming; it was also what he brought—bananas sometimes, candy for sure, always the "funny papers" with "Mule Maud and Si," "Buster Brown," and the very bad and often-punished "Katzenjammer Kids."

Usually in addition to those regular Saturday night gifts there was a surprise for one of us or another. Once there was a tricycle for me; another time a small red fire-engine for Clarence; and once, what Elsie wanted most in all the world, a pair of skates.

Each of these gifts eventually led to its own disaster. I was so proud of the tricycle that I couldn't resist holding my head high and leaning back like a lady in a surrey. Every time I did so, the tricycle was overbalanced, and back of my head hit the rough, hard brick sidewalk to the accompaniment of stars in my eyes.

Clarence thought he had found a perfect highway for his little red fire engine, the banister rail in the front hall. He sneaked up the front stairway, an act which in itself was entirely forbidden, set the little wheels astraddle the rail, and gave the engine a shove and a ting-a-ling. Down it went right into the middle of Mama's new red swinging lamp, her Christmas present from Papa. We expected the seat of the boy's breeches to blaze when Mama laid down the hairbrush, but he was able to continue wearing them, though not to sit comfortably.

Elsie's skates seemed always in a hurry, especially when she started down the sloping walk in the side yard. They always slipped out from under her and let her head hit the sidewalk. But that in itself seemed not too tragic to the rest of us until one day she fell, clumsy thing, right down flat on top of our little pet chicken which was following her. She mashed his insides out. It was such a sickening sight and heartbreaking occurrence that Clarence and I hardly forgave her for days. Elsie practically had to go to bed. She had major claims to the chicken, for it was into her hands that Grandma Ussery had placed it, and it was usually her privilege to gather up the table scraps and feed it.

But it was Papa's regular gifts that meant most to us—the bananas, candy, and funny papers. We felt that we couldn't possibly live through a weekend without knowing what Maud, Si, Buster, Mary Jane, Tige, the Kids, and the Captain were doing. So it was very handy that we had a Papa to come home on Saturday night.

❦

The Cap'n's Kids

Papa's crew of men lived all the week "on the road." They had a train of freight cars all fixed up for living. One car was the cook-coach and dining room, with Papa's office in one end. The other cars had bunks for the men.

One of Papa's big problems was keeping a cook, one who was satisfied to stay away from home throughout the week, and one who's cooking could please so many people. Keeping the men satisfied seemed easier than keeping the cook satisfied, for there was a rule in the cars that anyone who complained about the cooking had to take over the job himself.

The men called Papa "Cap'n." When we went down to the cars on Sunday morning they looked us over thoroughly and spoke of us as the Cap'n's kids. This made us very proud. Any time Papa was out of sight and hearing, one of the men would say to us, "Your Papa's a mighty good man, yes sir, a mighty good man." Dozens of times I've heard that expression in regard to Papa. But one night he seemed to have not been so good and that's a story that stayed with that crew as long as they were on the road.

Papa was trying to cut down on the amount of profanity used among the crew. So a ruling was established that any man who used an expression that he wouldn't say before ladies had to drop a penny for each word into a little tin bank. When the bank was full, it would be opened, and its contents were to be used to buy a Bible for the "cars."

All was going well. The bank was filling rapidly enough, for sometimes a good healthy oath would cost its exploder a whole nickel.

One night when a sudden rain came up, Papa got up to shut the car door and caught his finger in a quick pinch. He turned loose a big and dirty cuss word, then caught his breath—but not before one of the men had heard it.

The man got up quickly, roused up the whole crew, from one end of the sleeping cars to the other. They lit their lanterns, went back to the tool car, got a barrel and hand saw, turned Papa down across the former, and applied the latter. Then they made him put a dollar in the little tin bank. That midnight spanking of the Cap'n did those men more good than the Bible ever could, they said.

Papa died when I was ten, Elsie six, and Clarence three years of age. But Papa's porch chair with the bell on it continued to sit by the stove, always empty, but always as a reminder, until summer came, then the chair was taken out, and we could go out to play in the backyard or under the house.

∞

Playing "Mrs."

There was not much inducement to play in the backyard. It was entirely bare. And like Grandma Jones's backyard, it had to be kept clean, swept every Saturday.

The only things of interest in the backyard were two maple trees that must not be climbed; a plum tree which, also, must not be climbed except when Mama wanted the plums picked; a walnut tree which annually produced many caterpillars and a few walnuts, the latter of which must not be touched on account of their stain; and a dripping hydrant which kept the chickens supplied with water, and which also must not be touched except for drinking and handwashing.

But under the house was different. It was latticed all around and nice and dusty underfoot. By taking particular care of our clothes, we could sift the dust, make "flour," "sugar," "salt," and every imaginable kind of groceries. The lumps which were sifted out were imagined into apples and potatoes, and Clarence kept store and sold groceries to Elsie and me, who, under assumed "Mrs." names, kept house and raised our imaginary children. But we did have to try at all times to keep our clothes clean while playing under the house. Besides that, we had to crawl about and keep our heads bowed during the entire playing process, for under the house was not very high.

It was during these earlier years that Biddy became a part of our experience. Biddy owed her life to the fact that Company didn't come. The little black hen was bought extra for Sunday

"Company" dinner. The grocery boy brought her—her blue feet tied with twine—when he brought the Saturday morning groceries: prunes, dried beans, celery, and such. Mama intended to wring off Biddy's head, pluck her feathers, and rub her down with salt on Saturday afternoon. But the noon mail brought a card saying that the "Company" was not coming. So Biddy was spared for another week.

All that week Elsie, Clarence, and I devoutly prayed that something would happen to that company before the next Sunday. Our prayers were answered, and for another week, and still many others after, the little black hen was spared to us pet-starved youngsters.

൙

Afraid To Love

Biddy was not the first pet in our backyard. In the days before Clarence and Elsie were big enough to share him, I had owned a teeny-weeny pet guinea—a darling little fellow with a bell around his neck. Papa had brought him from somewhere "down the road," and Grandma had given me the bell to tie around his neck. That guinea was a large part of my whole life just then.

One afternoon I was invited to a party, a nice little party it was, with cake and ice cream; but there were games I didn't understand and boys and girls I didn't know; so I felt that I would much rather be at home with my guinea fowl.

I could hardly wait to get off my Party Dress before rushing out into the backyard to call my familiar playmate. I called, but he didn't come. I called again and again. I hunted in the henhouse, the woodshed, the shop—but no guinea.

Then naturally I went into the house to ask Mama. It was always a custom at our house, in any crisis, to "ask Mama." Mama answered as casually as though she were speaking of beans or potatoes: "Why, that guinea got to be such a nuisance out there in the backyard I decided to fry him for supper."

I don't know how I got out of the house. I don't know why I went to the chopping block in the woodshed. "If I could only find even his little bell," I thought.

Mama supposed it was too much ice cream and cake that kept me from eating supper that night; that it was too much party that made me toss and tumble all night in my trundle bed. I never did find even the little bell, and I never could ask about it.

After losing the guinea, I was afraid to love anything else. I didn't love the younger brother and sister. I didn't love Grandpa Ussery's horse, Old Nell. I couldn't bear to love even the little calf that came in the spring. I almost loved the little squirrel that Uncle Charlie gave me. In fact, I was thinking entirely too much of that squirrel; then one morning his cage was empty, and I was hurt again.

It was hard, however, to keep from loving Biddy, even though all three of us lived in constant fear that she would make a Sunday dinner. As it was, however, she became the pet of the whole family. Papa posed us with her on the back steps and took our picture. We took turns feeding her and eating her eggs for breakfast. One of Biddy's eggs was worth two from any other hen. Biddy was with us for years, but she belonged mostly to Elsie and Clarence. I had learned that a pet, no matter how much loved, could be fried for supper. From that time on I was afraid to love.

Mama took after her side of the house, of course, but she never seemed quite so precise as some of her relatives. You might guess her size when I say she could stand under Papa's outstretched arm with her hat on, and from the time I could remember, she weighed 136 pounds.

Mama was a model housekeeper and a very busy mother during the years I can first remember. I think most of all now of the pies and cakes she baked for Papa's homecoming on Saturday nights and Sundays, and of the weekly scouring and scrubbing she gave us three children on regular bath nights.

I remember particularly that we all had new Easter outfits for Easter Sunday mornings, and regardless of Easter weather, we wore them. In early autumn Mama made our fall dresses; mine was of dark blue and "serviceable" storm serge; Elsie's of the same material, but red. Both were trimmed lavishly with gilt braide and brass buttons. On the first Sunday of September, regardless of weather, we wore those new wool dresses.

Many times as I shivered along to Sunday School on a chilly Easter morning, in light blue mercerized gingham, or sweated it out in scratchy serge in September, I wondered why the seasons couldn't be swapped so we'd have Easter in September, and September in spring.

But the neighbors had to be impressed.

౽

Keeping Her Shoulders Up

From the time Papa died, Mama had a typical widow's problem of keeping up with the taxes and the grocery bill. Her main income was from dressmaking; she could sew and stay at home, and with three growing children she reasoned that she needed to be at home.

For long, un-numbered hours she stood at the dining room table and "cut out," or sat at her sewing machine by the window in the sitting room and stitched. But no matter what the hours, how long the days, or how tiresome and monotonous the work, Mama always "kept her shoulders up." That was her greatest pride. She was determined not to have "dressmaker's stoop." The neighbor's opinions were always remembered.

I was old enough and observant enough to notice what a hard time she had. I realized, many times, that she was wondering where the next week's provisions would come from, and how on earth she'd get the money to pay taxes, insurance, grocery bill, and note at the bank. She always managed though, somehow, and proved to be an excellent business woman and a good provider, considering what she had to provide with.

There were times when the grandparents or the uncles and aunts would or could help a little, but usually Mama was too proud ever to ask for help. She did however accept $10 checks as Christmas presents, and $5 bills as birthday presents. Those helped a lot.

I used to always remember Christmas and birthdays in my prayers, hoping that Grandma and Grandpa and the Aunts and Uncles wouldn't forget and asking God please to remind them. Also in my prayers I would ask him to make Papa's death not true.

I always expected to wake up some morning and find that his funeral had been just a dream. I'd always hang on the gate on Saturday afternoons hoping that he would again turn that corner with a sack of bananas in his right arm and a surprise package in the other, and the funny papers in his right hip pocket. I prayed for Papa's death to be a dream just as fervently as I ever prayed that my freckles would leave and my hair would turn from stringy and potato-colored to shiny black and curly.

My prayers were only one-third answered. The grandparents and aunts and uncles didn't forget.

My Prayers Were One-third Answered

CHAPTER 4

Family Album Glimpses

Album Glimpses

The South Side of the House—The Userys

Our grandparents, with their medium to large sized families, generously provided us with uncles and aunts of various types and temperaments, and indirectly with a goodly number of cousins.

Those were truly memorable days when Aunt Beulah, of the Ussery clan, made for us those beautiful batches of caramel candy. She always began that candy by burning sugar in a heavy iron skillet, then dissolving that melted sugar in cream—no short cuts and no short-comings in Aunt Beulah's candy-making.

Many people thought that Aunt Beulah was pretty. Others liked her clear, rippling, musical laughter, but the thing that I remember best about her was the loveliness of her snow white, waxy hands. They were as nearly perfect as those of the lady on the monument in the cemetery, and no less white. One of the most vivid pictures that hangs on the wall of my childhood memories is that of Aunt Beulah's graceful marble-like hands, pouring a golden wealth of caramel candy on Grandma Ussery's marble biscuit board.

Aunt Beulah's hands were often busy with other impressive activities. I have watched them holding a small brush, painting pictures on jars, glasses, plates, wooden plaques, and wooden trays—such as the ones that sausages came in. I remember watching her hands busy embroidering a turkey-red felt lambrequin with variegated yarn. And I remember them, too, turning, cutting, and tediously shaping crepe paper into flowers—carnations, tulips, but mostly lilies. Her hands were lovely with the lilies.

Aunt Beulah, as I remember, seemed always a good person to be about. In addition to her fair skin, her glossy black hair, her ringing laughter, her dancing eyes, and her beautiful hands, she carried with her a fragrance similar to that of the little rubber-bulbed perfume atomizer on her bureau.

I was not regularly a meddler, for Grandma Ussery had told me over and over again what a terrible thing happened once to a little girl named Meddlesome Matilda (Mattie, for short). She had opened her grandmother's snuff box and smelled it! No, I wasn't regularly a meddler, but somehow I never could pass through Aunt Beulah's room without squeezing that little squirt-gun bulb of the atomizer. Even at the risk of punishment worse than scolding, I would have done so. It seemed to make me and the room and the whole world smell like Aunt Beulah.

There was another aunt of the Ussery blood who had been married since before I could first remember, and she was living up town in a lovely big house. I used to delight in visiting Aunt Agnes. Everything was always so "just so" and so exactly right at her house; yet it seemed to require little effort on her part to keep things that way.

For example, she had sliding doors between her front parlor and her sitting room, and sliding doors were very proper and up-to-date then. She had also a parlor lamp that had brass filigree work around the bottom, and she had a marble topped brass pedestal for the lamp to sit on.

She had large pink roses scattered over her green velvety parlor carpet, and she didn't seem the least bit afraid that her carpet would fade. In fact, she dared to keep her parlor shades halfway up—the only person I knew who did that—and she kept her parlor door open even on week days and when she didn't have company. That matter of raised shades and open parlor door made Aunt Agnes seem different in my estimation from everybody else I knew. Then, too, she bought the first piano in the neighborhood; that set her apart from all other women.

Aunt Agnes had in her sitting room-bedroom a rich-looking bright red and dark red carpet stretched over the floor. She had more straw under her carpets than did anyone else in the whole family connection unless it was Grandma Jones in her parlor. Aunt Agnes's dresser, too, was different from all the others in the family. The mirror was very large, and the primping part was so low that I could see myself comb my hair without standing on a stool. This seemed the height of convenience and luxury.

❧

Button! Button!

I liked spending the night at Aunt Agnes's house, for she let me have the whole big front upstairs room to myself, and she let me sleep in her folding bed—what a promotion from the mere trundle bed I had at home!

Aunt Agnes had time to sit down and talk to me just as though I were another grown-up. She had time, too, to tell me things I didn't know, things that were interesting and important. She always was offering me good things to eat. She seemed continually to have cake in her china closet. She offered me a choice of white or dark meat when I had no idea which to choose.

One Sunday dinner Aunt Agnes though didn't have "white meat or dark meat." She had fish! A whole baked fish all on the table at one time! It was a big fish with slices of lemon all around it and sprigs of green stuff, which I know now was parsley.

To one who's former experience had been limited to tinned sardines and salmon, this seemed monstrous.

Both Aunt Agnes and her husband, Uncle George, liked to see little girls eat, and I liked to oblige them. They had a wonderful cook named Minnie. She was so smart that she mopped the kitchen floor every day after dinner, every day, mind you, not just on Saturdays nor twice a week. She mopped that floor after dinner every day, even on Sundays and in the winter time. I greatly admired Minnie's mopping and her muffins.

Aunt Agnes had much of Grandma Ussery's properness and up-to-dateness about her, and she had a much better opportunity for exercising and indulging those qualities than did her mother. I won't say that she worked harder at being proper and up-to-date than did Grandma, but she seemed to get more impressive results.

Furthermore, she dressed me in one of her own nightgowns, one that had buttons all the way down the front from collar to hem—with never a button missing. As Aunt Agnes was a tall woman, that gave me a long and more or less graceful train—which I tried, when alone, to handle like a lady. I also had dozens of buttons, to do and undo and to count "rich man, poor man, beggar man, thief." Never before nor since have I had so many buttons, so much train, nor felt so dressed up as in Aunt Agnes's nightgown.

Button! Button!

Aunt Agnes was considerate, definite, and very, very firm. She was horribly shocked one day to see me chewing a wad of gum when we chanced to meet on the street. I feared her so much that I threw away the gum before I had chewed even half the sweet out of it.

꙰

Big Black Box

How early does a child begin to remember? I can answer only for myself. I was two years old in June before Uncle Gillie, my father's only brother, was killed in February of the next year. But some things I remember—just snatches, I admit—about that loved and indulgent uncle, as clearly as if they had happened this morning.

I can remember being with him and Grandma Ussery in Grandma's garden. There was a grape arbor up the middle of the garden with herbs, calamus, mint, garlic, and such, on each side between and under the vines. I had always before walked along beside the herbs, but on this occasion, just as we got inside the gate and after Uncle Gillie had fastened it, he picked me up and set me on his shoulder. In this way we all went up the grape arbor. It seemed so funny to me to look down at the grape vines instead of up at them. I had never before known how an arbor looked on top.

We walked the full length of the arbor and on to the very small vine at the farthest end and on the left. That vine, it seemed, was the one we came to see. It was loaded with bunches of pinkish-purple grapes, and they seemed so large. It seemed funny to me that the littlest vine—this one was not more than waist high to Uncle Gillie—should have the biggest grapes. Another thing that seemed funny was the name of the vine. Grandma told Uncle Gillie that it was "Lutie." That seemed such an odd name compared with plain old "Concord." Uncle Gillie pulled the grapes off one by one and handed them up to me. I remember how good they were, and how important I felt to be so high.

Again, I remember sitting on Uncle Gillie's knee at the left of the fireplace in Grandma's room. The weather was cold, and he seemed to be warming my hands and feet; at any rate, he took off my shoes. Grandma was on the other side of the fire with some needlework, darning, I think, or knitting. I remember a dark, gray sock-like-looking something in her hand.

I remember, too, at another time seeing Uncle Gillie standing at the back door. He was looking down at me and smiling. I remember how tall and big he seemed, and I remember especially his dark mustache and tie against his white face and white shirt.

Then there was the day someone held me up to see him in the long black box. I remember how white his collar and forehead were, and how dark his mustache and his hair. That must have been in early February, 1898, as that was when he was killed in a railroad accident. I was three years old the following June.

ॐ

My Richest Poor Relation

There was another aunt on the Ussery side of the house who was always referred to as "poor Molly." Why the word "poor" was used with Aunt Molly's name was more than I could understand; for it seemed to me that she had a great many things the others hadn't. True, she had no husband. She had been a widow for years, but her other possessions made me think her the richest relative I had.

Take children, for instance: Aunt Molly had a good-sized flock of bright and healthy sons and daughters and they seemed the most fun of any cousins I had. Every member of the family had a keen sense of humor. When their jokes and laughter were turned loose at the table, in the cornfield, or around the fire on winter evenings, hardly a minstrel show could surpass them. Yes, Aunt Molly was rich in sons and daughters, and their laughter.

And then, Aunty Molly had Old Ned, and she could drive him and her rickety old buggy to and from town along the tree-shaded country road that had wild flowers blooming on either side. This seemed to me a rare and incomparable privilege.

Aunt Molly also had a farm. True, it was not a very productive farm, but it had a high hill on the far side with a chestnut tree on the very top, and from that hill one could look down on the neighboring farms for miles around. And down both sides of the hill were ditches deep with high crumbly clay banks. Those banks were more fun to slide down than any cellar door I ever saw. But I got such warm and thorough hairbrush applications from Mama for what that clay did to my petticoats—and such—that I haven't cared for ditches since.

And Aunt Molly had a Mortgage. It wasn't mentioned often, and for a long time I couldn't imagine what a Mortgage was. It seemed in the class with chickenpox and dirty hands—something uncomfortable and something that should be hidden. Years later when I had accumulated some experiences with mortgages of my own I realized how Aunt Molly must have felt about hers. I realized, too, that Aunt Molly had a great many things that a mortgage couldn't cover.

Consider Mary, for instance. No mortgage, not even one of the tightest chattel variety, could hamper Mary. Mary, at Aunt

Molly's house, was not the "being" that had the lamb; Mary *was* the lamb. And what a lamb! She was pet and nuisance, joy and sorrow, of the farm.

Because Aunt Molly always kept a flock of sheep, and because in the flock there were always ewes who lacked a sense of motherly responsibility, there was always a Mary, either orphaned or disowned, to "baa" about the house.

Yes, to my childish delight there was a succession of Marys. How we distinguished these lambs one from another, if we did, I don't know. We didn't call them Mary 1, Mary II, Mary Belle, or anything like that. Each was just Mary. And as a playmate she was all one could desire.

Aunt Molly's sons and daughters were older than I, and usually were out at work somewhere on the farm. Aunt Molly also kept busy. That left Mary and me to our own entertainment; we had the run of the farm, fields, woods, and barnlot.

But there were some places where Mary wasn't permitted to go, even though I was. One was the parlor, where the organ and the album were. One was the front porch where Aunt Molly's geraniums bloomed. Those places were taboo to lambs; yet, contrariwise, those were the places Mary wanted most to be, especially if I was there—most especially the front porch. Mary seemed to like geraniums as much as Aunt Molly and I did, but in a different way.

There were hickory trees in Aunt Molly's barnlot and persimmons in her pasture. There were cedar trees, large ones, around and over her pond, and those cedar trees had bluebirds. There was the old rock spring across the road and down-a-ways from Aunt Molly's house. That was where she got her water, except that which she caught in rainbarrels, used exclusively for "first suds" on washday Mondays.

There was the neighborhood school where Aunt Molly and her sons and daughters each in turn served as teacher. Next to the school was the little white church where her grandsons preached in later years as they moved on to minister to big city churches.

As Aunt Molly's was the nearest house to the church and school, it became more or less a community center. It was there the extra teacher boarded, when there was one; and there the Evangelist boarded when there was one; and there the visiting preacher spent the night. Aunt Molly was largely the community's heart and pulse, mother-confessor, and chief dependence.

Aunt Molly had neighbors, good whole-souled, neighborly, accommodating, borrowing, lending, visiting, country neighbors. They were not least among her riches.

Aunt Molly also had fruit trees, but especially apple trees. Somehow I always associated her with apple trees. She and they had so much in common. She loved them beyond compare. I remember standing with her one day beside a large and very beautiful tree in full fruit. She was saying, "I planted this tree myself when it was only a little switch."

One of the Best Things in Life is to Plant a Tree

Those were the words, and she said them very simply; but her tone of voice said to me that next to rearing a lovely daughter or stalwart son, one of the best things in life is to plant a switch or seed and to watch it week by week, year by year, grow into a beautiful and productive establishment.

Aunt Molly had an attic, just an unfinished attic. There were stored winter clothes in summer; summer clothes in winter; and old clothes at all times. That attic was an ideal place on a rainy day for "playing lady." There was even a cracked and speckled mirror leaning against the studding, and in this a lady could view her finery from her high heels to her frayed ostrich plumes.

In the attic was where Aunt Molly stored her herbs, her dried peas and beans, and her garden seeds. They were hung in bags from the rafters. Up there were also her quilting frames, loom, reel, spinning wheel, and bags of wool and feathers. Anything that wasn't in regular use, if it didn't need to be stored in the cellar or smokehouse, was put away in the attic.

Aunt Molly had a better understanding of how to make and cut homemade bread than any other housewife my childhood knew. That she was expert in baking bread there is no need of saying. All the people who traveled that road on Wednesdays and Saturdays knew by the aroma that Aunt Molly could bake good bread. But it was in cutting the bread that she excelled.

Her baking pan held five loaves crosswise. That made the loaves somewhat broader and shorter than the loaves we bought in town at the grocery. While her bread was still warm, Aunt Molly sliced it lengthwise, and buttered each slice to the outmost crust. They were not too thin, either, those slices. They were sturdy enough to stay whole when laid lengthwise in a child's two hands held with the tips of fingers touching (almost like a pack-saddle). They held a surprising amount of blackberry jam, grape preserves, honey, sugar-butter, molasses, or apple butter—the good thick kind made with spices and fresh cider!

And there were Aunt Molly's gardens, the large and some-what rugged vegetable garden, and the small well-loved flower garden. Fences were expensive, and her chickens were Leghorns; so that meant a long walk across a field to the vegetable garden which to me seemed very large indeed, especially on a July day when I tried to help pull weeds out of a bean row that ran the entire length of the plot.

I thought the plot must also seem very large to Aunt Molly and to Alfred, the oldest boy who was twelve years old when his father died. Aunt Molly and Alfred and Old Ned did all the plowing both in the garden and in the fields. Old Ned pulled the plow; Alfred pushed it, and Aunt Molly guided by walking ahead in the furrow leading the horse by the rein. Until Alfred and Ned were experienced enough to do the job by themselves, this was the way the family's food and clothing were earned, as well as the interest on the mortgage.

As I remember that vegetable garden of Aunt Molly's, I remember especially the cow-peas and peppers, perhaps because the peas were so plentiful and the peppers so pretty. Aunt Molly always stored bags and bags of dried peas in the attic for winter, and hung strings of red peppers and festoons of yellow popcorn on the kitchen walls.

I remember the sweet potatoes in that garden too. How their vines covered the ground five or six rows wide and the length of the whole garden. Their solid mass of green stood out in sharp contrast to the other vegetables that showed the thin brown earth between their rows.

That cloddy hillside garden might not have seemed productive to people accustomed to more fertile land, but by the use of labor, love, and barnyard fertilizer, Aunt Molly and her sons and daughters made it produce year-round food for themselves, and an extra amount for town relatives and country neighbors.

A Far-flung Garden

But the part and possession of Aunt Molly that was shared with the greatest number of neighbors, friends, and passers-by was her flower garden. The peculiar way in which the country road curved as it passed Aunt Molly's place left a triangular plot of rocky ground that hardly belonged to the road and scarcely belonged to the farm. This being a sort of no-man's land, you'd naturally expect a woman to take it over. That's exactly what Aunt Molly did. She made a brave effort at fencing the pigs and cows and chickens out, and prepared to plant flowers within.

The garden began in this way, she said: When her first baby had three-month colic, an old Negro woman, a neighbor named Nora Fox, brought her a bunch of catnip and set it out in the corner of the triangle nearest the house where it would be handy for making the baby's tea. Believing that a mother's soul needs treatment as well as a baby's tummy, Nora planted beside the catnip a flaming crimson double poppy.

When the poppy bloomed, the neighbors saw. Traveling then by horse or by horse and wagon, the flower-lovers stopped to admire and discuss and to ask for seeds of the bright blooming poppy.

In exchange they brought seeds, bulbs, cuttings, and plants from their own flower gardens. Thus, the roadside garden grew and spread. Every passer-by who had contributed to the garden continued to be interested in it.

In saving seeds for her own "start" each year, Aunt Molly always remembered other flower-lovers. One who visited her house in winter "to sit for a spell by the fire" would see her rise from her patchwork-cushioned rocker, and take from the mantel an ash-dusty shoebox filled with small packages of seeds wrapped in old envelopes and scraps of newspaper, tied with sewing thread and neatly labeled.

"These are seeds of Nora Fox's double crimson Poppy," she would say. "I want you to have some of them. Many times I have thought I had lost it, but always a stray plant shows up somewhere, perhaps in the fence corner, perhaps in the pigpen or chicken yard, or even out on the roadside, and I find it in time to save seeds for another year. The catnip is growing now, all over the place. It makes itself a weed, but I like it.

"These are seeds of Mary Nicholson's marigolds. You must have some of them. These are Sackie Jones's pink Zinnias. Here's a new flower that Mrs. Felix Sowell gave me. Here's a start of Anna Gray's verbena."

In this way flowers spread each year. Hers was indeed a far-flung garden.

In the matter of labor, Aunt Molly's garden was always a no-man's land. "Men don't know flowers from weeds, or just don't care," she would say.

And so, as long as she could make her frail, tired body move, she worked her flower garden herself. There were many times when a weak back permitted her to do barely more than sit on a stone and dig weeds with a butcher knife, but the thoughts of the flowers that would come when the weeds were gone, she said, kept her happy and hoping. Those thoughts and sunshine helped to heal both mind and body.

One afternoon, walking in the garden with Aunt Molly, I tried to count the number of plants and flowers and remember their names as she introduced them. Just inside the garden gate an oak tree sprang from an acorn that had sprouted in the lily bed. The gardener had spared, even cherished it, because, as she said, "Lilies do better with a little shade." There were several kinds of lilies in the bed; and next to them were a mass of four-o'clocks, baby slippers, feverfew, foxgloves, verbena, and mourning bride.

A black-eyed Susan was twining over a blanket flower, and climbing up a rustic trellis to join a spinsterish wisteria. This, Aunt Molly said, never bloomed. But she protected it forgivingly.

A bed of marigold, hardy sunflower, golden bell, and artichoke reminded one that all gold is not in mines and mints. Prince's feather and white and blue asters were about to hide the violets and dianthus underneath. Honeysuckles, woodbine, cosmos, and a yellow rambler rose were trying to outgrow a Jean Kerr dahlia which was tangled in their midst.

The things there were hanging on the next trellis I thought were dishrag gourds, but Aunt Molly declared that they were "the fruit of a new and rare foreign plant called "Bella Casa,"

and in their native country they are used for pickles and such."
I suspected she was quoting from the seed catalogue.

A volunteer asparagus plant and a yellow Texas rose stood in front of a hedge of lilacs. White and purple Jack beans were blooming in the mock orange and crepe myrtle bushes. Nearby was a clump of Angel's Trumpets—that may be just a glorified "jimson" weed to some, but despite its common cousin in the pig pen, it is really a beautiful flower, especially when spoken of by the name Aunt Molly always used—Angel's Trumpet.

Lavender petunias and yellow cannas made a pretty picture in the next rock-bordered bed. Two new hydrangea cuttings were getting a start under turned-over fruit jars, shaded by shingles with clods on top. There were a dozen or more varieties of cannas in the next bed, "A Popular Dollar Collection," Aunt Molly quoted again. In the midst of them flourished a little rose bush with rich dark leaves and briar-covered stems. Aunt Molly said that some folks always called that the Jackson rose, after the old General; but she thought of it as the Harrison rose, because it had been given to her by Dr. and Mrs. Harrison.

There were bachelor buttons, gladioli, chrysanthemums, wild roses, sweet Williams, seven-steps-to-heaven, hibiscus, Shasta daisy, bridal wreath, lady finger, bear grass, cacti—each plant with a story of its own, one that Aunt Molly liked to repeat.

Many things were buried in that garden, mostly cares and worries. Many memories clung to the plants in the rocky little triangle. There was a bleeding heart near the gate whose story she never told. There was a golden-leaf honeysuckle that made her eyes fill as she mentioned the daughter who planted it the year before pneumonia struck. There were other plants that had special significance, either as to the time of planting, or source, or person.

Floods covered the garden and droughts parched it, for it was low and founded upon a rock. Moles seemed most pestiferous, and calves, lambs, chickens, rabbits, field mice, bugs, mules, and stray billy goats—all liked that garden, sometimes to the point of exasperation for the gardener. But despite all those disasters, Aunt Molly's love and patience and ever-trying-again made the garden prosper year after year.

There is no measuring the spread of that garden. An editor in Washington wrote an editorial titled, "Memories of Miss Molly's Garden." A housewife in Texas cherishes a lily from there. Another in Oklahoma watches every year for her "Miss Molly" hyacinth to bloom. A pair of bereaved parents came each summer to get a bouquet from the garden for a little green mound. "Our child loved your garden so much," they would say.

When Nora Fox passed a flower on to a friend, she tossed a petal that started an avalanche of beauty, good cheer, and love. It may go on for a century or more.

Indeed I think that the aunt they called "poor Molly" was the richest relative I ever had. Certainly, despite much misfortune, a meager income, and a heavy mortgage, she proved to be our family's greatest philanthropist.

❧

The North Side of the House—The Joneses

On my mother's side of the house, of the good old practical Jones blood, we also had a variety of aunts and uncles.

PEACHES AND CREAM

There was the pretty aunt who, remarkable to say, was as lovely in disposition as in features, and her features were lovely indeed. Her skin was of the tint and richness of cream that came to the top on the crocks in Grandma Jones's milk house. Her cheeks were as pink as those of the peaches we brought in from the orchard—but they turned even pinker when they were mentioned. Her hair was a little darker than new molasses, and long, and just wavy enough. I used to enjoy watching her sit in the sun and comb it, or stand by the washbench and turn it white with soapsuds, then rinse, rub and sun it, and stand by the bureau and do it up.

This aunt had the most company and got the most letters of any member of the family. It was she who took care of the parlor, which was to be expected, for she used it the most. She had a great many beaux, some steady, some transient—she got three gold-headed silk umbrellas and two boxes of candy one Christmas. All that, I thought, was too much for anyone woman, especially one who didn't like to walk in the rain or sun and didn't care for candy.

I never could discover what became of that candy. She didn't seem to eat it, and she didn't seem to pass it around. It just stayed out of sight, mysteriously and curiously. The umbrellas: I lay awake at night trying to figure how she would ever get the use of them all. I knew that, being a Jones, she would have to. Perhaps she finally did. Ladies had to be protected in those days, and umbrellas and hatpins each served two purposes.

It was this aunt, Aunt Daisy, who did most of the dainty jobs around the house. Whatever she did seemed dainty. She was the only person in the family who could peel potatoes, cut up cabbage, and wash the dishes with an air of grace and artistry.

There was the aunt who was always greeted with "Aunt Mamie, tell us a tale!" She could spin the grandest yarns and could make them seem so real that we would laugh or cry or shudder as the story suggested.

Those were truly a great part of the good times when we sat at evening on the doorsteps beside Aunt Mamie and heard about Red Riding Hood, Bluebeard, or the Three Bears.

I am sure we could all have listened to her telling of the Three Little Pigs, and of Goldilocks and the Three Bears ten times in succession. Another story we liked was "Beauty and the Beast." Aunt Mamie made that so perfect in detail that we could almost see the frightful beast, and the sisters whose eyes were red from deliberate applications of onion juice. Secretly, I thought it took supreme courage to put onion juice in one's own eyes, no matter what the incentive.

There was another story also, about two men and a bushel, or was it a half bushel, measure? Anyway, it had glue smeared into the bottom of it. And there was a mother-in-law who was propped up in the buggy even after she was dead. The two men in the story were named Great Claus and Little Claus (or was it Claws, or Klaus?).

I remember only a few incidents of the story now, but it was one of our favorites then. Especially thrilling when Great Claus knocked over the dead mother-in-law and thought he was going to hang for killing her. There were a number of Aunt Mamie's tales that I never heard elsewhere and never saw in a story book. She herself didn't seem to know where she had found them. Perhaps, I'm thinking now, many of them "just growed." We three children were, I am sure, eager and inspiring enough to make stories grow in the fertile mind of a hard-pressed story teller.

Another auburn-haired, pink-cheeked aunt, was one whom I regarded as chief among feather-bed artists. She could make up a big fat feather bed with the squarest edges and smoothest pillows of any other woman in the family. She took care of the upstairs at Grandma's house, made the beds, swept the matting floor coverings, and kept the clothes in order. All dresses were spread over a line stretched across the corner of each bedroom and covered with a sheet to keep off dust and fading. Another thing I remember about her was that she saw to it that every member of the feminine part of the family put her hair-combings into the proper hair-receiver.

I looked forward to the day when all that hair would be untangled and made into switches. Saving combings was a proper practice in those days. That hair came in handy for "rats" and switches, which were used to bolster up the size of clubs, braids, or pompadours.

This aunt, like the older two, was married and taken away from home before I could remember a great deal about her as a member of Grandma's household. I do remember visiting her in her Nashville home, however, the summer I was ten years old, and riding for the first time on a street car; and also, just previous to the street car ride, having my first strawberry soda! Excitement, strawberry soda, and a jostling street car ride on a hot June afternoon didn't fit well together. I gave up the soda and to this day the very term, "strawberry soda," makes me uncomfortable.

Of the older aunts I knew little except that they were industrious, that they were ladylike, and that they liked to make pretty things with their fingers. Articles of handicraft all about the house were credited to them. The what-not, and many of its ornaments, we owed to them. One was the poetry-loving Aunt Ada who kept the scrapbook. She was the aunt who was "different." I suppose every family has at least one who is different. But both those aunts had died before I was born.

And of the uncles: there was first the Great Bear—he really wasn't so bearish as that may sound, but he was big and dark and hairy, and his voice was so heavy and his hair so bristly. I just used to play-like he was a bear.

Then there was the jolly, fattish uncle who would let us ride on his knee, his foot, or his back, according to how the notion struck us. His idea of fun was to romp with us on the floor or in the yard; or to catch and hold us and count our ribs with his stub of a thumb, and make us giggle and squirm and squeal— until, as he said, we "stole sugar." He also taught us some of the grandest games, "I Spy," "Fox and Goose", "Poison Stick," etc.

We adored the Jolly Uncle. We appreciated him even more in later years, and after we learned that he probably had more worries and heartaches than any other member of the family. But worries never showed in his face nor in his ways with us, as children.

Then there was the primped-up uncle. He was as handsome and as neat as the youngest aunt was pretty. He was kind and pleasant in disposition, but we children somehow always admired him from afar. We couldn't play with him as we did with the jolly uncle, and yet we didn't fear him as we did the bearish uncle.

The youngest uncle on the Jones side of the house we called Bubber. He was young enough to play with us, yet old enough to know everything, or so we thought.

He knew exactly how to cross the sticks to give a kite the proper shape and balance, how to tie and stretch the strings around these sticks, and where to put paste on the paper cover. He knew, too, how to mix and cook the flour and water that we used for paste.

He knew, almost to an inch, how long a kite's tail ought to be, and whether to lengthen or shorten the tail if the kite wouldn't go up. Moreover, he knew just what time of year to make kites, and which way to run so they would catch the wind as I, who was the tallest of his nieces and nephews, stood on tiptoe to hold high our homemade flyer.

One of the joy-peaks of my childhood was the day a kite actually flew. It flew the full length of the string—all the string we could buy at the village store with Sunday School money we had saved back for two Sundays.

It flew so high that one or two of the grown-ups came out in the orchard to see it, then a mere speck in the sky. But how tight that string was! Some of the family prophesied that the string would break and then we would lose the kite, cord, tail, and all. Whether it did or not, I don't remember; but I do remember wishing we could have had at least one more Sunday's pennies so we could have flown her out of sight.

Bubber could make doll furniture, just right for dolls the size of mine, and strong enough for them to sit on in the little cardboard playhouse he also made. He whittled out the parts for the furniture from soft wood and fastened them together with pins and small nails. He even painted one suite of furniture, the one he gave me for Christmas.

⟡

Uncle and a Steam Engine

Neither kites nor doll furniture were Bubber's chief interest. The ache of his heart and his principal efforts were toward steam engines. A steam engine at the time was his God, no less, and what was his God was mine. I have watched him sit for what seemed hours, staring at the picture of the toy steam engine in the mail-order catalogue, and staring at the black letters and figures about it, "Only $1.98."

As heartbreaking as anything I remember of my childhood was the way that boy wanted that steam engine. But the nearest he could ever get to it was 78 cents. With all his savings, and all my savings, and all our embezzlement of Sunday School pennies, that amount was all we could raise. That $1.98 seemed as far away as a million and ninety-eight thousand.

There seems an old law of nature which decrees that if we can't get our must-haves in one way, we will in another. So we two resolved that if we couldn't buy a steam engine, we'd make one.

I don't remember whether we began with the furnace or with the boiler, but we finally got the two together in a far corner of the orchard. We selected a spot that would be out of sight of the house, one that was well-screened by blackberry briars and sassafras bushes.

The furnace was made of field stones and some good stiff clay for mortar. To make our mortar doubly strong we got some ashes out of the kitchen stove and some salt out of the meat barrel in the smokehouse. With these we plastered the whole, just as we had seen Grandma patch the cracks in the oven of her box-stove. That mixture should make the furnace smoke-tight.

The boiler had started out being a syrup bucket. Grandpa always kept "bought" syrup on hand. Whatever this omniscient young uncle did to the bucket to put it into its final form was more than I can remember now, but there was a matter of cutting and soldering. I do remember that. I remember, too, that when he had it in place, it lay on its side instead of sitting on its bottom as I thought a respectable syrup bucket ought to do. But he showed me again the picture in the mail-order catalogue and convinced me that a boiler should be placed that way.

A salmon can, or rather a stack of salmon cans, made our smoke pipe. I was busy making blackberry jam in a sardine can

I found in the lane, but I helped Bubber all I could with the "engineering" by bringing articles and materials that he needed from the house, barn, and woodshed.

I didn't understand a great deal about what he was doing, or why, but I listened carefully as he explained, and I took great pride in the whole affair, especially the whistle. That was the part I understood best.

It had a "governor," I remember. It had some wheels made of Babbitt metal (I could remember that because it always made me think of rabbits). We melted the white metal and molded the wheels in a shoe-polish box. He pointed out that in some ways our engine was almost as good as the one in the catalogue. But to me the two didn't look alike. And looks counted much in my conception of steam engines.

Almost as Good as the One in the Catalogue

It seemed days before we were ready to start the fire, but at last the time came. I had a pile of dead grass and twigs and broken brush ready beside the furnace, then I was permitted to go to the house for matches. I got them off the mantel in the kitchen, after first seeing that Grandma was well settled with company in the front of the house.

The fire started off well, and we were jubilant. The boiler got hotter and hotter, but no whistle blew. We wondered if, when it did, the grown-ups at the house would hear it and come a-meddling. But we didn't have long to wonder. In fact, we never did know how loudly the little whistle might have blown if it had had a fair chance.

Just then Uncle Herman, the primpy uncle, came traipsing through the orchard with his rabbit rifle on his shoulder. He saw our smoke and bounded into the thicket wanting to know what in the world we were doing!

We tried to explain, but all he could understand was that we had put water into a syrup bucket, sealed it up tight, and built a fire under it—we were fixing to blow our heads off, he said. He kicked the bucket off the furnace, stamped out our fire, and went to the house to "tell Pa." That was Grandpa.

Even worse! He didn't merely tell Grandpa. I think that Grandpa would have smiled and understood. But tragic for us, especially for the machinery-loving Bubber—he told his Ma. And that was Grandma!

CHAPTER 5

Goin' to Grandma's

Messing with Dough

Women of my childhood were divided into two classes, those who would, and those who would not, permit a child to "mess with dough," that is, take the scraps left from biscuit-cutting or pie-trimming, roll them thin, and cut out little biscuits with a thimble, or make tiny pies in fruit-jar tops or in the tin lids of baking powder cans.

The women on the south side of my family tree would, but those on the north side would not. That may have been the reason I long felt that I had come from a house divided against itself and feared that I'd never be able to stand long in the same attitude on any particular subject. Not that I'm chameleon-like; just unstable and inconsistent. I'd find myself swaying first toward the north, then toward the south side of the family tree. Those sides were so different that the strain was hard.

Not only would the south side of the family—the Usserys—which was that of my book-loving Grandpa and my active-minded Grandma—permit a child, namely me, to mess with dough; they actually encouraged me; although when I did so I scattered flour all around the marble biscuit board and on the floor, and caused the cedar rolling pin to have to be scraped and washed all over again.

If Grandma Ussery was making the breakfast biscuits she would save the "trimmings," put them into the little cracked and handleless cup that she used for measuring buttermilk, and place them—with a saucer for a cover—over on the back of the kitchen table, ready for me to "roll dough" when I should come to her house later in the day.

If Grandma was not able to be in the kitchen, and if black Aunt Elviry was making the biscuits, Grandma would instruct her to do the same. Aunt Elviry, with her white apron and her wisps of kinky hair tightly screwed up on scraps of stocking legs, was a likable person, but not altogether tactful.

She frequently called my attention to streaks of gray in the dough I was rolling, and declared that she wouldn't eat any of my cooking "fer love ner money." Grandma never seemed to notice the gray, but she didn't eat any of my biscuits and pies. Only Grandpa Ussery, among all the grown-ups, seemed to have an appetite for child cookery. He and I together, up in the little office, could eat almost all the thimble biscuits that a cupful of trimmings would turn out. Grandpa would even taste my pies—not the mud ones, but the dough ones. If they chanced to be burnt or under-done, Grandpa would say: "Why, Tot, that's just the way I like them." It is probable that the limits of

Grandpa Ussery's endurance and patience with grandchildren were never reached.

However, Grandma Ussery was generous and indulging in other ways. Many times I have known her to take the thimble off her finger while she was busy darning, and let me have it for as long as I wished to cut biscuits. I strongly suspect that Grandma didn't like darning very much anyway. At least, she gave up the thimble willingly.

One day Grandma gave me a thimble all my own. It was very small and very light, but very, very precious. It was a present I treasured most next to my book. On the day I received that thimble, I felt that I had made a great step toward becoming a woman grown.

☙

The Snuff-Box Churn

Another industry which the south side of the house permitted, even encouraged, was my effort at churning. Not grown-up churning—Aunt Elviry did that—but snuff-box churning. Grandma saved all her snuff cans just for my churning. She even took to buying the largest sized snuff boxes available, the big dime-size tins, so that I would have larger churns.

While splitting kindling Grandpa would watch for straight pieces of soft pine or cedar which could be easily whittled into snuff-box churn-dashers; and when such a piece was found he would carefully lay it away on a high shelf of the woodshed.

On a rainy afternoon or chilly evening by the fire, Grandpa would whittle out a smooth little round handle and two small flat pieces to be crossed at the bottom of the handle and fastened in place with a shoe peg or the top half of a broken brass pin. When a hole had been punched through the snuff-box lid large enough for the dasher handle to slide through, I'd be ready for milk.

Aunt Elviry usually was willing enough to give me half a snuff-box of milk. I'd have liked a box full, but she advised against that. Sometimes it was "sweet" milk, sometimes buttermilk, but as I suspect now, rarely cream. Grandma, however, would even give me cream to churn in the little contraption, as she called it, but I don't remember ever getting enough butter to print. At times I used soapsuds for milk and, fellow churners, what a fluff was there. I took out suds "butter" by cupfuls.

Thus churning, crocheting, rolling dough, listening, and looking over old and new papers and books, were favorite pastimes when I visited across the street in the Ussery household.

Vacations on the Jones' Farm

When we went to visit the Joneses, who lived what seemed a hundred miles away, then matters were different. There we lived a wild and woodsy life, free as the wind and about as capricious (when we could get out of sight of the prim and precise grown-ups). We managed very well, however, for we had to be accounted for only at mealtime, naptime, foot-washing time, dark, and on Sunday afternoons.

First-cousin-to-Paradise to us three little town-lot youngsters was that small, edge-of-the-village farm of Grandma and Grandpa Jones. There was the big, grassy, front yard where we were expected to play all dressed up and very gently on Sunday afternoons in case any of the neighbors, the preacher, or passers-by might see us. There was the big, bare, backyard which we were expected to sweep with brush brooms on Saturday mornings, and there was the serene and darkened parlor of afternoon nap acquaintance. Aside from those places, all the rest of the farm seemed just about perfect.

There was the barn lot, which was always a source of interest, and the barn which we used to advantage on rainy days. We jounced in the haymow, borrowed a plowline from the gear-room, made a swing from the rafters, rolled and skidded down the corn pile in the crib; and, if you'll cross your heart you won't tell, ever, I'll confess that we were the "mice" that ate the pumpkin seeds that Grandpa had spread on a suspended board, high in the loft to dry.

He never could understand how mice got up there to those pumpkin seeds. By moving part of the haymow up under the board, we could reach them. After eating plenty and filling our pockets, we would move the hay back to its place again. I still think pumpkin seeds taste better than pumpkins.

There was the meadow, too, or the "lower field" as it was called. The clay in that meadow, especially in the deeper gullies, was perfect for making mud pies, cakes, and bricks, and for realizing other culinary and architectural ambitions.

It was in the meadow that the pound apple tree stood guard (or tempter) over the gate. I couldn't understand why or how that tree happened to be in the field instead of the orchard across the lane, but there it was.

There was the orchard prolific in apples, peaches, pears, saw-briars, birds' nests, sassafras toothbrushes, blackberries, dewberries, wild strawberries, quail, and crab apples. Also, there was the chicken-yard with its dense thicket of wild-goose plums.

There was the pasture field where we children rode Old Fan, all three of us on the dear, one-eyed, old nag. We'd manage somehow to get her blind side up close to the rail-fence corner, or up to the ladder-like pasture gate, then by "mane" strength and plenty of pushing and pulling, we'd manage to mount.

On the Dear Old One-Eyed Nag

Best of the well-loved places of Grandma 'n' Grandpa's farm was the Big Woodslot itself, with its crunchy leaves, mossy glades, clean woodsy smell, cool shades, bright patches of sun, tall trees to climb, numerous playhouse sites, rabbits to chase, birds' nests to spy into, pond, and spring-branch to wade, yearling calves to harness and ride, and its snakes and lizards to throw rocks at.

If the grown-up Joneses and our ex-Jones mother had any inkling of our darings, our outlandish (and to them heathenish) adventurings in that woods-lot, that natural and perfect playground, their hands would have been raised in horror, their hair would probably have risen straight up out of their psyche knots, and we would have been confined ever after to playing "Mrs." in the grassy front yard. Or perhaps to making whistles and popguns from the stems of the pumpkin leaves.

Who knows, we might even have been called into the house and taught to do embroidery—in the summertime! However, fortunately for us, they supposed, or we supposed that they supposed, that we were being nice children in the woodslot. Perhaps we were—as nice as wild young animals.

Getting Ready

That is all getting ahead of the story: First, there was the "goin' to Grandma's," the Great Adventure in its beginning. Out of every year we spent approximately three weeks during the summer at Grandma 'n' Grandpa's little farm. We spent the other forty-nine weeks either looking backward to the last visit or forward to the next.

From before the time school was out in May, Mama began getting our clothes ready for the big trip. Why she put so much work on those garments, considering the life we lived there, was more than I could understand. However, Mama had been a Jones, and the Joneses had ideas about impressing the neighbors. So I supposed she was trying to make us look as though she had married well.

At any rate, there were ruffles and laces and ribbons galore— a whole stack of new dresses and starched petticoats for Elsie and me. There were two-piece "little boy suits" for Clarence. They consisted of bloomers for underneath wear and box-plaited, embroidery-trimmed "dresses" for top wear. As Clarence grew a little older, he was promoted to dresses with sailor collars, or Buster Brown styles with fluffy black silk bow ties.

Looking at the matter through my Ussery eye (I suppose I did inherit at least one of my eyes from the unpretentious Usserys), I remember thinking that something to wear on the train; something that wouldn't show coal-dust; something to wear in the woods; something that wouldn't tear or show apple stain and mud splatters; and perhaps an outfit of Sunday School clothes for each of us, would have been all we needed. However, both Mama's eyes and most of her ideas had come from her side of the house. So we wore laces and stiffly starched linen to mud-pie makings, to grapevine swingings, and to sapling-steed tournaments.

There were weeks of cutting, basting, stitching, tucking, "trying-ons" and finishing before we could go to Grandma's. Even then there were in the big trunk, in the two big canvas telescope valises, in the little brown grip, and in all the extra bundles, barely enough clothes to last us the three weeks. We did look "stylish" during those three weeks, I am reasonably sure of that, even though fruit stains, saw briars, hay-mow skidding, and such, made a new wardrobe necessary for each of us when we got home again.

I remember that the immediate "getting ready to go" was truly an exciting and exasperating ordeal. It was a strain for the entire family except Papa, who was away all week at work on the railroad. He wouldn't begin his part of the visit to Grandma's until the last Sunday we were there, so Mama had the brunt of getting ready to go, and she seemed to revel in it.

When a neighbor had promised to milk the cow, feed the cat, water the flowers, and gather the eggs (Mama was always a backyard farmer); when the big trunk and two valises had been packed, strapped, locked, roped, labeled, and sent in the grocer's wagon to the depot; when the windows had been locked, barred, and nailed down; when the doors had been locked and propped with chairs (except the front one); and when all the shades had been drawn except the one nearest the kitchen corner bathing place and the one nearest the bureau in Mama's room where the last primping would be done—then Mama began the final steps of getting us ready.

She brought out the old Saturday night tub and put it in the kitchen behind the stove (we bathed behind the stove in summer as well as winter), then she laid out other bath appurtenances such as towels, soap (castile for that occasion and borax extra), pair of scissors for nails, box of talcum for necks and noses, and comb, brush, Vaseline, and hair ribbons. There was also a leg or sleeve from a suit of last year's underwear, which was cut into suitable size washrags—Mama had subtle ways of taking spite out on Grandma Ussery by never using on us one of the hand crocheted twine-string washrags which she supplied us lavishly on birthdays, Christmas, and other gift occasions.

Clarence was scrubbed first and hardest. There was scouring powder for his knuckles, knees, and ankles, and sometimes for ours. I remember one time after he had been given his very thorough bath, he was dressed only in his next-to-'ims (it wasn't nice to say drawers and drawer body) because you know what a three-year-old can do to a white linen suit if left two hours to his own devices. So semi-dressed he was put in the front hall to play while the rest of us got ready.

Elsie and I then had our ears gouged with a well-soaped washrag, and had our hair, long, fine and full of snarls, untangled to the accompaniment of yelps and tears. Usually Elsie's hair would have been rolled up the night before on strips of stocking legs, so it had to be untwisted and coaxed to arm-pit-length curls and topped off at the upper left with a large pink satin bow. My hair was brushed and combed and Vaselined, then tightly skewed into pigtails. Each pigtail was then tied with a piece of eel-skin which Aunt Ann had given me, as it "would shorely make a young'uns hair grow." My bows, one behind each ear, were always blue, when I so much coveted pink ones.

She Put A White Linen Suit on the Boy

After we had been talcum powdered and had donned petticoats, dresses, new patent leather "baby-doll" slippers, leghorn hats with flowers around the crown, streamers behind, and quarter-inch elastic under our chins, and after Mama was all ready except for putting on her soutache-braided Eton jacket and her rose-covered turban with its stiff maline bows; then she made ready to perform that next to last rite—put the white linen suit on the boy.

She walked out into the hall, but the boy was gone, drawers, drawers body, and all. We looked for him upstairs and down. We called and searched and wondered. Then we found that someone had left the high latch on the front door unfastened. Outside we began a wider search. He was not in the yard; nor at any of the neighbors; nor anywhere up or down the street. Could he have been kidnapped? Gypsies passed that way occasionally!

We were just about to call the police, when we saw a man coming from toward the railroad leading the little near-nudist underwear-clad boy by the hand. He had been in such a hurry to "go to Grandma's" that clothes hadn't mattered. He couldn't wait for us women folks to get primped up. Of course, we felt he had disgraced the family name running around in such an unclothed state, so it was good for our pride that we were leaving on the next train, or were hoping to.

Had it not been for that good old Jones' family trait of starting to get ready plenty of time beforehand, the delay caused by the lost boy might have made us miss that wonderful "choo-choo" as he called it, and as a result we would have been a day late in going to Grandma's—stark tragedy!

⚭

On the Train

But we made the train and once aboard there was a mad scramble for next-to-the-window seats. Once we were settled, each by a window, Mama heaved a deep sigh of relief—relief that we were all packed up, all dressed up (and certainly we were), and that we were on our way. Unless there occurred a cinder-in-the-eye catastrophe, or some similar upset, we would give Mama no further concern for some time. She had earned that brief rest.

I remember how impressed I was by how fast the telephone poles, fences, houses, and country roads sped past our windows. I remember exactly how each railroad depot looked along the way, and how the loafers on the depot platforms looked at the people on the train. We felt rather important to be stared at so.

I can remember how the trainman came through in his dark trim uniform, singing out the names of the stations:

"D-a-r-k-s Mill—C-A-R-T-E-R-S' Creek—Spring H-i-l-l —Thompson's Sta-tion—F-r-a-n-k-l-i-n—B-r-e-n-t-wood—

N-a-s-h-ville." I cannot spell the names as he drawled them, but you, too, know the chant.

Then the train-butcher's wares. The big polished apples, oranges, waxy delicious looking bananas, packages of chewing gum, and best of all were the little glass trains, lanterns, and pistols filled with colored candies. Only another child can imagine how we longed for those. However, after so long a time we knew it wasn't worthwhile to ask, or even to hint for anything in the butcher's basket. We could only look and wish. Mama always said that the "stuff on the train" was too high, cost two prices, in fact. So we never owned a glass train, lantern, or pistol, and never tasted a butcher apple, orange, or banana.

We always took our own food along with us, and such food! Eating supper on the train was the height of the trip. It was a watched-for moment when Mama rose from the red-plush seat, reached to the rack above and brought down the twine-tied shoebox full of food.

The top layer was of biscuits, some plain to eat with the ham, crisp and greasy. The next layer was of biscuits, some plain to eat with the chicken and some with piccalilli, or green-tomato chow-chow soaked through, and others filled with blackberry jam or pear preserves, syrup and all. On the bottom layer were thick slices of cocoanut, chocolate, and pound cake.

Tucked juicily in among the other delicacies were some of Mama's specialties such as peach sweet pickles, apple pie flavored with bits of stick cinnamon, egg-custard pie heavy with nutmeg, cucumber pickles, and salmon croquettes. By the time the box was opened, some hours after it was packed, all flavors blended. Eating supper on the train was the next thing to a Sunday School picnic.

It was no wonder that Mama found good use for the damp washrag she had brought along in anticipation, to clean those three sticky faces and six greasy hands, all embellished with bits of pickle, preserves, jam, and chocolate icing. Mama had the rag carefully wrapped in one of the many special packages. Sometimes it had to be re-wet during the procedure.

After supper there had to be drinks all around. Like little drunken sailors we reeled to and from the water cooler at the far end of the coach. Sometimes Mama tried to drench us by bringing what water we required in one of those little collapsible cups she carried in her pocketbook, but too often the cup collapsed before it reached its destination. Besides, we were sure that the water tasted better when taken broadside from one of the big tin cups that were chained to the barrel cooler. There we could drink just like everybody else.

⚬

Union Station

I can never forget how high the steps at Nashville's new Union Station seemed in those days when our legs were short, nor how much fun it was to slide our hands along the sooty hand rail although we were well scolded for doing so. That phase of misbehavior called out the wet washrag as soon as we were settled for our long wait between trains in the palatial "Ladies Waiting Room."

I could never see the need of changing trains in Nashville, but like other conveniences and inconveniences it was accepted as part of the Great Adventure. It was fun anyway to slide our new slippers over the glass-like tile floor, and to trace the tile patterns with the point of Mama's umbrella, which was among our other bundles.

Time after time we were shushed and told to behave ourselves or we would get a whipping, and all that sort of stuff, but it was hard indeed for us to sit still when we were so dressed up and going to Grandma's.

One important phase of the trip was gathering up all our bundles from the "baggage table" in the center of the waiting room and trailing with Mama halfway up the block on Nashville's busy Broad Street to a fruit market to buy two dozen bananas as a surprise for Grandma's folks. We rarely bought bananas except on this special occasion and they were always a great surprise to those that Mama called "the home folks."

Lantern Under the Surrey

We always arrived in White Bluff after dark. Uncle "Bubber" met us at the depot with Old Fan hitched to the topless surrey. Grandma's phaeton was never uncovered or taken out of the buggy-shed except on special occasions, and then never at night nor in bad weather. It was never allowed to travel in mud, and the night air was not good for its shiny finish. Besides, the phaeton couldn't be seen at night, so what was the use taking it out. That phaeton was chief means of impressing the neighbors on Sundays, at funerals, and on special occasions. At night the family used the rusty, rattley, mud-spattered old surrey.

In the dim light of the depot platform, with all our baggage, the sack of bananas, and the wet washrag, we climbed and piled into the old open surrey. We jogged down the town's main street, which was neither more nor less than a bumpy country road that seemed always muddy. This muddy appearance might at times have been caused by the light from the lantern swinging under the surrey, but usually there was real mud, especially in ruts and holes.

Often we had to "sooey" the hogs out of their mudholes in the middle of what was to become U.S. Highway 70, "the Broadway of America." One night, as I well remember, we ran over the rear elevation of an old black cow slumbering in the roadway. How she groaned, scrambled up, and jangled her bell. We screamed and clutched for something to hold to. Since the surrey had no top, we could catch only at the air and each other. As the old cow rose to her feet halfway between the front and back wheels, we thought the surrey would turn over for sure.

This would have been particularly tragic on that occasion for among our other bundles on that night was a decorated wedding cake for one of the aunts whose marriage was to be a special event of our visit. It was lucky for us and the wedding party that the surrey was soon down on four wheels again. The old cow sighed, and we did too. That frightening near-accident might not have happened if Fan hadn't been blind on one side, and if the old cow hadn't chosen to sleep on that side of the road.

Fido and Bugler were always first to greet us. We would hear them barking even before we started up the hill to Grandma's front gate. Then we could see the light in the hall, the silhouettes of Grandma and Grandpa, all the aunts, uncles, and cousins coming out to meet us. There were hugging and kissing all the way around, front gate to house. Then we went inside.

I can see it even yet, the lamp lit old "settin' room," couch under the window, double decked bureau, sewing machine with its head under a box-like cover and its damask scarf spread over it all. I remember the calendars of various ages on the wall; one with a picture of a race horse labeled "Dan Patch," one with a steaming train "The Dixie Flyer," and others of fruit, fish, and flowers.

However, we stopped in this room only long enough to lay down our bundles, take off our things, and open and pass the sack of bananas. After kissing us again all around, Grandma would declare that she knew we "poor things must be starved to death," and she would hustle us off to the kitchen and uncover the table for us to eat another supper.

I can never forget how that kitchen-dining table looked and smelled. Grandma's table was "set" at all times. All that was necessary to put it into service was to remove the "table cover," which consisted of eight flour sacks flat-felled together, and to turn up the plates. The plates were always turned face down over the bone handled knives and forks. All the spoons stood in a spoon holder in the middle of the table to hold up the cover.

Grandma had two tablecloths for everyday use. The red-and-white checked one was used one week, the blue-and-white one the next week. I was always glad if we could arrive at Grandma's during red-and-white-checked tablecloth week. Meals from that seemed more cheerful.

Back to supper: after we had been well filled with "cold vittles," which always made up supper at Grandma's house, it was time for one of the aunts to light an extra coal-oil lamp from the small table in the corner of the back hall and lead us off upstairs to sleep. Mama had a big feather-bedded four-poster in the company bedroom, and we had "Baptist pallets" on the floor around her.

We could hardly wait for next morning. Somehow we never cared to sleep late at Grandma's. There was too much to be seen, done, and tasted. Somehow, no matter how early we got up, by the time we got around to the fragrant old kitchen and back-hall summer dining room, it was time for breakfast. However, before we were permitted to come to the table, we were shooed out to the back porch to wash up. This seemed so unnecessary.

∞

The Foot Bucket

There we dipped the shiny tin wash-pan into the rain barrel under the eaves. After fishing out the wiggle-tails we would wash our hands and faces, or more accurately, dampen our palms and chins, and wipe them dry (and more or less clean) on the meal-sack roller towel which hung nearby. We never failed at some time during the ablutions to slide our fingers over the fragrant cake of pink "florescent" soap that Grandma always kept on the washstand. Then, if anyone doubted our cleanliness, we could let them smell our fingers and know thereby that we had been to the washstand.

Washings over, it was the part of etiquette (and compulsion) to pour the sudsy water into the wooden candy bucket, which we called the "foot bucket" beside the washstand. This was a bucket with a purpose, or rather with more than one purpose. First, it conserved used water for further uses. Second, it served as the place where we children would have to wash our dirty feet when we came in from play in the evenings. We would take turn about standing there almost knee-deep in the old wooden candy bucket (more or less conscientiously, but in either case languidly), scrubbing the top of one foot with the sole of the other, then reversing the process, and taking out first one foot then the other for inspection.

When we had either washed off or loosened up the worst of the grime we would step out and wipe off the remainder of the dirt and the dingy water on the foot-towel, which had been the face towel the day before. When the foot-bucket's evening work was done it was carried by one of the uncles to the front yard. There the washings of the day served to refresh Grandma's geraniums, the ones parading in whitewashed buckets along the cobble-stone and shell-bordered front walk.

Now back to breakfast. It was at the breakfast table that Grandpa's hospitality shown. It was the height of his pleasure to see us children eat. He sat across the table and watched us with much the same expression on his face that he had when he sat on the pig-pen rail fence and watched his fattening pigs champing their corn.

Besides the "bought grub" that Grandpa brought from the store as special treats for us as company, there was an abundance of food from the farm, garden, orchard, smokehouse, chicken-yard, cellar, dairy house, and Grandpa's mill. My grandparents could never have imagined a toast-and-coffee breakfast.

A typical, ordinary, everyday breakfast began with fried chicken and "wooly" gravy, and/or fried ham with marble gravy (no bacon—only po' whites and colored folks ate side-meat). Then there were eggs—fried, boiled, poached, or scrambled—on dishes piled high. In addition to the meat and egg dishes/here were bowls of fried apples, almost candied with brown sugar, fried potatoes, fried corn dotted with lakes of butter, cornmeal mush with milk or oatmeal or both, stewed peaches, apple sauce, plum jelly, pear preserves, jam, honey, molasses, and pickles (sweet and sour). (Those last half-dozen or so staples were kept on the table at all times.)

Then there were hot biscuits, one plate at each corner of the table with plenty of butter nearby, three kinds of milk (we had a choice of sweet milk or buttermilk on the dining table, or clabber from the thick white pitcher on the side table). There was a big pot of Arbuckles' coffee exclusively for Grandpa. He got up early in the morning, ground a cupful of the coffee beans from those that Grandma roasted every Saturday, and made a pot of coffee when he made the fire in the kitchen stove so the womenfolks could cook breakfast.

There was tea for Grandma, usually "tea-kettle," or cambric tea, merely hot water and milk. Ladies didn't drink coffee, and certainly children didn't. Coffee would make children turn black. Usually we drank clabber milk. That seemed the whitest of all breakfast drinks. Daily we watched for Grandpa's complexion to change.

After breakfast when we had washed the remnants of breakfast from faces and fingers, we had play-aprons tied about our necks, and sunbonnets or wide brimmed hats tied under our chins. We were warned to keep those on because sunburn was then almost a disgrace, and to be freckled was the next thing to being "common." Well-protected from sunshine, we were off to the fields and woods.

On our way to the woods, we stopped in the barnyard to watch Grandpa curry and saddle Old Fan to go to the mill and the shop. Then we watched Grandma turn out the newest calf and start the morning milking.

❧

Super Grade A Raw

Obtaining the family's milk supply was a ritual that Grandma trusted to nobody but herself. As people said about her milking, she was "particular." She really was, and was vastly proud of it. As she explained, milk at its best was dirty enough and there wasn't any need of putting extra dirt in it. The product that Grandma took to the spring-house after milking time would surely have rated Super Grade A.

Grandma took with her to the "milk place" three vessels besides the pan of water and towel for the old cow's udder. There were the bucket and strainer, which were sunned all day, aired all night, and scalded before and after each milking with boiling soda water. They were placed high on a fence post and covered with a clean wet flour sack. Also there was the ever-present Jackson cup (a half gallon tin measure with a lip on one side and a handle on the other) and it was this she used to milk in.

After giving the calf his suck all around, Grandma roped him off with a plowline and a cob. The cob went through the slipknot loop under the calf's jaw and kept the silly fellow from choking himself. After the udder (we always said "bag") was well washed and dried, the flank well brushed (with Grandpa's curry comb and brush), Grandma took her cup in hand (it had been hanging upside down on a fence-paling), and began to take her share of the milk.

No milking stool for Grandma. She stood, or half-stooped, at arm's length and made each spray bury itself in the exact center of the fluff of foam in that half-gallon cup. It was a marvel to me. I suppose Grandma never milked directly into a bucket in her life. No sir, that was a slovenly and dirty way to do, and she was particular.

Grandma's cows always had descriptive and distinctive names. There was Old Cherry, veteran of the herd (mother of most of the others). Then in succession, Old Red, Old Pied, and Old Brindle. All other bovine animals on the farm were called simply "yearlings," even though they may have been as big and as old as the milk cows. The cows all had bells, so they could be found if lost. They all had calves or near-yearlings, so they would come home at night. They all switched flies, and Grandma. We children would volunteer to hold the old cow's tail while Grandma was milking, and she let us take turn about.

Once in a while we'd let it slip—then, Boyee!—what a wallop Grandma got, right across the eyes. Cockleburs and all.

CHAPTER 6

The Piano That Wasn't

Friends

When the barnyard's morning activities had quieted down, the cows had been milked and turned out on the road to their grazing for the day, the last little galloping calf had been herded into his lean-to-stable and securely buttoned in, and when Grandpa and Old Fan were out of sight around the bend of the road, we were again ready to start on toward the woodslot.

First, we had to stop by for Maude and Pearl and Eddie who lived down the lane. They were regularly our playmates, and they knew a wealth of delightful games and woodsy secrets. Goin' to Grandma's wouldn't have been nearly the fun that it was without Maude and Pearl and Eddie. We would hop, skip, dance, trot, and canter up the lane between the orchard and the lower field. We climbed over the big gates. I can't remember when we tried to open a gate, a big one, that is. Those gates, with their well-spaced horizontal slats, were made to be climbed.

Near the big gate in the lower field side was the old pound apple tree with the biggest, mellowest, juiciest applies I have ever known. Strange to say, as many times as we went to

Grandma's that tree was never barren, the apples never scanty, sour, nor green.

I remember the time my brother wheedled Mama out of a highly prized pearl-handled lady's pocket knife. It was the one she kept in her letter box for special purposes like sharpening pencils, ripping seams, or trimming corns when Papa's razor wasn't at home. We well understood that it was something to keep our hands off. However, on that morning Clarence had managed to borrow it for "just a few minutes," but forgot to give it back.

When we reached the pound apple tree he nonchalantly drew the knife from his pocket and proceeded to peel an apple—a rare performance in our group—we took our apples straight and our peaches fuzz-first. Eddie envied him. I knew he did. We all did. Possession of a pocketknife in those days put a boy almost into the capitalist class.

The Biggest, Mellowest Apples

Anyway, about that time, Elsie discovered a nest of blue eggs high in the tree. Boy like, Clarence dropped apple, knife, and the straw hat under his arm to skin up the tree and see the nest. When he came down the knife was gone. Clarence declared that the hogs had eaten it. So we fearfully awaited the death of the guilty shoat.

I don't know how the thought of this impending tragedy affected the other children, but I actually lost sleep over it wondering what Grandpa would say about the loss of his pig, and what Mama would do about the loss of her knife. The dire possibilities were an overwhelming shadow to me. We watched and looked for days, but no hog died and no knife was found.

I'd rather not mention what the boy got for losing the knife, but will state that hair brushes were dual purpose in those days. The smokehouse was both jail and jury room. The smell of a smokehouse makes me sigh even today, and it's not altogether a sign of nostalgic longing.

If, in going to the woodslot, we followed the path by the potato-house or went by the cider shed and up through the orchard, we were certain to stop at The Playhouse. Many times our route was planned that way. The route also took us by the sweet-apple tree, the Hoss apple tree, (named, they said, for Old Bishop Hoss and not Old Fan's kin), through the sassafras bushes, the plum thicket, and by the crabapple tree.

The Playhouse was most important. How I pity children who have never known what it is to play "Mrs." in a real playhouse. It had a roof, which we could barely reach, walls, and a chimney just like grown-up houses. It had a window that would open and close, a door with a miniature latchstring, and a latch. In style it was much like a gingerbread house I had seen somewhere in a storybook.

The walls inside were papered with funny papers, which extolled the adventures of Mule Maud and Si, Buster Brown and Tige, the Katzenjammer Kids and the unfortunate Captain. There were pictures on the wall, too, of bright colored birds which came with the Arm & Hammer soda that Grandma put in her cornbread and biscuits and used in scalding her milk vessels. Pasted to the ceiling were pages from *The Youth's Companion*, which Aunt Ada took for a while. There were also these pages from *Godey's Ladies' Book*, *Delineator*, *Ladies Home Journal*. With all these decorations, if we became bored with our own company while in the Playhouse we could read our wallpaper, or try to.

The Playhouse had a real little front yard, one about the size of Grandma's Sunday dinner table, a real fence around it with gate and a latch, and real flowers growing in the yard.

The uncles and aunts had made this little playhouse and had planted its yard during their own growing up days. What a debt we owed them!

The playhouses that took most of our attention and time were the ones that we ourselves made in the woodslot around the roots of trees, on sand beds in gullies, on large flat rocks swept clean with brush brooms, but most frequently in the corners of the old zig-zag rail fences. The fence row corners were perfect for houses of many rooms.

~

Woodland Arts

And with us always were Maude and Pearl and Eddie. Maude was plump and ruddy, Pearl was thin and frankly freckled, and Eddie was just an ordinary little boy, even though he did grow up to be a banker.

Among them they knew many of the woodland arts, such as how to make a popgun for dogwood berries; where the best berries could be found; how to make a whistle from chestnut twigs; and how to ride down a sapling and make it behave like a wild and prancing horse. They knew, most of the time, which saplings to ride, but sometimes they made mistakes. Maude rode a sassafras once and it broke, so did the arm she fell on. One day Pearl rode a sapling of stubborn oak, or tried to, and got suspended in mid air. It took the combined weight of the five of us to get her close enough to the ground that she could turn it loose.

They knew how to make little furnaces and how to cook the products we could find in orchard, garden, and chickenyard. We tried to make jam in an oyster can, but had no sugar. We tried to fry slices of sweet-apples, but had no grease. From the amount of smoke that got in our eyes we decided that maybe the Indians didn't have such an easy time after all. Food that would cook well on an outdoor fire was hard to find.

We did have a rich haul one day, however. We found a hen's nest out back of the playhouse that we were sure Grandma didn't know about. Maude, Elsie, and I gathered up some of the eggs in our aprons. Pearl, Clarence, and Eddie brought up enough wood to replenish the fire. Not having sufficient cooking vessels to boil or fry the eggs we decided to lay them all on the tin shingle top of our little furnace-stove and let them bake.

It was not until the fire began to burn lustily that we realized that the hen who had owned the nest was about to become a mother. Well, we didn't eat any more of our cooking that day. And we hardly ate any supper that night either, despite the fact that Grandma had specially prepared egg custard, dressed eggs, and cornstarch pudding.

Better than anything else Maude and Pearl and Eddie knew how to make woodland playhouses, and with their coaching and our own originality, that became our favorite business, too.

Every mossy bank or shady grassy plot made us think of playing house. If there were several such places close together each of us set up housekeeping, and among us we established a "town." The boys, of course, had to run the store, the mill, and the blacksmith shop, but in our "towns" those jobs were not too difficult. Before the house sites could be allotted, there had to be a counting out with some such rhyme as:

"one-two-three. Mother caught a flea"

or

"One-ry, oh-ry, ick-o-ry, Ann."

Sometimes we didn't count; we just drew straws, broken leaf stems, or blades of grass to see who got the shortest straw for a choice of locations.

Once a space was allotted we would sweep the floors of our respective residences with brush brooms, leaving neat the bright moss, the smooth grass, the rough stone, or the bare ground. Then we locked our houses with a tick-a-lock, tick-a-lock clucking sound we made with our tongues, and fared forth in search of furnishings.

&

Imagine

If a stone or plank was found that could be imagined into the shape of a bureau top it was hurriedly placed in a bedroom which, by the way, was partitioned off from the dining room with rows of stones or broken sticks. Those made effective walls. We had walls of the same kind around our houses, and one was honor-bound not to cross such a wall without the unlocking procedure with the proper key and tick-a-lock sound.

It was not always hard to find a rock shaped somewhat like a bed. Of course, a bed might have five sides instead of the conventional four, but we overlooked such small defects. We could "imagine" one side off.

We found flat, square-like stones sometimes that could serve as pillows if propped up at the heads of our beds. Wild grape leaves made pillow shams. All the good housewives we knew— our mothers, grandmothers, and black mammies—had pillow shams. We imagined that ours were embroidered in turkey red to say "Good Morning" or "Good Night."

Large flat stones with smaller stones under them were tables. Acorn cups and hickory-nut hulls were dishes. Frequently we found large empty acorns that would serve as vases or jardinières for the yellow sheep sorrel or pink oxalis "lilies."

House furnishings for those play-like villages required all of our ingenuity, much imagination, and considerable searching. We roamed the woods, fields, and roadsides looking. Occasionally one of us would be extremely fortunate. Being fortunate meant finding such a prize as a piece of broken colored glass, a blue fragment from a quinine bottle, a brown one from a bitters bottle, or a green one from we didn't know what. At any rate, the glass-possessor became the envy of the other five.

What we couldn't find or imagine, we were obliged to make. That was where the clay in the lower field came in. With generous lumps of this mud, stingy little dabs of water, dipped and toted from the nearest hog-wallow, or transported in whatever containers we could find from the chickenyard-trough (formerly a stove door), or from the pond or spring at the far end of the woodslot, we tediously met many of our household needs with clumsy mud-covered fingers, or with little paddles pilfered from Grandpa's kindling shed.

We made bowls, cakes, bricks, and vases. I tried to make a cedar water bucket like the one that held place of honor on the washstand, but having no bail and no brass bands my bucket turned out to be just a deep clay bowl. Eddie said it looked like a salt gourd, and I wouldn't speak to him the rest of the day.

We attempted to make from mud any household furnishings we needed except, of course, our lace curtains, bed "kiverlets," chair tidies, and our table cloths. These, like certain articles of our apparel such as belts, caps, bracelets, and aprons, were made of leaves using stems to "pin" them together.

Maude was the oldest of us, the one who could outdo all the rest with both accomplishments and ideas. The last summer we played in the woodslot she was thirteen. I had just turned twelve, but I felt twelve-and-a-half when I was with her. Often I harbored a slight grudge because of the fact that I hadn't been born sooner so I could be as old and important as Maude. Anyway, when she got a bright idea, I tried to get one too.

One day Maude found a sort of humped-up rock that she called an organ. She began at once to make a parlor for the prize. A parlor like the ones our mothers had. One that would be so fine that she wouldn't use it for anything except company, courtships, weddings, and funerals. One of the boys, she said, would be the preacher and could come to her house, eat dinner, and hear her play the organ. Both the boys were five years old so they made small protest.

~

The Piano

Well, if Maude had found a piece of blue glass, one of brown, one of green, one of red, and piece of broken mirror besides, I couldn't have felt worse about them all than I did about that brown stone organ she had placed on the green moss carpet of her rail-fence corner parlor.

All the rest of the morning I searched the woods, the pastures, and even the lane, orchard, and cornfield for another humpbacked rock, or better still, one that could be imagined into the shape of a piano—a piano like the one we had at home in Sunday School. No such rock could I find.

That afternoon Maude and Pearl and Eddie had to go to the church to practice for Children's Day. Not being native we didn't have to go, or as the other children said, we "couldn't be in it." So after dinner and naps we went back to the woods. Again for the umpteenth time I searched for a piano-shaped rock. I didn't find one that even my imagination could con-scientiously use. At last, disappointed, but not down, I went back to my rail fence residence, next corner to Maude's. I took an imaginary key from my imaginary pocket and turned it in the lock. I made a click with my tongue and went into my house to sit down and think.

Hadn't I met other difficulties? Hadn't I made vases of clay when I didn't find acorns large enough? Hadn't I made skillets and bowls and buckets? That was it. I would make a piano of clay. I'd go into seclusion and not let the others know what I was doing no matter how hard they might beg. I'd make a piano just like the one at Sunday School.

The piano was not completed until after the other children had already gone home for supper. I was brimming with pride. I admired its slick brown sides, spit-polished top, almost well-shaped keyboard, and even its little lion's paw toes, which I added as an afterthought. These made it look more stylish and really more parlorish than ever. I lifted it gently out of the ditch and placed it cat-a-cornered in the mossiest spot of all in my zig-zag residence. Then I took one more admiring look and walked out. I turned the key again in the lock that wasn't there, put the imaginary key in my pocket of like kind, and danced and trotted down the lane to the house, thinking how I would gloat over Maude the next morning.

That night the rain came down like public opinion. It rained so hard that Grandma had to get up during the night and come upstairs with the dishpan, washpan, two pudding pans, and a slop jar to put them under the chronic leaks so the water wouldn't circle the straw matting on her bedroom floors.

Next morning the whole world was wet. The barnyard was a loblolly mess. We were delayed somewhat in getting off to play because Grandma said the grass was too wet and the lane too muddy for us to be out. We finally got away, scrambled over the big gate, and skipped up the lane toward the woodslot. I could hardly wait until we could get to the playhouses, but first we had to stop for Maude and Pearl and Eddie. They hadn't finished their after-breakfast chores. While we waited, I confided to Elsie and Clarence that I had an enormous secret, but I wouldn't tell them what it was.

At last the others were ready, and we all hustled off to the woods and our rail-fence village. Proudly I led them to my house, but I didn't turn the key in the lock. I saw, we all saw, that my beautiful piano had melted. All my art, all my afternoon's efforts, all my cause for exaltation had settled down into a lump of sticky clay mud.

All My Art, All My Afternoon's Efforts

CHAPTER 7

Chalkdust

Double E, Double F, O, C

Much of my education was acquired before and after the days of school attendance. Of course, by benefit of taxes, I did learn some things. But I began on the three "R's" before I started to school and I've never finished them.

My first reading was done from the family high chair placed beside the kitchen table. That doesn't prove that I was a precocious youngster. My sister wasn't born until I was four years old, and she didn't need the high chair until I had reached the age of noticing the letters on the oatmeal box, the coffee bag, and the newspapers which Mama put under my plate to save the tablecloth and floor.

It was probably to keep me out of other mischief that she would let me sit in the high chair beside the kitchen table while she rolled biscuits with that fat white rolling pin and board, or frilled pie crusts for Papa's coming home on Saturday nights.

As she worked, I asked questions. In later years she said I'd never get forgiveness for all the questions I asked as a child.

The first literary peculiarities that caught my attention were the two "E's" on the coffee bag. They looked like little white three-legged stools lying on their sides.

"Who turned the stools over?" I asked Mama.

She had to explain that the two little marks were not stools at all, but E's, and that they helped her to know what was in the coffee bag—as though she couldn't tell by smelling!

Next I asked about the turned-over stools with broken-off legs. These she said, were F's, and they also helped her to know what was in the coffee bag.

I soon learned the O; and then the C, which seemed like the O that wasn't all there. Then I knew how to read COFFEE—except that I read it always EE FF O C. It seemed more natural and interesting to begin with the turned-over and broken-off stools, then the whole O, and the broken O, or C.

OATS was my second accomplishment. I was attracted first by the O, which was already familiar. Then the S which was funny and crooked. The A looked like a chicken coop. And the T was a post with a plank on top, like the trellises in Grandma Ussery's grape arbor.

But all my reading and querying were not done in the high chair. There came to our house in those days two periodicals, *Hearth and Home* and *Comfort*. I learned to spell the titles of those, and in the daily papers too, I could frequently find letters that looked familiar—O's, E's, A's, T's, F's, H's, and other capitals. The small letters were just an uninteresting mass.

My first real accomplishment in reading, the first time I was able to spell out two words and put them together, came one day as I was lying on my stomach on the floor near the stove in Mama's room. Mama's room at our house was sitting room, living room, everyday reception room, family room, dressing room, and bedroom. On this day it was also sewing room and library. And from the odor of "middling" meat and white beans boiling on the "air-tight" heater, it had aspects of a kitchen also.

Mama sat at the sewing machine near the window while I sprawled on the floor over a newspaper, laboriously searching out letters I could recognize. Finally I found a whole group of familiar shapes and spelled out slowly, "F-O-R S-A-L-E." Mama told me what the words were, but she had a harder time explaining what they meant.

I had, however, as I thought, learned to read the newspaper; and as soon as the newsboy came each afternoon I ran out to get *The Herald*, spread it out on the floor, and hovered over it, searching out every insertion of the words, "For Sale." Advertisers would have been flattered by my early tastes in reading.

ॐ

Lead Pencil Publications

Shortly after learning to read, I learned also to write, or rather, to print. With a penny pencil, heavily chewed, and scraps of wrapping paper salvaged from the kindling-box behind the kitchen stove, I began making newspapers, books, and magazines—their total contents running something like this: "FOR SALE OATS COFFEE HEARTH AND HOME COMFORT."

Wobbly printing it was indeed. And Grandpa Ussery was my sole subscriber, and only reader!

At some time during my very youthful youth, I wrote a poem. It came about this way:

One day in my usual fashion, lying on my stomach in the middle of Mama's room floor, I was perusing my periodicals, *Hearth and Home* and *Comfort*. By this time I had learned to read even the letters that were not capitals, and to print in the same medium.

Near the back of one of the magazines was a page of "Songs and Poems Requested." This department was very interesting to me, and more readable than any other part of the magazines—except the ads!

In one issue a reader asked the editor to print a poem entitled "The Dying Girl," beginning—

"Raise the window higher, Mother;
Air can never harm me now."

The editor regretted that he did not have a copy of the poem.

My sympathy for editors and readers must have begun there. I would, I thought, obligingly write a poem that the editor could print for the dear lady.

So with stubby brown pencil and a piece of pinkish grocer's paper, I began:

"Raise the window higher, Mother;

Air can never harm me now."

What else I wrote will never be known, but I remember thinking at the time it was a very good poem. It had rhymes, some four line stanzas, and everything. And according to the development of the idea, the girl finally got the window up, even though her mother, like mine, was afraid of what the night air would do for sick folks or well.

After much deliberation and continued pencil chewing, the poem was finally completed. Then I ventured to try to read it to the only available audience, Mama, sitting there at the sewing machine.

I started reading, but had no more than finished the first stanza when—I don't know whether it was the telephone or the doorbell or the beans boiling over—there was an interruption, and before Mama ever seemed to realize that I was reading a poem of my own making, she was called from the room.

When she returned, I waited quietly but eagerly for her to ask me to continue reading. But she never did.

After a long time I crept away to the dining-room closet, the dark place under the back stairs, thinking I'd bury my unappreciated masterpiece there. Then I remembered that in the spring Mama would surely clean out the dining room closet; so I was afraid to leave it there.

Instead, I decided that the safest thing would be to slip that bit of paper up under the drawstring of my blue calico sailor-waist blouse. For days, even when I changed to the black and white sailor waist, that poem reposed in my bosom.

After several days I gave up hope of ever finding an audience or being asked to read my poem; so sitting on a stool, alone by the stove in Mama's room, I took the poker, fearfully pried open the stove door, and made a burnt offering of my literary creation.

❧

A Formal Education

On my first day at school I learned, or was told, that the teacher "saw a cat." I couldn't understand, however, why she thought that was so important; or why she continued standing there by the black wall printing words and talking all the time about how she saw a cat, a hat, a rat—when we knew she didn't.

But I didn't. So I wouldn't.

Then she tried to get me to stand up there by the black wall and say, "I see a cat." "I see a rat." But I didn't. So I wouldn't! Grandma Ussery had told me I mustn't tell "stories." And certainly there was neither a cat nor a hat in the room, much less a rat. I was beginning to get ideas about that teacher. And she seemed to be getting ideas about me.

At last she told me to go back to my desk. She seemed to think that by doing that she was punishing me. But I didn't mind because that was where I had left my wrapped-up lunch— ham and biscuits, jam and biscuits, pickle and biscuit, and a big red apple. So I didn't mind at all.

I settled down in the too-high seat, swung my feet for a while, looked around at the other girls with their pigtails and their striped and checked dresses; then I remembered the apple! I took it from my blue denim satchel, rubbed it slick on my sleeve, and proceeded to bite sweet juicy chunks from its reddest side.

Well, sir, that teacher, rest her soul, stared at me, raised her hands, in horror, and looked as though she had never before seen a little girl put food into her mouth!

She swooped down to my desk, snatched the apple away, and began saying things about not eating in school, and other things. She said so much and looked so frightening, I felt hot all over and put my face down on my arm to cry. I wondered why we had to have school and teachers anyway; and I wanted to go home to Mama.

Once I got up from my seat and started home. But that woman caught my arm and marched me back to that old desk again.

Unending hours, it seemed, I sat there in agony and embarrassment, wondering how much longer I could endure it. Each time I raised my head, the teacher looked hard at me, and the girl across the aisle, the big one with two pigtails and a plaid dress, crooked her finger at me under her desk and whispered, "Shamey, shamey, Cry Baby." Then I'd start crying all over again. I hadn't cried so hard since my rag doll, Susie Jane, was washed off down the gully.

I wanted Mama, and I hated school. But there seemed to be little I could do about either my wants or my hates.

The longer I was there, the more I wanted to go home. At last, when it seemed that I couldn't possibly endure it any longer, the teacher opened the door and let us go outside. What a relief!

The out-of-doors had never seemed so welcome. I set out as fast as I could in the direction I thought was home and Mama. I had not gone far when I came to a fence, a high fence with no gate. Then indeed, I began to cry. I cried and ran, blindly following the fence, and calling as loudly as I could, "Mama, Mama, Mama!" I know how a lost lamb feels.

Then a bell rang. That frightened me even more. So I ran faster and faster, and cried louder and louder, calling for Mama and hunting a gate. Just as the gate came in sight, and as I doubled my speed toward it, two of the bigger girls ran up and caught my arms, one on either side, announcing that it was not time to go home—it was only recess! Another word to be stored among my dislikes was that word, "recess." A word that cheated!

Indeed, like a lamb to the slaughter, but not a meek lamb, I was dragged back to the schoolhouse between those two "Judas goats." I'm not sure I ever liked either of those girls as long as I knew them.

That was my first day of suffering. Others followed until I became actually ill. How much of the illness was mental and how much was physical, I don't know. But it was welcome as long as it kept me away from school. My first grade education was acquired in a matter of a few misery-filled days.

In the second grade I must have become either callused or interested. At any rate, I seemed to bear up better. In the second grade I scored one on the teacher. Although I had learned in the first grade that a little girl mustn't eat in school the apple she brought to school, in the second grade I learned that it is all right to eat the apple if you can do so when the teacher isn't looking. The girl across the aisle taught me that and helped with the eating.

It was in the third grade that I memorized the states and their capitals. A long and monotonous process that was, for I had no idea what states or capitals were. I got them down, however, from Maine-Augusta, to California-Sacramento. I could sing them off like multiplication tables, and I understood them about as well.

That state chant, however, was an awful nuisance. Every time company or some of the kinfolks came, Mama would call me into the house, no matter how busy I was with mud pies or doll houses, to say over and over again the states and their capitals. My school-acquired knowledge was a wearisome burden indeed, a distinct liability!

☙

The Playwright

In the fourth grade I wrote a play, not that the teacher could be directly blamed for that; fortunately or unfortunately, she never knew. Some of the older girls—I always played with older girls—thought we ought to have an entertainment; but they bemoaned the fact that we didn't have a play, and the teacher wouldn't get us one. I didn't know much about what a play was, but I felt sure I could make one if I could understand what it ought to have.

I had, remember, made a piano.

They finally explained how one ought to go; so after much hard thinking, I filled four pages of my tablet with "play writing" and passed it over to the other girls, Lola, Maggie, Mabel, Louise, and Frances. There were six of us in all, and the play was made to include the crowd.

I had planned that each one of us should be dressed in a long-waisted white dress with stand-out skirt, a very much stand-out skirt. We might have to wear as many as four petticoats to make our skirts stand out as much as I had planned.

Each of us would wear a crown of daisies on her head, and a chain of daisies around her neck, and we would hold hands! I think I had seen a picture like this somewhere. I drew some pictures along with the play-writing to show the girls just how we would look with our daisies and wide, short, stand-out skirts.

But alas, the poor play never had its "first night," nor even its first Friday afternoon. None of us had the courage to show it to the teacher.

No "First Night." No Friday Afternoon.

The Lie

It was in that same fourth grade that I accomplished my first lie—the first I remember; the last I admit. Nellie Mai and Chester, two of the classmates who were more friendly and understanding toward me than most of the others, had acquired some wonderful animals they called guinea pigs. And guinea pigs, guinea pigs were the talk continuously. They were shocked that I had never seen any guinea pigs.

I must have suspected after I admitted that I hadn't, that honesty might not be the best policy. But the real lie evolved eventually and indirectly.

Each afternoon Nellie Mai and Chester begged and pleaded with me to go by their house and see those pigs. "It wouldn't take more than a minute, certainly it wouldn't," they said. Their house was hardly a block out of my way, and the guinea pigs were right in their front yard, near the sidewalk. I could look over the fence at them. It wouldn't take a minute.

I hesitated long before yielding. It must have been several days, perhaps a week that I refused. I knew well, for Mama had told me many times that she watched the clock from the time school was out, and she knew how long it ought to take me to come home. And if I didn't get there by the time I should, she'd know I'd been fooling along the street somewhere, and when I did come in I'd certainly "catch it!"

It never did occur to me to tell Mama about the temptation and how very much I wanted to see those mysterious animals. Mama just didn't seem to be the kind of person who could appreciate a guinea pig.

Finally, the tempters won. And circumstances seemed to favor us. We were dismissed a few minutes earlier one afternoon, and Nellie Mai, Chester, and I agreed that the fates were for us, although that isn't the way we thought of it or expressed it. We ran every step of the way in order not to lose any of the precious tell-tale time.

I arrived. I saw. And I thought the sight was worth whatever "catching it" I'd catch. But a guilty conscience told me all the way home that I'd stayed too long, I'd be found out. I'd better think of some way to fix things up. I thought easily and quickly.

The minute I put my foot on the first step, my excuse for being late left my lips.

"Had to stay in," I announced nonchalantly.

"What for?" Mama asked.

I hadn't thought of a reason, but one came easily. I was supposed to take a new reader-book to school that morning, but the books were all sold out before Mama could get to town and buy one; so I glibly replied, "Because I didn't have my new reader."

That excuse was ideal. It would put that old teacher in a bad light with Mama, I reasoned. Then I gaily went on to the kitchen to see what was left from the noon meal.

I didn't know until later, but Mama went straight to the telephone to "bless out" the teacher for keeping in her child for not having a book when there were no books in town.

The teacher suavely explained that the precious child had not been kept in, but, on the contrary, had actually been dismissed several minutes earlier than usual.

Oh, boomerang lie!

And, oh, the look on Mama's face when she summoned me from the kitchen to her room. Whether she used the hairbrush or razor strap, or whether it was "peachtree tea," I don't remember. But I do know I caught it. I was forced to explain.

Then I caught it again. I got some extra for the way Mama felt about blessing out the teacher.

It didn't help matters any when Mama explained that it wasn't for seeing the pigs, but for telling a "story" that I was punished.

Nevertheless, I've never been able to look comfortably at guinea pigs, even to this day. And I never could read "Pigs is Pigs" after I heard that it contained twenty millions of the creatures.

It was in the fourth grade, also, that I vowed: "If I live to be eighty-nine and have a hundred daughters, never, never will I make one of them wear a "nice little white dimity pinafore apron." Never should a child of mine wear an apron.

You see, my mother, like other mothers, was determined that her child should have the best of everything, especially the things she wanted when she was a little girl, and most especially the things she didn't get.

So early in my fourth year of school, just as I was beginning to bear with teachers, and as I was beginning to feel ever so slightly that I might become somewhat like the other girls, about that time Mama made up a year's supply of nice little white dimity aprons with ruffles and lace and Hamburg embroidery and straps over the shoulders and strings for bows at the back. Along with these she made a generous supply of nice little white sunbonnets with ruffles and starch and even splints of cardboard slipped into tucks to make them stiff, and strings to tie chokingly under my chin.

However willingly or unwillingly, I donned that apron and fresh white sunbonnet the first morning, I never again donned them willingly. All the other girls who didn't have aprons and sunbonnets—a sum of one hundred percent minus me— laughed at my sunbonnet and apron and called me, Grandma! Grandma! Grandma!

Of course, I rushed home in tears. But Mama merely sniffed or sort of snorted when I told her. She explained that the reason they laughed at me was because they didn't have any pretty white aprons and sunbonnets. Wasn't that just what I had been telling her? They didn't have any. And I didn't want any. I didn't want to wear things that the other girls didn't. I didn't want to be different.

But no. Mama had made those aprons and sunbonnets for me to wear to school. They were just like the ones she had wanted when she was a little girl. They were pretty. They were the very things for little girls to wear, and I was to wear them. She was determined on that. I might as well forget that foolishness.

But I could forget nothing. My tormentors saw to that.

"Grandma! Grandma! Grandma!"

In the fifth grade I learned that a noun is the name of anything. And to me it was a name, merely that and nothing more. Then I learned that an adverb modified (I called it "mortified") adjectives, verbs, and other adverbs. I learned, too, that a verb "denotes action, being, or state of being." But I didn't understand any more about the "state of being" than I did about states and their capitals.

Oh, education is an awful ordeal when you are very young or very stupid; and it is painful indeed when you are both! Let those who will sing of "happy school days." I cannot join in the chorus, for I must have missed the happy ones.

In the sixth grade I learned that the blond young man across the aisle was very good to look at. In the seventh grade it was a brunette in a blue shirt. He seemed even more pleasing in appearance. And never, never shall I forget the day he offered to carry my books as we walked home from school. Not to be described was the thrill I had when he took my elbow to pilot me across the mud at the street crossing. I could show you that exact street crossing, even today!

In the eighth grade I learned that Henry the Eighth had six wives, or was it Henry the Sixth who had eight wives, or was it seven? I heard it emphasized, too, that Caesar built a bridge—in the fourteenth or seventeenth chapter, I forget which! And that he crossed the Rubicon; he came; he saw; he conquered; and fell in love with Cleopatra.

I was also exposed to a course of spelling and arithmetic, and to one on how to sprinkle commas and semicolons among words. But those courses, like my smallpox vaccination, didn't seem to "take."

CHAPTER 8

Yellow Jasmine and a Hope Chest

A Hopeful Despair Barrel

Certain parts of my education were really broad. But neither Caesar's bridge nor his conquering seemed very important to me then. By that time, you see, I was desperately in love. First it was the blond, then the brunette, then a sandy haired dandy.

During high school days I had a number of love affairs, although in most cases nobody knew of them but me. It was usually the handsomest young man in the class that I admired from afar, and most unobtrusively. I am sure that not a single object of my affection ever suspected that he was so honored. There seemed in those days no really ladylike way of letting a young man know he was admired. And, poor, timid maiden that I was, I suppose I should have died outright if I had thought that anyone suspected how deeply and irreparably in love I was. More suffering in silence. For half a dozen years or more, I had one heartbreak after another, all of the silent kind.

Summer vacations between school terms were not too exciting. Mama usually kept a few boarders who were in for the morning and evening meals. I was roused out of bed far too early in the mornings and assigned to the duties of putting wood into the stove, making biscuits, and setting the table. After breakfast came dishes, floors, and beds. What monotony!

I was trusted to peel and stew potatoes and make hoecakes for lunch. Mama never would risk my cooking ability too far, but as a special treat she did let me make myself a chocolate layer cake for my birthday. After lunch each day I lay down in the parlor to take a nap, because all the family agreed that I seemed generally "run down." At supper I again peeled potatoes, put wood in the stove, set the table, rolled pie crusts, and cut biscuits. After supper, dishes again, and so to bed.

This program was varied sometimes by a Rook game with some of the neighbor girls in the evening, or with sitting in the front yard in the summer afternoons crocheting pillow-slip edging for my Hope Chest—or Despair Barrel, as kid brother Clarence called it. There were few beaus or dates, for Mama was strict, and she let that be known throughout the neighborhood.

Occasionally the neighborhood girls and I were permitted to "go out walking" on Sunday afternoon. The most thrilling place we had to walk to and through was the cemetery. I think we memorized the inscriptions on every monument there. We knew more people dead than living. But the nicest thing about going out walking to the cemetery was coming back home by the depot. And there was plenty of life there when the late afternoon train came in!

Of course we girls were occasionally allowed a slumber party, just a small one of course, where one or two or three went to spend the night with another one or two or three. Of course, there was very little slumbering done at such parties. Mostly just giggling.

But the most fun of all was going to the Fair in late summer. Again we traveled in packs; and did a little flirting with the young men who also were traveling in packs. Of course, we had opportunities every Sunday to go to Sunday School and Church, and to the young peoples' meetings in the early evenings. And occasionally one of us would pull a "walk home" date. But all of our parents were "strict."

⚬

What Goes Around…

In the late fall after the summer following high school graduation, it was decided that I must try school-teaching to get a little experience in the wide, wide world, and to help out with the family income. I was still not quite half past eighteen, and certainly I couldn't have been trusted with a school of my own. But Aunt Molly and her daughter Edi' Mai had contracted to teach a three-room school down in Georgia, and I was to teach the third room. Aunt Molly taught first and second grades; Edi' Mai sixth and seventh; and I had that very interesting group of third, fourth, and fifth.

The locality was in the south-central part of Georgia, at Dexter near Dublin, and the county of Laurens, one which the school superintendent said "paid out more money for Tennessee mules and Tennessee school teachers than any other commodities." From the time I got my first monthly paycheck of $30.00, I had little doubt as to which "commodity" was considered more valuable—even though there did seem to be more children than crops.

My clearest recollections of those days are of the charred pine stumps in fields of white sand; sweet potatoes fresh out of the hill; juicy cane stalks that the children brought to the teacher in lieu of apples; the nostalgic odor of fatty pine knots burning in stoves and fireplaces in late evenings and early morning; ribbons of green that were cotton rows; beauty of yellow jasmine and blue and white violets blooming in the piney woods; the flavor of peanut-fed, fresh pork, hoecakes; fat biscuits (tender and flaky); cane syrup; white and fluffy butter; and grease-soaked collards.

I remember well my most embarrassing moment. I wanted very much to make a good impression on our new landlord who had agreed to board us three teachers for $11 a month each. Mrs. Faircloth needed some water in the kitchen and to show her how smart I was I grabbed the wooden bucket and rushed to the well to draw some for her.

Somehow in my hurry and enthusiasm I let the chain slip through my hands too fast and dropped bucket, chain and all, right down into the well! In my misery I felt that my reputation, my career, my chance of continued teaching in Georgia all went to the bottom of the well with that bucket. I knew I was sunk, for Mr. Faircloth was sitting on the porch and he had seen the whole performance. And Mr. Faircloth was on the School Board!

I felt that I could read his mind as he sat there leaning back and puffing his cob pipe—that the Buckhorn School Board wouldn't want to keep a teacher that couldn't go after a bucket of water and come back with even the bucket.

But Mr. Faircloth, as I learned later, was really a prince of a man. He acted as though dropping the bucket in the well was an everyday occurrence for everybody. He reached up to a nail on the wall and brought down a hayhook attached to a plowline. With a little fishing he brought up bucket and chain and made no unpleasant comment.

From then on I would have been his slave. In the afternoons after school I would help him and his daughter, Miss Naomi, with whatever chores they would permit me to do. I helped shuck corn for the shoats; I helped seed some special cotton that he didn't want to send to the gin; and in the evenings by the firelight I sat in the family room until bed-time and shelled peanuts by the pan full. Those peanuts were for seed, and had to be carefully handled. And when the time came for a new turn of meal, I shelled corn until my thumbs were blistered. Indeed I paid well for that dropped bucket.

The fact that most of the girls in that neighborhood were married at fifteen or younger made me in my nineteenth year practically a spinster. In fact Edi' Mai and I both might have been considered "on the shelf" in another community, but there, girls were scarce, and boys were plentiful; and after all we *were* the new teachers. So every swain who bought a new buggy or broke in a new mule tried the same out with us.

We went to candy-drawings, tent meetings, play-parties or folk dances, neighborhood singings, funerals, sitting-ups, quiltings, and just plain "out-drivings." There was little or no monotony.

Jasmine and Violets

As much fun as anything else were the Sunday afternoon "out-drivings." Most of the time we had a different young man, a different new buggy, or a different young mule. But as spring approached and Valentine's Day came and passed, I was more inclined to go out-driving every Sunday afternoon with the same young man. That same young man also was more likely to be he of the steady date on Wednesday night, as well as Sunday night. Yes, springtime became an era of "specialization" as to dates.

Sometimes on the out-drivings we'd let the mule pick his way slowly along the sand-boggy country road; sometimes to a neighboring town for ice cream; sometimes to a community singing or church service; more often we let him choose the beautiful old Swamp Road, with its masses of green bay leaves and wild honeysuckle, yellow jasmine, and other woods flowers; and with gray Spanish moss overhanging from pine, live oak, or cypress "knees" in the bog.

The yellow jasmine was a great favorite with me, I loved to string the blossoms on long strands of wire-grass and make romantic little haloes, necklaces, or bracelets. I felt sure they must enhance whatever girlish beauty I might have, and the young man of the afternoon, whether "steady" or not, never did argue that point as far as I remember.

Of course, the flower I love best in all the world is the shy and timid violet, lovely in its daintiness and delicious in its fragrance. The most violets I had ever seen were in the piney woods of Georgia. Especially in the swamps which have a violet of their own, an enormous and gorgeous white one.

Imagine my surprise one evening to receive from the "date of the day" a very large bunch of white swamp violets. I thought they were the loveliest I had ever seen, and said so. The stems were so long and the blooms were so large the bouquet was as big as a bowl. Ecstatically I buried my face in the depths of beauty! Imagine my shock to learn, not that the lily had been gilded, but that the violets had been scented—and scented with the cheapest and commonest kind of baby talcum! Much as I love the deep purple garden violets, or the paler blue woods violets, I don't think I could ever again look a white violet in the face without a shudder.

Monday mornings we three teachers set out rather early to wind our way toward school. Monday mornings in Georgia were generally fair, and usually Friday afternoons were rainy. Mr. Faircloth said Friday would always be fairest or foulest, and usually he was right.

❧

The Children Were Precious

When the weather was dry the white sand along the road ruts would sift into our shoes, so there had to be stops along the road to take off and shake shoes. And at every rambling farmhouse or cross-roads a group of children joined us, until by the time we got to school we had most of the pupils in train. The children were very precious, sometimes rather mischievous, but mostly well-behaved and much interested in attending school.

It was my luck, good or bad, to have among the third grade pupils the neighborhood's "worst little bad boy." He was a problem child, and proud of it; in fact his family and all the neighborhood seemed proud of his naughty accomplishments. Our private war began on the first day of school; and if I must admit it, he seemed to win just about every battle.

He was big as boys in the third grade go, and he was genuinely an artist at being bad. I tried persuasion, ignoring, diversion, every manner of managing an unmanageable youngster that was in my poor slim bag of school teaching tricks.

Finally I kept him after school one afternoon and resorted to a thorough and complete spanking. My hand burned for the remainder of the day; but next morning the erstwhile bad little boy brought to school a big juicy stalk of sugar cane from his parent's cane-bed, and ever after we were fast friends. He was always the first one who volunteered to get me a switch if another child was misbehaving; and best of all, he passed his grade that year. For the first time in three years he got out of the third grade. We both thought that was an accomplishment.

He Stood Six-feet-two

A pupil in the fourth grade was one who had never been allowed to go to school when he was of school age. He always had to stay at home and work with the crops. However, on the day he was twenty-one and "a man of his own" as he expressed it, he started school. At the age of twenty-four he was in the fourth grade, and in my room.

He stood six-feet-two, and must have weighed nearly 200 pounds. His teacher was a fraction under five-five, and weighed not more than 103. I lived in constant fear of the day when that fourth-grade pupil might miss his lesson or be a bad boy, and need a switching. But I never had an excuse to even keep him in after school.

After those few delightful months of school-teaching and out-drivings in Georgia—when the yellow jasmine had finished blooming and cotton was ready for the children to stop school and chop weeds, we three teachers pulled ourselves away from Georgia's paychecks and romances and returned to Tennessee.

I settled down again to potato peeling, crocheting, and Rook-playing, and Mama's strictness. Mama never could have understood the romance of going out-driving down a swamp road with the white sand underneath and Spanish moss overhead, and bay leaves, white violets, and yellow jasmine all around—or would she?

∝

My Education Continued

Sunday School and Church activities relieved the monotony somewhat, but even a Sunday School picnic in Tennessee was not so much fun as a candy drawing or a play-party in Georgia, not to speak of the sitting-ups (with sick or dead), or the dates with young men who had new buggies and/or spry young mules. In the fall of that year I was old enough to start trying to be a city school teacher in my own neighborhood, and my "education" continued.

Again I taught third, fourth, and fifth grade classes—the overflow pupils from the regular grade rooms. And you can imagine the kinds of pupils the regular teachers picked out to send to the "Overflow Room."

As I got better acquainted with the children, it seemed I had been given the smartest and dullest, the badest and the goodest in school. Each seemed extreme in one way or another. Each child seemed "special" in some way or another, and I didn't feel that I was specialist enough to meet the job. In the afternoons I would feel too exhausted to climb the stairs to my room at home. I'd have to lie down in the parlor, usually, before I could get up and help cook supper.

All too soon, to my way of thinking, it would be time to get up, change clothes, kindle a fire in the kitchen box-stove and start peeling potatoes or mixing biscuit dough for the boarders' supper. Mama always tried to keep a few boarders for two meals a day. They did help to pay the grocery bill, she said, and they could give me some spare time employment potato-peeling and dishwashing before and after school.

Most of the consolation I got, outside of the fun with the children, was thinking about how much money I was making!

In Georgia I had made $30 a month. From this I paid my board of $11 a month, sent Mama $10, and skimped essentials and my home-bound railroad fare out of the remainder.

But in Tennessee, I was paid $40 a month. Half of that went to family expenses, for, as I said, I was living at home. Ten dollars each month went into the bank to pay for going to summer school; and the remaining $10 was splurged on clothes, books, knickknacks, or whatever a young girl's fancy dictated. There were times, I admit, when the dictates had to be slightly pinched because the city school required better clothes than had been necessary for the country one.

But every day my "education" was continuing. Those "special" pupils taught me a great many things that my own former teachers had neglected, overlooked, or hadn't even learned.

I remember one bitterly cold day. In those days the teachers who arrived too early were permitted to go right on into the warm building. They were supposed to go in, open up, and be ready for the children. But the pupils, poor little shivering mites, had to stand outside in the street until the bell would ring.

I confess it now; I always felt like a first-class heel every time I entered that gate, trudged up the hill and into that warm building before the children did. However, I was too scared for my job ever to mention such a thing to the Principal or Superintendent.

When the doors were opened each morning after the bell had rung the children rushed in like peas poured out of a bag. Bringing up the rear one day was a very small, chubby, black-haired first-grader, with a very red button nose, and fat stiff blue-red fingers. His eyes and nose were running but his feet were not. I guessed by the way he was stumbling along that those little feet must be almost frozen. I didn't know the little fellow's name but a family resemblance led me to believe he was a member of a certain biggish family. If so, he had trudged about nine blocks on that zero morning. Quite a trudge for a little fellow like that, I knew, for I myself had trudged eight.

I led him as close to the radiator as I could get for the other children crowding around; rubbed his stiff little fingers and did what I could about the nose and eyes. Then I remembered the feet. I drew up a chair, took him on my lap, pulled off his shoes and his snow-wet socks, and began to play "Piggy went to market" with his toes.

Years later, a voice on the telephone reintroduced me to this lad. He was by then a famous writer and if there should ever be any gossip about my playing games with his distinguished toes, the entire matter was due to circumstances and weather beyond our control—as you might well understand if you have ever stood out in a chilly street waiting for that old school bell to ring.

Having had little scientific training in teaching, and scarcely any coaching in child psychology, I think I merely acted on instinct, and instinct led me to try to feel and be just one of the children and to try to understand just how each child felt about his surroundings. This, I hoped, would lead to a more complete understanding between teacher and pupils.

That understanding was less than complete I learned when time came for the first quarterly examinations. During three hectic months I had been giving all that was in me toward putting the prescribed geography, history, reading, 'riting, arithmetic, and even spelling into my fourth grade group, as well as into the third and fifth grades.

We were using Frye's big old blue-back geography book, and I had been conscientiously following the book, explaining each sentence, using my handy roll-up wall map to back me up on locations.

On this first exam I took the first question in the Map Questions in the Geography Book—one we had rehearsed for weeks. The children had been well drilled on the Northeastern States, I was certain.

That first question on the fourth grade's first examination was: "Give reasons for the dense population in the Northeastern States." The answer that one of my well-coached pupils gave, in all sincerity, was:

"The reasons for the dense population in the Northeastern States is that most of the people come from somewheres else and they brung dense with them and give it to the population."

In the afternoons after school I generally walked along with whichever of the pupils went my way. But when a rainy day came I could nearly always look out the window about time for school to be out, and see a sleek black horse and a shiny new buggy. Then I knew I wouldn't have to walk home in the rain.

As time went on, sometimes I'd see the black horse and that less-new buggy waiting in front of the schoolhouse even on days that were not rainy. Sunday afternoons there were "out-drivings" with that same black horse and his driver, a sturdy, steady, and persistent Scottish farmer.

Finally, and especially after I had graded that particular examination paper, I decided that I had done enough harm to the teaching profession, and it might be, after all, a good time for me to "reform" from teaching, and get off the path to old-maid-dom by accepting an engagement ring. There seemed to be just one way to get rid of that Scots's persistence, so I promised to take the chance.

He set out to find a farm, one with plenty of rich, plowable land; I redoubled my efforts at crocheting, trying to fill that Hope Chest to the hinges with lace-edged pillow slips.

Out Driving With The Same Young Man

CHAPTER 9

Matrimony and Mulality

And then we were married.

There were several reasons why we didn't take a honeymoon trip after the ceremony. On our wedding night the temperature was seven degrees above zero. Two or three nights later it dropped to thirteen below. That seemed reason enough for staying at home, especially as our only mode of traveling was by horse and buggy.

Another reason we did not make the trip was money, or the lack of it. After we bought our wedding clothes and furniture, and made a down payment on a farm, which we called Knoxdale, we scarcely had enough left for garden seeds—and garden seeds were very important.

There were other reasons, of course: a house to furnish, a farm to plow, not to mention a family to start; and, of course, there might possibly have been at the back of my mind an idea that I didn't relish getting too far away from home with "that strange man."

We started housekeeping during the worst winter our part of the country had known in years. Snow was nearly a foot deep, and that was unusual for Tennessee, especially if it stayed on the ground for more than a day or so. And this snow did. It was plenty cold and our "new" old farmhouse was not built for sub-zero spells.

A big, bleak house it was: a thirteen-room colonial, nearly a hundred years old, with rooms eighteen feet square, high ceilings, big windows, wide doors with plenty of air coming in all around, six hungry black-throated fireplaces, rough floors with a creak in every joint, and oh, so full of vacancy!

Lucky we were that during that January honeymoon we had accumulated nine quilts; and I also felt very fortunate in the fact that the bridegroom was a good wood-cutter. We had four to eight inches of snow over everything most of that winter and all our wood had to be dug out from under it and dried before burning. Don't ask me how we started the first fire to dry the first wood—probably with wedding-present wrappings and corncobs from the ramshackle old barn, bless it.

My farmer-husband had bought the farm because the land was good. The house just happened to be thrown in as an after thought. It was an old plantation manor house built during slavery days and seemed designed to keep slave labor continually employed. I thought many times as I wrestled with the dirt in the cracks and reached for the cobwebs on the ceilings that if Abe Lincoln had ever tried to clean up that house, he might have been tempted to join the Rebels.

A Stove, A Bed, A Hopechest

During some cozy pre-honeymoon evenings, poring over the mail-order catalog, we had selected and ordered all the furniture our budget would bear after the farm's down-payment had been made. And we had been expecting that furniture to arrive weeks, or at least days, before the wedding. But because of the unusually bad weather, shipments had been delayed, and we were obliged to set up housekeeping with a few pieces bought on credit locally or handed down from relatives. We had barest necessities, and not many of those.

Those necessities, however, became the mother of numerous inventions. We did have, fortunately, a cookstove, bed and blankets, a few pots and pans, and several wedding presents, which included four sugar spoons, six butter knives, three pairs of salt and pepper shakers, some linen dinner napkins, four cut glass vases, and a set of silver.

However, we found ourselves woefully lacking a table on which to use the linen and silver, and chairs to use around said table, or anywhere else. Worse, we had no biscuit cutter! And my new husband was one of the kind who must have biscuits three times a day, especially at breakfast. Even if he had toast (or even a hoecake) for breakfast, he wanted a biscuit to eat with it, so I pressed the smallest cut glass vase into service as a biscuit cutter.

The cedar hope chest, which Grandpa Ussery had made for me in teen-age days, was placed in the middle of the big kitchen and used for a table. For chairs the bridegroom used an up-ended soapbox, and the bride sat lightly on a decrepit lardstand.

Necessity mothered around until she helped us find a use for most of our wedding presents except the butter knives and sugar spoons. We carefully wrapped three sugar spoons and five knives in Irish linen napkins, and stored them away in the hope chest as surplus assets.

The house seemed so big and so empty I felt obliged to fill in some of the spaciousness while we waited for the delayed furniture. And a hope chest table with soapbox and lardstand chairs contributed little to artistic meals. So I began rummaging around in basement, barn, and buggy-shed.

The families who had lived there before had obviously done a thorough job of moving. I did, however, find a pair of broken-down carpenter's "horses"—one a little taller than the other—and some old boards that had been used for shelves in the basement; and with a brick for a hammer—almost like a woman of the stone age—I fashioned a table. Rickety though it was, it would display our bridal linens and silver—although there was no one to see them but ourselves. Weather was still too bad for visiting.

Meanwhile my husband had taken ax in hand and gone to the woods to rustle up fuel for the hungry fireplaces and the omnivorous cookstove. That was the meanest cookstove that a woman ever wanted to put her foot under and kick out the door. Before the second meal was cooked we admitted that we had probably been victims of super-salesmanship. Besides, stovewood dug out from under the snow wasn't conducive to the baking of light biscuits.

I had believed before I was married that I really could make good biscuits, but that stove soon taught me otherwise. It sputtered and sobbed and remained sadly cold for an exasperatingly long time after the fire was kindled. Rarely in less than an hour could I get it hot enough to raise the biscuits; and rarely indeed, and then only if the wind was in the right direction, would it condescend to give them a tint of brown.

How I ever did it I don't know, but for a long fifteen years I worried with that old stove. Just because we had paid $42.40 for it, we thought we had to use it. (We really were that "scotch.")

A Town Girl Copes

"Well, they say Alex married a town girl!"

That, I suppose, is the way our wedding was announced among his rural friends and kin.

What the town-bred kinfolks on my side of the house said was probably something like this, "I reckon she's done right well; he seems to be a good sort of fellow, practical, sturdy, steady, and a Christian gentleman."

What his family really thought of the marriage I am not sure, but would suspect that the consensus (with a sigh of relief) was, "He's the one who'll have to live with her."

One thing, at least, I knew quite well when I said, "I do," and went to the farm. I knew I didn't know anything about farming. My farmer-husband fortunately knew a great deal and he delighted in teaching me.

Nevertheless, there seemed a stigma attached to my ignorance. I imagined that the entire neighborhood, and especially the in-laws, were pitying the poor farmer who had married a town girl. "She doesn't know how to do a thing," I imagined they were saying when I was barely out of earshot. So I thought I'd show them. I'd make them say, "What a smart woman! What an industrious housewife! She can do anything! She works all the time! Isn't he fortunate!"

So I Thought I'd Show Them

So, like the woman in Proverbs, I arose while it was yet night to give meat (and biscuits and gravy and hoecakes and hot coffee) to my household. I always took pains to look at the clock so I could tell people what time I got up that morning. I always put a lighted lamp in the front window (not under a bushel), so the neighbors could see I wasn't lazy, not early in the morning, anyway.

☙

Mail Order Education

This may or may not have been the reason I planned to make my garden on the side of the house nearest the road. As soon as the snow had melted enough for the mail carrier to travel our country lane, I sent off a batch of penny postcards ordering seed catalogs and government bulletins. They were to help with my agricultural education.

I got bulletins telling how to raise poultry, cucumbers, tomatoes in greenhouses, treat diseases of fruit trees, make cows give more milk, build iceless refrigerators, remodel kitchens, cure sick calves, make pickles, use tankage for hogs, smoke meat, bake bread, and grow corn. As I remember, there were seventy-one bulletins in that first package. Others followed.

I read and studied those bulletins carefully. Much of the time while Alex was out cutting wood, feeding stock, turning land, fixing fences, and doing other jobs an old farm must have done, I was reading and re-reading how cucumbers ought to be trained, how poultry ought to be fed, how pigs ought to be nurtured. I accumulated such a store of information that soon it was my turn to do some telling, and my time to be laughed at for the impractical things I had found in books. "Book farmer," he called me, also "Book cook," "Book housekeeper," and later I became a "Book mother."

℞

The Most For My Money

One of the first projects that the government bulletins and I tried to carry out was a crop of cabbage. The seed catalogues too were partly responsible for this idea. Is there anything that will fan the flames of early spring garden fever faster than a stack of seed catalogs? These I had; and then, too, I had a skeptical audience.

In the catalogues we got that year the tomatoes were magnificently red; the beans preponderously long, the peas exceedingly fat. But, ah! the cabbages! Such heads I have never seen before or since—except in later catalogues. One head was so large (in the picture) that the gardener, who was admittedly a small man, had to use a ladder to climb on top of it.

So I decided that would be my major crop. Alex laughed at me as much as a Scotsman can laugh. "A man couldn't work on a diet of cabbage!" Then I explained that my cabbages would go to market. He wouldn't have to eat a single head unless he specially wanted to, and even then he'd have to get tolerably cabbage-hungry before I'd put any on the family table. My cabbage growing was to be a business proposition. I intended the cabbages to help raise the mortgage.

Well, who did I think would buy the cabbages, he scoffed. Anyone who wanted cabbage to eat could grow his own, and folks in town who couldn't didn't care about the stuff anyway. There wasn't any need to try growing anything on a farm to sell except corn, mules, and hogs, and perhaps a few potatoes.

But I thought differently. The government and I had ideas about cabbage growing and I had ideas about cabbage marketing, and the seed catalogue bore out both. The plea I made to him was that if he and the mules would plow up that little patch of ground adjoining the garden I would take care of growing the cabbage, and the merchants in town would sell them. I had already investigated that and had a promise of $1 a dozen heads for what they could sell of the earliest crop.

He plowed the ground and I ordered the seeds, three attractive packages of highly recommended varieties: early, mid-season, and late. Then I made a seedbed in a sunny spot under the kitchen window, covered it over with one of my hope chest sheets. And thus the cabbage project began.

Meanwhile there was the home garden to start. The seed catalogue and the government bulletins helped with that. I studied carefully everything that each booklet said and tried to follow directions. Alex did the plowing and enjoyed the fresh vegetables, but there his interest stopped. Gardening, to him, was a sissy business.

We had a full garden that first year. I planted vegetables I had never before heard of, vegetables that appeared only in the seed catalogs. They were so new to me I didn't recognize them when they came up, or couldn't distinguish them from weeds, many of which were as new to me as the vegetables. This lack of intelligent discrimination undoubtedly brought about the destruction of most of my rhubarb, chives, chard, endive, and other rarities. But even then we did have a very good garden.

And the cabbage patch, be it noted, was very productive indeed. All told, the market took enough heads to give me $75, most of which went for door and window screens, for furniture, and for fruit jars. The fruit jars were filled, according to government directions, with blackberries, wild plums, seedling peaches from the fence rows; beans, pickles, tomatoes, and sauerkraut from the cabbage I couldn't sell. Those three packages of cabbage seed spread themselves out very well even though I never did have to use a ladder to climb up and sprinkle on the bug dust.

And it all was so much more fun than teaching school!

Mulality

Before, during, and for some time after World War I our home county, the limestone-bluegrass band of Middle Tennessee, was noted for its donkeys—or more accurately, its sons and daughters of donkeys: mule-colts. For a long time, it seems, the farmers didn't know, until the mules showed them, these little brown pebbles and slabs of phosphate mingled among the bits of hay and pasture were building an uncommonly good strong "bone" in young mules.

The same nourishment that builds "bone" in young mules also builds "bottom" for maturity, and "bottom" in mule men's lingo means sturdiness, stamina, and endurance—in other words, mule power and will power to pull a heavy load to the end of a row and back again, or to the end of the road.

We were married in the midst of a mule boom. Mules made a deep and lasting impression on me in my early years of matrimony. For one thing, they made it possible for my husband to take a wife. For another, they were the backbone of our farming, and our main cash crop.

To me, mule men rated next to preachers and doctors. Preachers saved souls, doctors saved bodies, and mulemen were the saviors of our pocketbook. The trick was to buy weaning mule colts in September, hold them for a couple of years, then sell them back to the traders for enough to buy twice as many. Alex started with a little money from his corn crop, which he invested in a single mule colt. From there he built up his mule capital to 23 at one point (although the arithmetic does not quite figure), and sold most of these for the down payment on the farm.

Our early years of near poverty were like the bit in the mule's mouth. We were held in check by it and guided along a narrow path. Everything we had was tied up in the young mules. We could not buy furniture, clothes, farm equipment, or anything else except by selling mules. They existed for us, but it seemed that we also existed for them.

That first year of matrimony, I was not unaware of the economics of all this, but I had too many things to learn about the farm and setting up a household. Even so, there was not all that much to do since there were just the two of us to cook and wash for and we had little furniture to dust. While Alex worked in the fields, I found time to ramble about the farm, to look for wild flowers, or sometimes just to sit quietly in the shade crocheting or tatting lace for sheets to match our pillowslips.

On one of those quiet lazy afternoons, Alex was plowing Old Kate, Blue, and Brownie just out of sight on the other side of a hill. I had taken him some water and was sitting under a tree at the far end of the field. All of a sudden I heard a loud cry from a place just out of sight around the bend of the furrow. It meant, "Come quick!" Frightened, I dropped what I was doing and ran along the furrow as fast as I could.

What a spectacle! Man, mules, harness, and plow were so mixed and tangled that I could hardly tell where one left off and the other began. It seemed that somehow in the process of turning a corner, a lever had hung, a harness strap had broken, or something had happened that made the mules fall backward over one another, and the big heavy plow had been upset on top of them. How the man escaped I don't know, but when I got there, he was trying to hold the mules down to keep them from struggling and cutting themselves on the plow.

What he wanted me to do was to hold those three floundering mules quiet while he got the harness loose and turned the plow over and off them. It seems that as long as a mule's head is down, the mule must stay down, too. So all I had to do was to sit on the heads of three frightened, struggling animals while harness and plow could be removed. Nothing in my government bulletins had prepared me for this.

When we finally got them untangled, we found that two of the mules were not badly hurt, but Brownie, our lead mule, who had been on top of the other two and immediately under the plow, was badly injured. The disc of the plow had sliced into her flank in several places, and the two levers of the plow had gouged deeply into her hip and side. She was trembling in pain and fright.

Alex ran across the field to a neighbor's house to telephone a veterinarian. I led Brownie and trailed the other mules to the barn as best I could.

My First Degree

The doctor did not believe—and Alex and I hardly dared hope—that she could live. The vet suggested a treatment that *might* save her. Alex believed that it would be better to shoot her. If I'd had any sense or known my condition (somewhat pregnant, if it's possible to be "somewhat" when there are no signs you are yet), I would not have pleaded her cause. But I didn't, so I did. I argued my dubious husband into letting me care for her since obviously no one else could do it. He gave in with the understanding that he was not to be bothered with her, no matter what.

Nothing in my past experience prepared me for the role of mule nurse. But with the courage of fools who rush in ahead of angels and a naïve will to succeed, I took on a new chore. It turned out to be a long, painful convalescence both for her and me. But I think that we each learned something.

Although the vet had prescribed the treatment, the technique of restoring her to health was left strictly up to me. And on this I had no person or reference book to fall back on. So I improvised, calling upon the best of motherly instincts, and happy in a sense that it was a mule instead of a person who had been so wounded in the accident. Brownie seemed to understand I was trying to help her and put up with me even when I was awkward and clumsy.

What I did was to go first to the stable next to hers. Then through the cracks I would feed her a few ears of corn to quiet her down. After that, as my husband had left the bridle on her, I could lead her gently into the enclosed hall of the barn. She liked to have her nose rubbed and at the same time I would talk to her. When we reached the right spot, I tied her head up high to the corn crib door.

While she was eating, I had mixed a solution of Creolin disinfectant and water, according to the vet's instructions. It made a milky solution which I set in a nearby feed trough. Then I took a big syringe with a long pipe on one end and filled it. I needed one hand to pat her and two to operate the syringes. I always needed a third hand.

She had blinders on her bridle and could not see what I was doing. But she felt in her bones what I was up to. Her side was so torn that I had to put the syringe way up into the wound to do any good. She flinched, but never once kicked or dodged despite the pain. She just stood there and shivered. I started with the worst place and went on to four or five others. This happened three times a day—after breakfast, dinner, and supper. It went on for several months before her side was healed.

During that long, hot, anxious summer, Brownie and I did a lot of thinking together. I guess that was when we had the best chance to study each other, and concluded which had the "person-ality" and which had the "mul-ality." Observing the way she met her misfortunes and endured my crude treatments, I became certain that she must have more than human personality. And I rather believe that from the way she observed my determination that she should get well, especially when both my husband and the vet were so doubtful…well, I imagine she suspected I had a certain degree of mulality; at least she seemed to respect me as a fellow creature. Witness that never during all that time did she ever twitch an ear or lift a heel.

Now I believe that you will have to admit that in a mule—a sick, suffering, and bewildered one—that is something. At least, when our "Graduation Day" came, when I laid the syringe of Creolin solution forever in the feed trough, patted the patches of white hair that would cover the scars and mark her for the rest of her days as a blemished mule—when I patted her nose declaring her recovered and awarded myself a degree of "Mule Doctor"—she lightly, ever so slightly, switched her tail. As it was December, there were no flies around, either, and if you know mules, you must admit, "That is something."

I thought Brownie's mulality was beyond bravery and courage. She had been so critically cut, slashed, gouged, and sliced on her side and hip by the overturned hillside disc plow that she must have gone through terrible pain. My treatments with the huge syringe of Creolin shot into and around the raw flesh three times a day must have hurt even more. But I was sure that more than all the rest, she was hurt by being kept in the dark stable alone while the rest of the mules were in the field working. A mule is a sociable animal who wants to be with her kind. How slighted she must have felt when all the other mules were taken out of the barn each day and she was left alone. Brownie could not tell her troubles to anyone, and she suffered in silence, patient, alone, uncomplaining for all those long months.

Anyhow, it was our considered opinion, mine and Brownie's (which had developed during that eventful summer), that neither mulality nor personality are a sudden something. It must begin with ancestors and be a long time agrowing— nurtured by man, nature, and a lot of other things we don't or didn't understand.

Some man, I believe it was, perhaps trying to be poetic, made a much quoted statement that a mule is "without pride of ancestry or hope of posterity." As to Brownie's ancestry, we both believe he was wrong. Although neither of us ever knew her father, he must surely have been one of the finest of imported Spanish jackasses. Only a jackass can become the father of a mule, and breeders know well enough that the best can be imported only from Spain. George Washington's own account books are said to prove that! He spent a great deal of money for Spanish donkeys, it is said. Others have done the same, many breeders' bank accounts agree.

Her mother must have been one of the best of mares, probably a Morgan, or a "dowager" Tennessee walking horse. Now ancestors like those, in my book, are not to be sneered at or sniffed at either.

As for posterity, the men who wrote the dictionary took care of that when they put it down in writing that "mules are usually sterile."

Now about my own ancestors and what they might have to do with such qualities as stickability—which must be a quality of both mulality and personality—I can only suspect that it took a great deal of something to get great Grandpa Adam through his "recovery program."And I still believe that the only reason Mother Eve reached up and pulled down that apple was that she got tired of waiting for Adam to do it. I doubt also whether she ever got more than the peeling and the core for her trouble.

ℛ

Not So Dumb

Once I earned my self-awarded M.D. degree in mule doctoring, I found that I could not stop there but would have to go on for an advanced degree. For this period of my life, during the First World War, the Government kept men traveling in our part of the country just to buy up mules. Prices rose by leaps and bounds, until one mule might bring as much or more than two fine horses, or a matched team, up to $1000.

We started matrimony with three mules and increased them to nearly the number Alex had before he made the down-payment on our farm. When the war ended and the mule market broke, we lost what was our main, and for a while, our only cash crop. But in the meantime, I earned enough more about mules and mulality to award myself an A.M. degree—Admirer of Mules.

My favorite mule was Kate, our "cotton" mule.[1] She was a lady. She reminded me of my dainty Aunt Daisy who made the hoecakes. Kate was precious and understanding. Whenever there was anything tedious to do, we called on her and she could be counted on. When it came to drawing a harrow, she was our lead mule. Once off in the right direction, all one had to do was follow her along. She could hold a perfectly straight line across the field and knew just when and where to turn. She led the others and as long as she was leading, there was rarely any trouble. I thought of Kate as the mule whose hand would always have gone up first in the grade school classroom if she had been a little girl instead of a mule.

Old Tobe was the opposite of Kate in every way. He was a big "sugar" mule with a tremendous amount of brawn (bottom) and consecrated listlessness. He hated to leave the barn and was

---

[1] Mules vary greatly in size depending on their breed. There were five mule types based on size, which dictated the use the mule would be employed at. The smallest was the pack or mining mule, as little as 500 pounds. Cotton mules were the next size up, sired by a burro on a pony, then the farm mule. Sugar and draft mules were the same height, about eighteen hands; the sugar mule was lighter in weight, about 1,150 pounds, and the draft mule weighed-in at about 1,300 pounds—they were the largest and heaviest mule breed.

always ready to come back. It was a battle of wits on how to use him to suit his mood (mulality). If you put him on the inside of a four-mule team drawing a disc harrow, he would draw the three other mules, me, and the disc harrow out of the ground and dash back to the barn. If he got hitched up on the outside, I found that I could never turn in the opposite direction.

It was a struggle to get him out to the field, to put his strength to work in any helpful way, and then to get him back without having him run off or upset the others. From him I think I caught some of my most remembered glimpses of mulality and what it could result in.

I found the best way to handle Tobe when he wouldn't work was to tie him up at the far end of the field and put Maude, our buggy mare, in his place. She wasn't very strong and was annually in foal, so she could not be worked much. But Old Tobe, who hated work, hated being alone even more. He wanted to be with the bunch. So he would complain: "Hee, Haw, Hee Haw!" until I would gingerly unleash him and put him in Maude's place. You never could get more than a half day's work out of Old Tobe.

One way to deal with mulality, I learned, was to put it off by itself and ignore it. Eventually, it would find its own cure.

Blue had a kind of nondescript muleness. She got along reasonably well with everyone. Mostly she kept her mulality hidden, but it would appear in fits of sulking and pouting. She was really just a third mule with no outstanding characteristics.

She was not likely to get into trouble; neither was she likely to do anything that would set her apart as something special. I remember her as I recall faces in a crowd—just one of many.

There were mules I adjusted to first in our early years of marriage. They were succeeded by countless others, some of which I remember clearly, others of which have faded into a vast formless image of the species mule.

I guess I would have preferred not to have "gotten involved" with mules if I had given the matter sufficient thought. But that was a luxury for "liberated" women of a later era, not a farm woman of my time. I had to take my husband's place when he went to town or had other work to do. So I learned to cope with them, substituting brain for brawn sometimes and outclassing them in mulality at others.

When Alex was with the mules, I usually stayed out of the way. Except perhaps in "breaking" a young mule, two at once were almost always one too many. My husband really got his dander up a few times when he was in the barn with the mules and I came suddenly upon them. This might be just enough to cause one or more of them to start kicking in diverse reverse directions. Since he was closest, he was sometimes known to be a little upset in my direction.

If no one interfered, he and the mules seemed so much alike that they got along well together. He didn't have to talk to them, coax and cajole them as I did. However, I developed a psychology for dealing with them when it was my turn that made up for the lack of rapport with them that my husband had. As a matter of fact, I soon found that the same sort of psychology that would work with him would work with the mules!

I noticed that if Alex was "on the outs" with me or anybody else, he would take it out on the mules. If he got angry with me, he might whip all his mules. Maybe that was why I always had more trouble than he did in handling them. They could have blamed me for making him angry enough to whip them, so they got back at me by being balky when I ordered them about. Or so I thought sometimes.

ॐ

Getting Up the Mules

I'm in a quandary about whether to tell you this shaggy little dog story and let the pros and cons fall where they may. (We could call the story "Getting the Mules Up," or "Getting Up The Mules;" I never could decide which was better.)

It was a sort of ceremony or drama which was likely to take place after a long wet spell, when the mules had been out running loose in the back pasture and the weather looked like the ground might be ready to plow in the afternoon. Getting the mules up always seemed so easy for Alex.

To start with, we had realized that while somebody ought to get the mules up, somebody ought to go to town (we needed perhaps a little flour or sugar or salt or coffee, perhaps). We might have been keeping the buggy mare in the barn during this bad weather because she might not have been able to take the rough weather like the mules could. I might have thought things out a little better if I had really tried, but during that first year on the farm I was dumb enough and game enough to try almost everything Alex suggested.

Alex well knew (and I knew how well he knew) how much I hated to go to town. It would almost always take me a whole day. I was still trying to make folks in town think he had married well, so it took a long time for me to dress accordingly. First I took a long and thorough bath, dried off; then drew on my long lisle stockings, straightened seams, and supporters. Then I put on those beautiful high-topped gray suede wedding shoes, laced and tightened them, then that pesky, misery-making straight-laced size 22 corset and tightened that down to twenty-four inches—I still didn't want people to know how married I really was. Well, I didn't want to go to town, especially when Alex volunteered to go and he could hitch up Maude and be there and back in a couple of hours.

So that was the way we worked it out: he struck out for town and the dog and I started out for the back pasture. As I said, getting the mules up always seemed so easy for Alex, but then, as I conjectured later, when he got them up it was usually when Maude was with them.

He would merely toss a few ears of corn in the feed trough, stick a couple of ears in his back pocket, pick up Maude's bridle, jangle it a bit and walk back to the first little hilltop from which he could see and be seen all over the farm. Once there, he'd give a shrill whistle, jangle the bridle a little more, hold out an ear of corn, and corrupt the English language a bit with a "Co'up Maude, co'up Maude."

Maude, as expected, would lift her head, nicker in his direction, walk slowly up to him to accept bit and bridle, and travel toward the barn and more corn. Exactly what Maude did, except for the bit and bridle, the mules all did likewise. So easy ...

So easy for him. But not for me. First of all, the pockets in my stylish, well-fitted Hoover wrap-around apron would not hold ears of corn. Second, I didn't want to bother with jangling an old bridle when I went for a walk. I would never dare try to put a bridle on a mule unless she was in the barn and I could stand up in the feed trough. Ears on a 16-hands mule are rather high, especially when she chooses to hold up her head. Besides, I'd been warned many times that a mule may be a "fool about her ears." I was a grown-up woman, but only a little over five feet high, so I would not try bridling a mule in the pasture.

Besides that, we had visiting mules in the pasture, and they might be difficult. The reason for visiting mules was because of the weather and the lay of the land. In the spring, and especially after a long wet spell, our high sunny south hillside of phosphatic-limestone loam would dry out and warm up early and put forth a lush growth of pasturage.

But our neighbors down the creek bottom who had a heavy, rich, but boggy soil could not turn out to pasturage. So we swapped spring pasturage for late summer pasturage. Therefore strange mules.

Undoubtedly the worst handicap I had in "getting up the mules" was that they were without Maude. Both they were, and I was. When a mare, or spotted pony, or white filly stays with a bunch of mules for a few days, they form a sort of mother image of her. They will go anywhere or do anything she does. So if you lead, drive, or ride the mare, you've instantly got all the mules in hand.

I didn't think I would miss Maude so much for I had our dog Queen. And what Maude couldn't lead, Queen could drive. At least I thought so, and Queen thought so, too.

Queen had come to us a rolly polly collie shepherd pup at that cute age just under three months. She had been given to me by Gertie Bennet, who didn't like me too much because she thought I sort of had the Big Head over my five years of Latin. But she had too many pups and she thought every farm ought to have a dog. Why Alex named the dog Queen I don't remember. But inevitably she grew up to earn that name.

At about this time we had a neighbor in the nearby village of Bigbyville whose name was Mister Charley Thomas—known as Mister Charley.

When he went to town he traveled as he thought a gentleman should—always on horseback and usually across country.

As our farm lay in his "as a crow flies" route, he frequently crossed our farm twice a day, always being careful to leave the gates as he found them, either open or shut.

Mister Charley developed quite an admiration for Queen, and he told me many things about dogs and mules and men and horses and neighbors that I had never known or suspected. Many times, he'd stop and watch Queen about her maneuvers, and he frequently told me, and the neighbors, that that shaggy collie shepherd can "read, write, and recollect." I always admitted that at least as far as he was concerned, she could recollect. So much so that when she had enough pups to replace herself and had been kicked in the head a few times, we let her go live with Mister Charley. And so far as I know, they lived happily ever after.

But, goodness gracious, Miss Agnes! Alex and Maude would be back from town before Queen and I could get up the mules from the back pasture if we didn't get a move on. We walked back through the growing rye to the first little hill from which we could see and be seen. Queen trotted along in front to stir up snakes and I carried a stout stick in case she succeeded.

When we arrived at what I thought might be the proper place, I took my stand, drew a deep breath, and emitted my shrillest whistle. But I guess my teeth were too close together or I'd not had much practice. At any rate, not a mule's head was lifted and not an ear twitched. I took another deep breath and coaxed "Go'up mules! Go'up mules!" Not a budge from the low ground.

Then Queen took over, or as the 'coon hunters would say, she "opened up!" All heads jerked up at once, and all heels took to the air. In one fast-action move they took off toward the top of our highest hill and the big rock fence next to Stone's high wood.

There they took one backward look, turned all faces to the wall, turned all heels toward us, and formed a most animated and impenetrable barrier.

So much for me—and Queen—getting the mules up!

My Degree in Philosophy

When the First World War ended the mule market collapsed. A mule that during the war could be sold for $350 was worth only $25 once the war was over. After the mule had helped win the war, no matter how much "bottom" he had, the bottom dropped out of the market. Texans came up and bought the Jacks imported from Spain. They were uneconomical to keep in Tennessee. It was a period when most of the asses went to Texas.

We still kept Maude for a buggy mare and saddle horse. We did not always breed her because she would work like a mule. We did not want any more mules or Jacks then because they were not worth their feed and keep. There is nothing more ornery and useless than a Jackass if you are not going to breed him to a mare.

Thereafter the market never did come back from the peak years of World War I. For a while in the Thirties, the Chamber of Commerce tried to revive the mule boom as an anti-Depression measure. This was when Maury County Mule Day celebration again made the scene.

But with the coming of tractors in the Thirties mules could not compete, particularly for the youngsters. Our son insisted on a tractor when he was old enough to plough the fields and we had to give in.

A large part of our social as well as economic life circled around First Monday. If a young man lived south of town and his young lady lived north of town, there was an inconvenience. But it was sure to resolve itself on First Monday. They could meet at the drug store and drink ice cream sodas or lean against the counters at Woolworths, or share a hot dog on the street. Two or three girls walked arm-in-arm down the street dressed in better than Easter clothes. Boys stood on the corner watching the girls go by or whistled after them.

During First Monday in September, when the young men had saved their money to buy a couple of mule colts, they could spend what they had left on their girls. Once they bought their pair of colts (preferably matched ones) they would tie the animals to a hitching pole in the jockey yard. Then they would go to the ice cream parlor or walk hand-in-hand until it was time to take the new colts back to the farm. Of course, they could not start out too late because they wanted to get the mules home before dark.

Springtime was a slightly better time for courting. A young man could sell his work mules early and then with the money for his crop of young mules, he could spend the rest of the day and evening courting his best girl if he so desired and she desired and could get permission.

The tractor proved to be no bed of roses, however. With mules you could blame your own mistakes on them, but there was no way a tractor would take this sort of abuse. We got deeper and deeper in debt for various reasons after we got the tractor and were not at all sure for a long while whether it was working for us or we were working for it. Actually, we did not begin to get out of the Depression until our cows became more profitable. By then we were selling milk and cream.

But before we left the era of mules, I climaxed my studies with a Ph.M. It came from the traders I knew and from what I saw in the mule's eyes. It took me into the philosophy of mules and made me a philosopher of mulality. To one much in contact with mulality the significance can be readily overlooked. (Many farmers I knew paid no attention to it philosophically, although they dealt with it pretty often.) However, to me it spoke a many-faceted tongue and invariably had something to say worth listening to. To wit:

I have always believed that there is extra-sensory perception between man and mule. That is, the mule has it, if not the man. A mule knows if a man is nervous or afraid of her. She knows if the man is her friend or her enemy. She can foresee what the man is going to do and how he is going to do it, sometimes before the man knows himself. Thus, the mule acts accordingly. So if a man blames a mule for a negative attitude or bad behavior, usually the fault lies not in the mule but in the man himself.

To my way of thinking, the mule is the world's greatest creature for tilling the soil. Although tractors are a little more predictable, I rather admire the adventure of working a mule. The trouble with a tractor is that it breaks down more often. It also uses gas and oil and smokes up the atmosphere while a mule's pollution has fertilizing value and enriches the soil.

Mules are just as good as ever in the past, but the energy of men is less. They are no longer satisfied to get out behind a mule. A tractor depreciates when it is not being used. But a mule appreciates until it is eight years old. An eight-year-old tractor is ready for the junk heap, but an eight-year-old mule is still in her prime.

You need a special temperament to handle mules. You need to like what you are doing, working with the underrated mule, and have more sense than mules do.

Mules are not sociable in the same way that dogs are. When a mule tries to express pleasure to her master she might be awkward, even dangerous. Her very bulk might be a handicap to that expression.

I never knew storied Nip and Tuck, and I do not know their color or conformation. But from their reported behavior I guess they had that most desirable way of socializing—that of a matched team, a unity much to be desired in mules and married folk.

A balky mule elicits interest and often respect. When a mule balks, the whole neighborhood gathers. Then she gets attention. Everybody comes off his porch to twist the mule's tail. A last resort is to build a fire under her. She will move just enough to get away from the fire, but no further. Her balkiness is bound to continue until she is ready to end it. After human endeavors fail, after pondering a bit, the mule in her own sweet time will move on. She will know in her bones when that time has come. She should be ignored and treated with tender neglect until she is ready.

Now a mule, because she is "without pride of ancestry," should not be accused of inheriting anything other than her ears. Most of her traits are learned from man, or from other mules that learned them from man. An old mule trader I knew insisted that there was no such thing as a mean mule—there were only mean masters. I agree with him, of course, for I can walk up to a mule and tell you in a minute what kind of master she has had. If I raise my hand and she flinches, I know her master's personality.

So whatever they are, personality and mulality are to some extent interchangeable. I believe that people who have never known mules may have mulality. Properly recognized this may include wisdom, humility, and other positive virtues (as in the case of Balaam's ass in the Bible). Mules, for instance, are often sensitive, hardworking animals and good with children. Usually they are much quieter and more placid than men. However, the form of mulality known as Jackassery is dangerous.

It was not the mood or disposition of my husband to try to cultivate that harmonious mulality among his mules. He wanted them, I think, to grow fat, work, and go to market. They were allowed to run together or apart in the pasture. He did not work them in any particular order. He had no sentimentality for mules, or other animals, I thought. The togetherness that made a team worth more than its individual members was not something he sought to cultivate. He sought to cultivate the willingness to pull a load. Perhaps if I had handled them it would have been different, but then my mulality was different from his.

I considered personality an indescribable, indefinable something, usually found in a person. Some people were chuck full of it, as others seemed to lack it. The ones that made the biggest impression on me seemed to have the most of it. The ones who left me feeling cold, indifferent, or unaffected were deficient in it, as I saw it. Those were the fish-eyed "bureaucrats," no matter what their profession.

"Mulality" then is something of the same amorphous substance usually found in mules. While some people might think of it in terms of stubbornness and blind bull-headedness, it carries a connotation of other ingredients like "grit" and "guts." Mulality may even include a tendency to be generous and broadminded until crossed. It is sometimes confused with balkiness, which means to be pushed so far and no farther.

❧

Old Peck and Scratch

Along with gardening a country woman must learn poultry raising, of course; so during that first year came some memorable experiences with chickens.

Mother Knox had given us, among other household and farm necessities, a dozen assorted hens that had been roosting in her barn and making raids on her corncrib and garden. They were vari-colored and as self-sustaining as any dozen old hens could be. And they gave abundant promise of supplying us with eggs, fryers, and pullets for the next year's laying.

Enthusiastically, we cleaned out the old hen-house, put in new roost poles, nest boxes (old orange crates filled with straw), and shut the hens inside until they could get acquainted with their new apartment. They paid well for what they ate that spring, but not for what they scratched. Nevertheless, we enjoyed them and had high hopes.

At last one old hen went broody, and a worse tempered old hussy never sat on straw. I was sickeningly afraid of setting-hens anyway, and she was certainly vicious. I was determined, however, that we should grow some chicks that year, and that old hen seemed the most promising medium. So I filled my lap with eggs and gingerly approached the old hyena with a stick of stovewood in hand to ward off her pecks.

It was no good. With one hand to hold the lap and one the stovewood, there was no hand left to place the eggs where they ought to be. I went back to the house, put the eggs in a basket, gathered up a heavy bath towel for a shield, and tried again. Once more, no luck. The hen was nervous, and I was more so. It was night, finally, before I got that hen muffled enough with that bath towel (a wedding present) so I could slip under her breast those fifteen pencil-marked eggs intended for hatching.

A Twenty-one Day Battle

There followed a twenty-one day battle between me and that vicious black hen. We used mostly beak and bath towel as weapons. My most effective strategy, I learned, was to completely envelop her in the thick towel, and lift her off the nest with both hands. That gave me an opportunity to count the eggs and see if she had broken any (or if the other hens were laying with her).

When the chicks began to hatch the war began in earnest. That old fanatic seemed to have an idea that hers was a superior race, and that no chick but black should survive. Every white or yellow chick, or even pale gray one, was henpecked to death as soon as it allowed itself to emerge from the black feathers. What could I do with the old cannibal?

Of course, I removed the off-color chicks as rapidly as I could and put them with a bottle of warm water in a box behind the stove. But that did not permanently solve the problem. That night, after excitement of new motherhood had subsided in her bosom, I thought that the hen would relent. But not she. Next morning she was pecking chicks again as hard as her beak would thrust—and well I knew how hard that could be.

I took the vari-colored chicks out of the nest again, spoke harshly to the old buzzard of a perverted mother, then sat down on the henhouse doorstep, and cried. But that didn't help matters either.

I took the little orphans to their nursery again, put in another bottle of warm water, and set out to the nearest neighbors to ask what to do with a hen that pecks. Mammy Stone did not laugh at me, but neither could she advise. All her chicks were of one color and all her hens sweet-tempered and motherly. She did say, however, that she had read how some poultry raisers trim the beaks of chicken-fighting hens; just cut off the outer tip of the upper beak enough that the hen couldn't nip the two parts together. I went home to try trimming.

Again with my bath towel armor, I managed to get the old hen well in hand, her body between my knees and her crow-like head tight in my left fist. I tried scissors first, but no go. Then I reached for my best and sharpest kitchen paring knife, but that also was too dull. Next I "borrowed" my husband's razor. With that I proceeded to work, but her tough old beak wouldn't trim. It had to be cut, and cut hard.

I don't know how it happened, but it seems that down toward the outer edge the beak was not so tough after all. At any rate, the razor slipped. It went through quickly and on into the ball of my thumb. It was a mean gash, made with main strength and a sharp edge. And the sight and feel of it didn't help my regard for the old black hen, especially since she began again to lambaste those poor little off-color chicks as soon as I turned her loose.

That operation was anything but a success. The hen could still peck but she couldn't eat! I felt remorseful, sure enough. The poor old idiot would starve to death. She could not even drink water, it seemed. And there I'd be left to bring up a whole crop of orphans, black, white, and multicolored.

Repenting, I removed the unwanted chicks from the coop and decided to let the intolerable old sufferer die as unworried as possible. She didn't. She managed to eat and drink somehow and to bring up her own black babies according to her standards of chick culture, while I clucked ineffectually over the whites, speckles, and yellows. And, if I must confess it, she did a better job of raising her chicks than I did mine. Maybe hers was, after all, a superior race. Or maybe she just knew where the best grubworms grew. She helped considerably with my poultry education, but it was a painful process to have to take lessons from a fighting old hen and nurse a sore finger and a hurt pride at the same time.

A few years later I had learned enough, or little enough, to buy an incubator, a couple of brooders, and some reputedly high-bred birds. I had a terrific case of chicken fever, one of the worst you can imagine. I took chickens to shows and won prizes, sold hatching eggs at fancy prices (a few), advertised in the poultry journals, and read and wrote for those journals. But for all that and even more I never did learn to do a better job of raising husky, frisky chicks than the hen mothers themselves.

At last, after roasting an incubator full of hatching babies and letting the brooder catch fire a couple of times, I decided that after all the hens knew best; at least they can do better in their own particular vocation. So within a year or so, I managed to turn the business of chicken raising back to the old broodies and I put more time, thought, and effort into bringing up my own babies. The hens continued to teach me, however, and kept me marveling.

I am reminded of what that wise old writer of proverbs declared, "There be three things which are too wonderful for me, yea, four which I know not: the way of an eagle in the sky; the way of a serpent on a rock; the way of a ship in the midst of the sea; and the say of a man with a maid."

And if Solomon had been a farm woman, he might well have added the fifth mystery—the way of a hen in the grass. Now, an old dominicker hen is not a mysterious looking creature, but she does have some methods and accomplishments that mystify.

She'll saunter out into the crab grass in the cornfield, fence-row or thicket, scratch around, snuggle down, flop a little, whirl and flutter until she has swished the grass and leaves and trash into a dish-shaped nest such as human hands cannot duplicate; and then she will lay an egg.

Next day another egg; and next, another. And what is an egg? Just a yolk and a white with a shell round it, we'd say. A little water, lime, protein, albumen, the scientist will tell you. A handy bit of custard-thickening and a potential omelet, the cook will say. But the old hen knows better than scientist, cook, or casual observer.

When the time is right she will settle down and put her heart on those eggs; there she will stay through day and night, rain or shine, cold or heat, for exactly twenty-one days.

Then comes forth life. That is what is really in an egg; and the old hen knew it all the time. But how did the old hen know?

Indeed, the ways of the eagle, the serpent, the ship, and the man are all wonderful; but the way of a hen, warming eggs into life? That is wonderful, too.

℘

Investigated

One evening, just at the edge of dusk, Alex and I were poking in from the dairy barn, he with a pail of milk and I with a tobacco stick walking-cane to help my tired self along. Alex was walking along in front, farmer-fashion; and Eve-like, I was tagging along after him, when all of a sudden he stopped and exclaimed, "Look at those pretty polecats!"

Well, I didn't look for cats at all. My first thought was to take cover and I made a quick shift to reverse. I don't know yet what became of the tobacco stick. That man just kept standing there exclaiming how pretty they were, and he was not usually the exclaiming kind.

Now I am an admirer of beauty, but I hate the thought of holding my nose to look at it, so I continued to reverse. Then Alex said, "They're coming your way and they are the prettiest little fellows you ever saw." That word "little" gave me courage.

"Are they babies?" I asked.

"Oh, about half-grown," he said.

By that time they were right at my feet. Oh, they were pretty. I was wearing sandals and the cats were giving my toes a going-over. Then they looked me up and down thoroughly and trotted back to Alex, giving him an investigation.

Meanwhile the family dog had arrived and was evidently doing some wondering himself. When the kittens spied the dog they decided to investigate him also. He stood it until they got under his nose, then he gave them his heels and some dust besides. Can you imagine a full-grown, dignified, and sensible dog being chased by a team of baby polecats?

They kept up quite a game of it for several minutes. The dog would run, then turn to look, then run again. And the twin kittens just trotted along up and down the path after him. He made his way back to us and they followed. I was still too paralyzed and amused to climb over the fence, but I don't think a wire fence would have been much protection anyway.

When they came back from their frolic with the dog, I thought of the bucket of milk. They might have smelled that, and they might possibly take a little swig. We didn't know whether young polecats have any more understanding of milk than they did of folks and dogs, but Alex poured out a little into the top of the bucket and I set the improvised bowl before them. They weren't interested; they gave the three of us, Alex, the dog, and me, another good looking over and sauntered off together down the ditch whence they had come. We watched for them each morning and evening after that, but never another sight nor smell of them did we have. Evidently their curiosity was satisfied in that one twilight.

I Just Love A Village

Early, too, in married life I found I loved our neighboring village of Bigbyville—from the general store at the cross-roads to where the sparks flew from the blacksmith's anvil; its hominess, its neighborliness, its humanness, its foibles, its warmth, and its personalities.

Among the leaders of our village there was the clergyman. He was always looked to for comfort and guidance, especially in times of stress and trouble.

And the village doctor! Bless him! He saw our children into this world and was expected to see us all out of it. Every physical ailment beyond a growling tooth or a broken finger was taken to his office. Volumes could be written of him, except that praise embarrassed him.

The village school teacher. Dear only knows what that person had to bear. Dear also knows, as few others do, what a tremendous influence the village teacher had on the generations that come and go.

It should be a source of great satisfaction to a teacher to know that if she couldn't have her way in the present, the future was hers. She was molding the village of ten to sixty years from then.

Ranking high in importance in our village was the merchant—or let's just call him the store-keeper. He was more than that—much, much more, but I just like to call him store-keeper. I like that word better than merchant, and I notice that most villagers did too.

His activities and his services to his people were as varied and as valuable, perhaps, as his conglomerate stock of "general merchandise."

The term "general merchandise" is a fascinating expression; so much so to me that if Santa Claus ever started doing impossible things for undeserving people, I should like to send a postal card some Christmas and ask him to leave in my stocking just a country-store full of "general merchandise." I believe I'd get more entertainment out of spices and hams, oilcloth and dippers, nails and calico in reality than I would out of the Spring-Summer or Fall-Winter mail order wish-a-log.

The village store-keeper was so much more than a mere merchant. He was in our nearby village the hub around which much of the everyday life of the village moved. He was the one from whom the village drunkard borrowed the price of a pint 'til Saturday night. He's the one who might advance the dressmaker enough for her taxes until her pension came in. He frequently was the one who heard troubles that wouldn't be "fitten" to tell the preacher. Frequently he dispensed castor oil or turpentine to cases that were not quite bad enough to take to the doctor. If the telephone messages he relayed were laid end to end they would make a unique formation.

The village dressmaker—we cannot pass her by. All kinds of garments from layettes to shrouds took shape under her busy fingers. Trousseaus were her specialties, as well as shirts for the man whose arms were too long or whose front was too broad to be covered comfortably by ready-mades. The village dressmaker knew secrets by the score. She might tell them or not, according to the kind of person she was or what she thought of you. But don't forget this: she knew.

Ah, but there was one person in the village who knew more, much more, than the dressmaker, preacher, doctor, teacher, or merchant. You've guessed it! The telephone operator.

Why, I wonder, hasn't some intelligence specialist tested the know-it-allness of a group of village telephone operators?

She had Information deluxe. I would merely say: "Central, ring Miss Lydia."

The small voice in the telephone replied: 'Why, she ain't home. She's gone over to Miss Susie's to spend the day, but I'll ring her there for you."

If you wanted a doctor, preacher, weather forecast, hog market, or wanted to know the time of day, or whose barn was burning, all that was necessary was: "Just ring Central."

Then there was the village bachelor, the "professional" one I mean, the one who made a bee line for every new girl who moved to the neighborhood or dropped in somewhere for a visit. His heart affairs were many. They were quickly on and quickly off, leaving him perennially the village bachelor.

And there was the village half-wit, or quarter-wit, or three-quarter wit. You know the type, even if you weren't always able to specify the exact fraction. He might have been just a nit-wit whom everybody pitied or loved or tolerated. He might have been good natured and harmless, or a more tragic character.

The mechanic, the flivver-fixer, or perhaps he was considered the village blacksmith in less modern moments. The village tinker, he must not be left out, the whittler, the jockey or trader, and the squire, of course. I don't know how I let him get so far down on this list. There might also have been a constable, a Senator, a sheriff's deputy, or a representative of the law in some form. Maybe there was a banker, or a retired capitalist-fisherman. It had all kinds and sorts of folk—all interesting if you knew them. We just loved our village, and depended much on it.

I almost left out the combination furniture dealer and undertaker! He just sat there day after day waiting for people to wear out their stoves, tables, or bodies. He was a valuable asset to the community; as was also the "good old soul" who went to every distressed family to set up with the sick or lay out the dead, or the good brother with his pick and shovel whose regular neighborly tribute was to go to the graveyard and help dig the grave.

There is something very personal about living in or near a village.

I have wondered many times how in the world large cities ever get along without the kind of people who live in villages. I suspect cities are made up of villagers too. The differences in the city and village populations are probably quantity, not quality.

CHAPTER 10

A Daughter and A Son

Margaret and Jack

In the second year of our marriage our daughter, Margaret, came. Two and a half years later our son arrived. Within an incredibly short time the two of them were undertaking the great responsibility of bringing up a couple of parents.

There was little trouble in finding a name for Margaret. She had been named from the time I was in the fourth grade. At that time, in naming my Christmas dolls, I had one name left over. So I decided to save it for my own little girl, when (not if) she should arrive and need a name. From that time on, I saved my prettiest paper dolls, several special toys, a crocheted lace yoke, a scrapbook or two, and a number of trinkets. They had been packed away all that time—first in a shoe box, then in a larger box, and finally in the bottom of the hope chest that Grandpa Ussery had made me.

Our son's name had been harder to choose. Being the boy he was so important that several of the family connections wanted to put an extra word into his name. At last we compromised and gave him one name from each side of the family tree, and compromised still further by calling him by a nickname that had little reference to either name. We called him simply Jack.

Margaret always seemed a series of surprises to her new father. One surprise was that she had her eyes open the first time he saw her. The next was that she could make so much noise about a few minutes difference in her feeding time.

To me that first baby was a series of thrills. First was the flattering way she gripped my finger that first time it was extended to her. Another was one day in her third month, when lying on the bed kicking and gurgling, she announced, "Ah goo! Ah goo!" It sounded exactly to my admittedly partial ears as though she had said plainly, "I good."

And she was a good baby, no denying that. She got into plenty of predicaments, and she very likely started her parents' hair graying; but no more so, I suppose, than would the usual run of youngsters.

She gave me some surprises as well as she did her Dad. One day in the spring of her second year, I had her with me in the garden. And I was trying to get the weeds out of a row of very fine early beans. In our neighborhood the first "mess of beans" and the first ripe tomatoes were accomplishments. I was hoeing and pulling weeds along the row with my face turned southward. Margaret, in a little pink-checked apron, was behind me playing between the rows, or so I thought. When I turned around, Margaret was pulling, too, not weeds, but beans. She had cleaned that row so completely that we didn't have beans till mid-June—almost a disgrace in our neighborhood. And our garden was next to the road!

Jack was considerable of a problem baby in more ways than name selection. He had nine-month colic or its equivalent in incentive to exercise lungs. Every afternoon about the time I needed to be starting supper, bringing in wood and water, and fastening up the baby chicks—about that time Jack would take the colic. There was no place he could be comfortable except on his mother's hip. It was that way for at least nine months, maybe eleven!

From that time on, Jack was an explorer. He didn't exactly discover a new world every day, but he could certainly discover a world of mischief to get himself embroiled in.

There was the time he doused himself in fresh buttermilk by trying to pull up to the churn. There was also the time he upset a gallon bucket of sorghum molasses into his lap and all over the floor around him. There were other episodes equally exasperating.

❦

A Dark Coiffure

Margaret took care of her part of the mischief, too. I was to cope with one incident for days. Baby Jack's hair was red, a bright, golden auburn that drew attention and comment every time we took the children out. We didn't realize that those comments were having their effect on Margaret. But one day while they were playing in a little enclosure we had made for them out on the front porch I heard her say over and over again: "Now oo hair bwack. Now oo hair bwack."

Finally I went out to see how they were getting along. Never so long as there are zebras shall I forget what I saw there. Margaret, then aged three, had found a full new bottle of black shoe dye, and had proceeded to spread it on the baby, on herself, and on the porch, lavishly, and skillfully.

She had probably begun with the offending red hair. And indeed it was then "bwack." So were the streaks that ran down the baby's cheeks, neck, and little white dress. She had painted his elbows, too, and the palms of his hands. Then, for some unaccountable reason, she had given him a military stripe down the sides of his chubby legs; had painted the bottoms of his feet to match the palms of his hands; had then decorated her own little legs and feet; dotted her dress, as well as his; and with the remainder of the very good shoe dye she had made railroads, stripes, dots, and splotches on what had been my clean and newly-painted porch floor.

A psychologist might have been interested in the lines and scrolls that the three-year old had accomplished. But I was no psychologist; just a hardworking housewife; and at that time too much like a certain practical grandmother to be interested in baby-made scrolls, railroads, and designs. Then, however, and for days later, I was astonished at the stability of a certain brand of shoe-dye.

We gradually grew into a bona fide farm family; practically a non-profit organization—for our main crop was corn. We fed it to the pigs; and the pigs died. Or, if we managed to keep cholera out of the swine herd, the prices went down. Sometimes it seemed as though the mortgage grew faster than anything else on the farm.

We did, however, find a lot of LIFE in living down on the farm; and with the garden of cabbages, tomatoes, potatoes, onions, and so on, and poultry and eggs, and milk from the old red cow Mother Knox had given us; the flour and meal we swapped our grain for—we managed to live quite well. Mammy Stone would give us an occasional basket of apples or jar of honey from her adjacent farm. We'd find peaches, plums, and berries growing wild in the fence rows, so our cellar shelves were fairly well stocked.

Daddy's Mama's Garden

Necessarily our life was very practical. With that greedy mortgage hanging over us we felt obliged to make every movement count in dollars and cents. However, one year Margaret announced—and just at corn-planting time—that she wanted a flower garden "just like Daddy's Mama's." With her Dad, Margaret's word was law; so while the mules rested at noon that day he hustled into town and brought back a roll of chicken-wire and some assorted flower seeds. I got the spading fork and started turning over sod and clods, while he put in posts and stretched the fence. Margaret sat on the steps and watched while Jack collected worms.

"Daddy's Mama's Garden" was indeed an ambitious idea for us to try to copy, but Margaret decreed it must be done, so we bent our backs and tried. Making that kind of garden included fencing in the area immediately around the front door, so chickens and calves couldn't share it, and the planting helter-skelter, here, there, and everywhere within that enclosure all the seeds, plants, bulbs, vines, and bushes we could acquire took much of the spare time we could hardly spare. From a landscape architects' viewpoint that garden was an atrocity, but from our vantage point on the front porch it was an overflowing bowl of pleasure. We had violets, sunflowers, roses, marigolds, zinnias, lilies, and as many other varieties as we could buy or beg. Margaret's garden became a family pride.

I'm not by nature an early riser; many times I've felt that I'd rather sit up all night than get up next morning; but during the season when those Shirley poppies were in bloom I'd get up and go barefoot out to the garden in gray dawn to see what colors were open each morning. For a while I thought someone was pulling our beautiful poppy blooms—then I discovered that when the sun came up they disappeared. One must rise early to enjoy poppies.

In the evenings we enjoyed the fragrances from the garden; some odors we recognized, but one was a mystery. The children said it must be the kind of perfume that St. Peter sprinkled around the Golden Gate. I thought I knew most flowers by sight and fragrance, but this was beyond detection. However, on one of those early morning jaunts to the poppy bed I decided to stop and pull some weeds. This bed was an assortment of unknowns from a mixed seed packet. I had been afraid to pull anything out of it except lambs' quarter, plantain weed, and nut grass for fear I'd pull some strange new flower.

On this morning, however, I gathered up a handful of non-descripts and started to throw them away when I caught a whiff of the strange perfume. I sorted the dew-wet plants and smelled each one individually. At last I found it. An insignificant, rusty-looking little cone of florets, and I had broken the plant off right at the top of the ground. We'd enjoy the fragrance of that plant no more in the evenings, and we didn't know what the flower was, so we couldn't get another start of it.

Then came a search of seed catalogs for a picture or description that would identify the plant we had lost. Finally we decided that it was mignonette, and from then on we planted some of it every year. About every other year we'd either pull it up or chop it down because it looked so much like a weed.

But in the seasons it was spared we loved it and enjoyed its fragrance to the fullest.

Petunias, too, gave a great deal of pleasure and fragrance for our evenings on the porch, or lying on a quilt on the grass in the yard beside the little garden.

From this vantage point not only the garden but the whole countryside was our joy. The trees on the hilltops surrounding our valley embroidered a scalloped edge for the horizon. A cowbell would tinkle far over to the east; and over to the north we could hear the regular whacks of someone cutting wood. They'd probably be frying ham for supper. A dog would bark down at the creek.

Far, far over the hill on the highway we could hear the world roaring by—that buzzing sound might be a bus; the heavy pulling an over-burdened truck; the shrill horn, a young man in a hurry.

The evening air would be so sweet to breathe. A mockingbird would rehearse in the hackberry tree. A squeally pig down at the barn would be quarreling about his supper. The horses and mules shuffled their hay. The dogs and cats romped for our pleasure. And the hum and buzz of insects added to the pleasure of evening.

It was from digging in our small daughter's flower garden that I learned to think of the earth as "good"; even though its goodness might be only skin-deep, or mud-deep. I realized from seeing caves and underground streams that down below the earth might seem "cold-blooded," but the mellow topsoil I worked with seemed warm and friendly. I enjoyed being just a sister to the clods.

I suffered with fields that froze in winter and with those that parched in summer. I rejoiced with those that seemed happy in full production. To walk over land that is broken with gullies or scraped bare of topsoil hurt me to the quick, almost like broken skin on my body, like chapped hands or scraped shins.

I learned to love the earth and to cling to the promise, "Dust thou art, to dust returneth." And as I crumbled the clods that I am but a sister to, I felt that I could welcome being laid back into the arms of Mother Earth; my mould entrusted to fingers of green grass, my soul in the hands of the Maker of Earth.

❧

Measles Visits

Some take measles; some acquire measles; some have it thrust upon them. Margaret, acquired measles; went to bed willingly; and nobody had to tell her to stay there. But Jack, poor little kid, had measles thrust upon him time after time before he condescended to accept.

From the day Margaret went to bed I began to watch Jack closely. Every time he sneezed, every time his cheeks were flushed, I would say; "Son, that sounds, or that looks, like measles; you'd better take off and go to bed. You mustn't take any cold, you know." Jack would obediently (most of the time) go to bed, but by the next morning he would be up and ready to play again.

After two weeks of repeating such performances, Jack came in one day and said, "Well Mother, I guess I won't disappoint you any longer. I guess I've got 'em this time."

"But you are not coughing or sneezing," I said.

"No'm, but I'm tired and I haven't done anything to make me tired. I guess it's measles."

He went to bed that afternoon, and next morning he was ready to get up again. "No," I insisted, "you are already settled down in bed and are good and warm, so you may as well save yourself the trouble of getting up and down so much."

That night he slept fitfully, and ere long that hard, dry, stomach-soring cough set in. The sneezes came, and the reddish eye, and runny nose, and that terrible measly taste, and eventually Jack was all broken out with a full-sized rosy crop of measles.

ᕦ

A Bringer-inner

I wonder if a woman is ever entirely comfortable in her mind after she becomes the mother of a son? She will be happy many times, of course, overwhelmingly happy. But being entirely comfortable in her mental regions—that's different.

I have wondered, too, why the person who analyzed boys and found them made of "scissors and snails and puppy dog tails" didn't complete the job. He would have found, upon further analysis, I am sure, that boys also contain abundant other surprises.

At least that is what I observed from our boy, and he seemed not very different from others. From the time Jack could toddle about the yard in pincheck aprons until he strode over the hills in size 11½ shoes and 32-34 overalls, he was always a bringer-inner, or more explicitly a walker-outer and bringer-inner. Sometimes we were quite unprepared for the surprises he brought in.

One Sunday afternoon nobody else would have been prepared either. In each hip pocket of his bulky overalls he toted an adolescent skunk. Well, I thought I would have to leave home. But you never can tell. Boys have a way of doing things with mothers, and by the second day he had me feeding the creatures with one of my company best silver teaspoons. I couldn't stand to see the little things starve, we could not turn them out with the cows, so what else could I do?

On a drizzly day, a snowy Sunday, or an idle afternoon, Jack would always get restless and as he called it, would "go out walking." And dear only knows what he might bring when he came back. It might be a terrapin, a toad, a sunfish. It might be the first redbud or dogwood, an elder-flower as big as a dishpan; the tooth of some prehistoric animal, an ancient

Indian's arrow-head, spear, or hatchet; a baby crow, buzzard
or lizard eggs, a frying-size rabbit, a squirrel. Or just a wilted
bouquet of nameless weeds and wild flowers which, for some
reason, had interested him and which he wanted to share with
the rest of the family.

One of the chief worries with a boy, you never can tell what
he'll do next. A girl—you know she'll play paper dolls, ask for
a new dress, lose herself in a book, or want to go to a picture
show, but a boy is as full of surprises as his pockets, especially
if he has fields, woods, and streams from which to draw these
surprises.

When Jack would come home quietly, with one or both
hands behind him, when he would go upstairs or down to the
basement and bring out a sturdy box or the old canary cage, I'd
begin to feel apprehension rising in my nervous system.

One evening he strode quietly through the kitchen and
performed all these preliminary maneuvers, but instead of
bringing down the regular canary cage, he brought in the
smaller and more closely woven wire cage, the one in which
we had reared baby birds.

He put as large a pan of water in the cage as he could push
through the door, then slipped in half a biscuit, and something
else. That "something else" had me so curious and uneasy that
I let two griddles of our supper hoecakes turn too dark. When
Jack had completed his mysterious arrangements, he stood up

and with hands on hips, said, "Mother, come over and meet Old Gold's Rival."

At first I couldn't imagine what he meant, or just who or what "Old Gold" might be. But when I looked in the cage and saw a frog slightly larger than a special celebration postage stamp, I remembered that one summer California had a frog jumping contest in which a green-back named Old Gold had set something like a world's record by covering twelve feet in three jumps.

Jack went on to explain that although he wasn't sure whether this stamp-size frog was a bull frog or a tree frog (having found him halfway between the pasture pond and the thicket), he was practically certain that with patience and proper care and a balanced diet, this particular frog could be trained to out-jump all other jumpers, including even those from Florida and California.

That night he searched the encyclopedia and read everything he could find about frogs. He looked through our old farm and nature magazines for further information on the care and training of champion jumpers.

"Dad," he asked, "did you ever hear of people feeding race horses raw eggs to make them long-legged?"

"I've heard of feeding them raw eggs, but I think it's to make them long winded."

"Well, do you s'pose if I fed The Rival raw eggs it would make him long-legged?"

At last he went to bed, but evidently not to sleep. For just as I had dozed off into that first sweet slumber, I heard a voice: "Mother, Mother. Are you asleep?"

I grunted an inquisitive answer.

"Mother, what was the name of that frog that got fed on buckshot? Was it Daniel Webster? Who wrote that jumping frog story? Do we have a copy of it here? Mother, don't you think Daniel Webster would be a good name for my frog? Or do you like "Old Gold's Rival" better? What do you think of naming him Flash, or Omaha? Mother, who was it wrote that story? What county did he live in?"

I grunted a "Wait 'til morning," and turned over to sleep again.

But next morning the frog was gone. Jack had left the cage in the usual animal nursery behind the kitchen stove. But the occupant had escaped, and who could tell where?

Of course, I wouldn't be afraid of a little thing like a stamp-size frog, even if he were named Daniel Webster, but I did feel apprehensive all day, never knowing when I might be jumped at. I searched the house upstairs and down. I looked under rugs, behind pictures, in the bookshelves, and even down-cellar, hoping and fearing I'd find him.

It was not until two days later that we began to suspect that Daniel Webster, Old Gold's Rival, would never jump again. Our noses told us that Old Gold no longer had a rival, that Calaveras County still had the champion tall frog tale.

Fireplace Dramatics

The "very nice" housekeeper would not do such a thing: sweep trash into the fireplace in summer and leave it there a day or two or until a convenient time to burn it and remove the ashes. I must admit that I did such a thing. But I don't any more. This is the reason:

When a day came around that seemed the proper time to burn the trash, I turned the contents of my waste paper basket into our big black kitchen fireplace and proceeded to start a blaze.

As the smoke and flames rose in the chimney, part of the burning paper and the trash began to move, not up the chimney, but out into the room toward me. As they moved, I moved—toward the door. I still kept my broom in hand and my eyes on the apparition.

At last, one large lump of dust-covered trash seemed to separate itself from the burning paper and to come even more rapidly toward me. It was making a scratching sound as it hustled along. I saw what looked like a snake's head peeping out from under a derby crown, and four legs and a sprout of a tail coming along too. That tail could belong to nothing else but a terrapin.

As my paralysis began to loosen up, I remembered Jack had said the day before, "Mother, Buppo and I found a terrapin up in the field and brought it to the house for you to see, but you were not here."

I called to mind a practice that Buppo and Jack made of bringing anything they found of interest, whether it was a white blossom of the haw tree, the first wild rose, a cluster of "coffee-berries," anything they found in their ramblings for me to see. If I was not there it was left on my desk or in my chair.

The terrapin probably had been left in one of those spots and had been forgotten until it dropped into the waste basket.

Boys and Dogs

Boys were always beyond my understanding. When Jack went to the back field to "cut bushes," he would take his rifle instead of the ax. When he went to the creek bottom to sow clover, he would take fishing hooks and lines, but not a seed sower. Boys are peculiar beings, their ways beyond understanding.

Dogs are as mysterious as boys. In fact, their ways are somewhat alike. They seem sometimes to work "in cahoots." Just as I would get Jack down to weeding onions in the garden, Buppo would start up a terrible racket in the woods. Jack would stop and listen. He seemed always listening for that dog, especially when he was at work in the garden. He would listen and then say:

"Bup's treed."

I'd say nothing.

Then he'd say, "I'll bet it's a groundhog."

I'd say nothing. I didn't like groundhogs anyway. Too greasy.

Next he'd say, "It might be a squirrel."

Then he would begin a brief discussion of how good squirrel and dumplings would taste for supper.

I'd still say nothing.

Next: "I wouldn't be surprised if it's a rabbit. Say, Mother, don't you have another jar of that good Creole sauce that makes rabbit gravy so good?"

I'd weaken. He knew that the pride of our table is Creole rabbit, and it was the time of the year for young rabbits to be at their tenderest.

I'd finish the onions alone. It was the penalty I paid for being the mother of a son and the endurer of a dog.

❧

Squeal and All

On Saturday afternoon the old red sow found eleven little pigs back in the field by the straw stack. It was a chilly day, so Dad went back there and erected a temporary shelter of tin scraps and boards to protect the mother and her babies.

Sunday morning he went back again to see about them, and as he moved one piece of tin, the whole structure rattled to the ground. One little pig squealed, the old sow huffed, and eleven little pigs scattered in eleven different directions. You know how baby chicks will run and squat in the grass at the least sound or sight of danger. Well, the pigs behaved in the same way.

It took ever so long for Dad to get those little squealers, at least the first ten of them, back to their places; and one simply couldn't be found. So Buppo was called. As it was a misty morning, the old dog was dozing under my desk. But at Dad's call he willingly rushed back to the straw stack.

Dad explained to him, as clearly as a human being can explain to a dog, what had happened. And Bup started smelling around. He sniffed and trailed, and trailed and sniffed, he rambled back and forth through the orchard, through the crimson clover, up a ditch, down a ditch, over one terrace, then another, until Dad thought the dog had forgotten the pig and was hunting rabbits instead.

But not that dog! He scouted out to the middle of a 15-acre rye field—rye can grow thick and tall when unpastured in the spring of the year—and there he found the lost little pig, ears, tail, squeal, and all.

CR

Boys Plus Dogs Equals Trouble

Among other things to be learned on the farm is the fact that the commonly accepted rules of arithmetic do not work when applied to boys and dogs. If you have two peaches, you have two peaches; the same rule works with apples, radishes, and pennies. But with boys and dogs it is different.

For example: if you have one boy, you have one boy. That's granted. But if to one boy you add another boy, then, so far as work is concerned, you have only half a boy. And if to one boy and one boy you add one dog and perhaps another dog—then you have exactly zero for help with chores. You may, however, add them all in another manner and, forgetting the chores, multiply the fun.

One summer we borrowed a boy named Bill. Bill was one of those young Americans with four parents and lots of relatives. His mother and step-father lived in one city; his father and step-mother lived in another; and his grandparents and uncles and aunts and cousins were scattered here and there. All this and other circumstances made it convenient for Bill to stay with us, and he was the pet of the farm. All the folks and animals, even the wild things, seemed to love Bill. From the time he lifted his curly head from the pillow in the morning until he turned up his tired little toes in the evening, he was a continual source of interest and pleasure.

Bill's age that summer was somewhere near half-past-eleven, but he always said he was going on twelve. One of the first friends Bill made after coming to the farm was the old red mule. He learned to ride the mule back and forth to the field and pasture, looking rather comical perched high up on the ambling Old Red.

Then he made friends with the bull yearling, the one we called "Little Fool," a rascal just young enough to be fun and old enough to command respect. Bill and the calf could be seen almost any day romping about the barnlot.

Then Bill adopted the pigs. He seemed a natural swineherd. There is an art in driving pigs, and Bill was that kind of artist. But his best pal was Jeep, a nondescript pup that had been bestowed upon us by relatives in town.

Jeep was a born discoverer.

One of her first discoveries on our farm was a very dead frog, one from which Jack had removed the legs a week or so before. Jeep insisted on bringing it into the house just at supper time.

She found many long-forgotten old shoes—but no old stockings. Every stocking she discovered was new, although it didn't in any way look new by the time its rightful owner found her with it!

Jeep's favorite outdoor activity was discovering grass-hoppers. You'd scarcely believe a grasshopper could be so fascinating unless you could watch Jeep bouncing through the weeds or tall wheat, chasing first one then another nimble grasshopper. Jeep would also get nimble, so nimble in fact that sometimes she would forget herself, and seem not to realize that when she jumped she must land on earth and on her own feet instead of on stalks of wheat like her quarry.

On one occasion we saw her land in a puddle of water deep enough to bring her out of her ecstasy of bouncing for a few minutes at least. But she was soon back to chasing grasshoppers.

Bill alone might not have been so bad. But Bill and Jeep, added to Jack and Buppo—two boys and two dogs—well they made a zero that was indeed a problem. They were likely to attempt anything, likely to bring in anything, and at anytime.

One morning, hearing war whoops down in the lower field, I prepared myself for a surprise, but not for the surprise that really came. They all came marching single file up the path, Bill, Jeep, Jack, and Buppo. Bill was in front holding high the trophy: a very much alive half-grown polecat.

"Bill!" I screamed, "He'll scent you!"

"He's scented already," was the boy's reply.

And he had. Two boys went into the pond over their ears. Two pairs of overalls were buried. And two dogs were forbidden to come near the house.

Indeed, arithmetic does not work accurately where boys and dogs and skunks are concerned. Two boys, two dogs, and one skunk total five—and one big scent.

Fun on a Farm

For a long time there had been a very lonely and unloved little farm on the south border of Knoxdale. For years it had been passed back and forth among renters, tenants, and absentee landlords, until at last nobody would live there except one unparticular old cat.

It was part pity and part greed that made us decide that we could buy the place for a song if the loan company would sing the song. So we acquired an important looking paper containing a lot of "whereases" which denoted that we had a right to cut bushes, fill ditches, plow corn-rows, and pay taxes on another 37½ acres of land.

Dad and the part-time hired man had all they could do, of course, to manage the homeplace. So Jack and I took over the orphan farm, and Margaret adopted the little four-room house, the fireplace, the yard, and the cat.

Of them all, the fireplace seemed in the best condition, but it needed a new "face" and a new mantel-piece. The house had lost nine window-panes, and that made it look like a snaggle-toothed old hag. It had not had a coat of paint in the memory of man, and the yard was the only place on the farm that wasn't grown up in "shrubbery." Very likely the only reason the cat stayed there was the fact that the last family who had lived there had thought it bad luck to move a cat.

A stubby old broom was standing behind the door, and a box of salt was on the shelf—more than likely all left for the same reason. The broom we used to brush out the house and over the yard. The salt we took to the cows in the pasture. But the cat stayed on. Each time we went there we took it a pone of bread and a little bottle of milk. We hoped the cat filled in with mice between our visits.

When weather was too bad to work outside, Jack and I helped Margaret with the house. It was remarkable how the plain little thing responded to treatment. With lye soap, sand, rainwater, and the stubby broom, we scoured the floors until the grain of the pine smiled through. We cleaned, patched, and painted around the windows, then draped them softly with some left-over tobacco canvas on cane poles. We put in some window screens; dressed up the fireplace; applied paint inside and out; planted shrubs, bulbs, and vines all around; sowed grass over the bare spots in the yard; hauled off the trash to the gullies, and generally had a good time.

As for the farm, Jack thought that we could clear off the bushes, fill up the gullies to prevent more erosion, and grow enough hay crops and a few cash crops to pay the taxes and keep up the payments on the mortgage. If we could pasture some livestock, grow some clover and lespedeza to build up the land while he was going to high school; then by the time he was ready to go to Agricultural College, the little adopted farm might grow enough corn and tobacco to pay his college expenses.

He talked over some of his plans with the County Agricultural Agent, and together they developed some bright hopes for the place. The first problem was to stop the soil from going to the sea; the second, to trim off all unnecessary and undesirable bushes and thus give the native bluegrass a chance. The County Agent said that on a small farm one needed to make every inch count. And that was exactly what Jack planned to do.

Every Saturday the boy would work there all day with grubbing hoe, shovel, and ax. Margaret would be busy working on the dirty little orphaned house. I'd fix an early lunch for Dad and me, and then I'd take the children's lunch to them, which they would warm up and eat before the plain little fireplace if the weather was cold.

I'd take along a rake or broom and some gloves; and would get so interested in the project I couldn't get away to get back home and do my own work.

I couldn't help much with the grubbing hoe, but I could certainly help a lot, Jack said, by dragging the bushes out of the way as he cut them, and piling them into the raw, gapping ditches. I raked the dead grass and weeds and trash off, too, and found that they all made very good ditch-fillers.

I don't know when we ever had more fun on Saturday afternoons, or on any other days, than we all did in nursing that little farm back to smiling health.

At Jack's suggestion, I always wore a pair of overalls. It wasn't any job for dresses, he said. And we certainly did have some jolly tussles with those bushes and gullies.

When we would start on a new ditch we would first select the likeliest places for our dams. Narrow places in the gully worked best, we decided. There the banks would be close enough together to help give strength to our small dams.

We would make a bed of dry grass in the bottom of the ditch in the spot we had selected, pile weeds on top of the grass, then rocks on top of the weeds to hold them all down. Small brush came next; most of it with the bushy part pointed upstream. We'd pack that down as tightly as we could, and weight it with more rocks. And the big brush came next, and Jack and I had to put all our weight—his 135 pounds and my 115 pounds—on top of it all.

We'd scramble up on top of the brush, reach out and catch hands, and as Jack would yell, "Ride 'im, Cowboy!" we would both start jumping up and down with all our might and pounds until we had that brush packed down as tight as we could into the narrowest neck of the gully.

You can scarcely imagine the equilibrium required to "ride down" a brush pile into a gully unless you have tried the stunt yourself. It is a sport I can heartily recommend to anyone who is stout of heart and strong of muscle, this game of rehabilitating a bit of neglected land. The thrills that come as the game goes on are not to be compared with those from mere spectator sports.

Of course, we were not fooling ourselves when we bought that little, rundown farm. There would be many whacks of the axes and many shoves of the shovels between the farm as it was, and the farm we hoped to make—a neat, trim, well-groomed, well-fenced bit of earth. There would be an inestimatible number of backaches and muscular pains, and hundreds of scratched shins and thorn-stuck fingers between us and our goal. We knew well how heavy and rough were the rocks that had to be moved; how pesky were the roots and bushes that had to be cut; how hot the hayfields would be in July; how pitiable the crops would look during droughts. We knew all that and more.

Way back in my mind and deep down in my heart, I knew something that Jack hadn't figured out. If he would stick to the project, fill the ditches, cut the bushes, mend the fences, build the barn he planned, if he kept on using his head, his muscles, his Scots determination, and the advice of his Dad and the County Agent, he would make the little farm support itself. He would pay his way through Agricultural College and—what is more—he'd be a "real farmer."

Many times he'd come home, dog at heel, flop down on the back doorstep and say, "Well, I liked that little old place pretty well before we traded for it, but seems the more I do for it now, the better I like it."

I could understand very well what he meant. Margaret and I put our hopes of winter coats and summer dresses into that little old place and Dad took some rather proud walks over it, too. Any time he and the part-time hired man could be away from jobs on the home place they would go over and help with the rehabilitation project.

We decided that the place should have a name, and finding one for it was like trying to christen a new baby. Finally, because there was a leaning old apple tree in the front yard and a shaggy old one in the back yard, we decided that the name should be "Apple Rest," although as Jack said, so far as he could see there'd be few apples and no rest on the place for quite a while.

Jack at that time was indeed a son of the soil. He loved the feel of the dirt beneath his feet, the sight and touch of growing things. Farming, in his estimation, ranked somewhere up near football and fishing, and he frankly announced that he would rather spend the summer with "Oscar," our tractor, than go to New York, London, Hollywood, or South America—not that there was any prospect or opportunity of his going to any of those places.

Jack never did enjoy Algebra or English composition too much, but he did love to take a grubbing hoe and knock a prissy little persimmon bush to Kingdom Come. And it so happened that the little new farm needed ax and grubbing hoe more than math or English.

Saturdays, summer days, school holidays all found the boy, with dog at heel, tramping across a field with an ax, rake, briar-blade or shovel, and carrying a sack of seed, either grass or clover. "Just going over to groom her up a bit," he would say.

Early mornings and late afternoons would find him rambling up and down fence rows with hoe in one hand and a bucket of walnuts in the other, looking for rich pockets of soil where trees would be likely to grow.

But it was not always work. There was fun, also, in that formerly unloved farm.

❧

Mis-carried Christmas Trees

There was disagreement in our family at along about this time. It was all on the subject of cedar trees. Something there was in me that loved a cedar tree more than any other tree or shrub. I don't know what this love dated from—whether it was from memories of the twig of cedar that they dropped in Papa's grave; or whether it was from the cool shade and fragrant smell and the beautiful shape of the little cedar tree in Grandma Jones's back yard, the one where we children made a cemetery and buried with appropriate ceremonies every dead mouse, bird, doll, mole, rabbit, cat, or deceased object we could find.

But at any rate I loved a cedar, any kind of cedar, and Dad detested cedar, any kind of cedar. Cedars and rocks were his pet abominations, symbols of dire poverty, and he was determined that none of either should grow or rest on his farm.

I didn't realize how strongly he felt on the subject, or even how strongly I felt. But at any rate one Saturday afternoon, the children and I loaded Jack's little red wagon with a grubbing hoe and several tow sacks and went to the woods to hunt cedars to fill in some bare spots in the yard.

Strange, but it seemed that the prettiest little trees had the deepest roots, and were in the most inaccessible places. We searched long and dug hard. Finally we had acquired and wrapped the roots of thirteen handsome cedar specimens and one thrifty looking "beech," taller than either of the children and almost as tall as I. We planted the beech that afternoon, and left the cedars for Monday's planting—but be it said here that the beech turned out to be a dogwood—something we would never have tried to move if we had known, for we had heard that dogwoods were hard to move. But we tried it, succeeded, and had blooms for our efforts.

We didn't mention the cedars to Dad. Somehow we didn't think he'd attach much importance to them. We knew he didn't like them much, so we hadn't even asked or expected him to go cedar-hunting with us, much less cedar digging.

That afternoon when we returned we kept the roots carefully wrapped, put the trees, sprouts, sacks and all, in a tub of water in the basement in a dark corner. Monday we started setting cedars. We'd have plenty of Christmas trees by next Christmas, we thought. And we did do some really hard digging that Monday—I was still sore from Saturday's digging. We got our trees out before Dad came home from the field. But somehow we still didn't mention them to him. We thought that if we didn't say anything maybe he wouldn't notice. And we figured that what he didn't notice wouldn't distress him.

But cedar trees began to disappear. Disappeared completely. We couldn't think that the earth had opened up and swallowed them—although we had made those holes rather deep. We couldn't see that they had been dug up or that they had been chopped down.

We never mentioned the loss to Dad, nor did it occur to us that he had any knowledge of it. He just never had seemed to notice our small trees. He didn't seem to pay much attention to our diggings about the yard and garden. He was too busy farming.

But one Sunday afternoon the secret came out. We were all walking in the field next to the road, and there we came upon a sad looking little pile of cedar trees. There were all our little trees, or rather twelve out of the thirteen. The thirteenth was still by the kitchen door. Perhaps we had watched that too closely. But it turned out that Dad had made and followed a practice of taking with him one little tree every time he went out to that field. He just couldn't stand cedars and rocks, if he could help himself ... and he could.

CHAPTER 11

Morning and Evening Were a Full Day

Daybreak to Backbreak

You can learn what skilled work is if you follow in your mind a farmer's wife of the Thirties as she went about her daily tasks.

Try to cook beans that taste like those she put on the table. Bake a cake like the one she took to the Church Social. Or put out an eighth of a mile clothes-line of clean and starched garments from a very full hamper of very much soiled clothes. And while she was doing the wash she kept the baby quiet, answered the telephone, dismissed a book-agent, and at the same time got dinner ready for the menfolk so that everything would be just right and on the table, ice cold or piping hot, when they come in from the hayfield, tired and hungry, at noon.

The farm woman's motto may have been, "I'll have to put off 'til tomorrow what I can't do today," but she could cram just about as many completed tasks into a day as there were flakes in a box of rolled oats. There were two eight-hour days in her every working day, seven working days in every week, or at least six-and-a-half, fifty-two weeks in her every year—or maybe fifty-three, for the week before Christmas might well count two. I knew women on farms who hadn't been away from their homes for a week's vacation in as many as fifty-three years.

Day in, day out, that was the life of the country woman. She came about as near being a living example of perpetual and effectual motion as one might find.

This is what her day's work might have been:

Arise at 4 or 4:30 A.M.—some get up earlier, but few farm women later than 5 A.M. even on Sunday or in the wintertime. Dress, make the fire; go after a bucket of fresh water, cut and bring in some extra stove wood, feed the chickens and give them water, slop the pigs, and clean up around the back door, all while the stove is warming up.

Back to the kitchen, turn the damper, put more wood into the stove, put on water to heat for cereal and coffee, slice the meat; sift the flour, mix the biscuits, cut them out, and put them in the pan ready to shove into the stove as soon as the pesky oven gets hot.

Chances are that the wood is green (green wood is easier to cut), or the wood may be wet. The stove may be one of the cussed kind that won't draw—there are fewer good stoves in country kitchens than you imagine. And a contrary cookstove can make one madder than anything on the farm unless it be a roguish old sow. So if the housewife has a poor stove, or if the wood is green or wet, she may have time to hustle about and shuck and silk a few ears of corn or peel potatoes and get those on to cook while that stove is getting around to fever-heat.

In those days some farmer's wives were still "doing business" on one of those flash-cooking little box stoves—I suppose they called them "box" because they are so near the size of a shoe box. When a woman with a large family had a stove like that, she had to cook one thing at a time and that undone well, set it off to get stone cold while she put on something else to cook.

A woman who can be patient with a stove like that in rushing times like these, and when an impatient farmer and hired man are waiting for breakfast—a woman who can be patient with a stove like that with wood like that, should be taken right on to Heaven before the stove gets cold, but she rarely is. By the time breakfast is done she has to start dinner.

There may be interruptions, such as a neighbor calling to say that the cows had broken over into his cornfield, and would we please come and get them out. Cows know, somehow, the most inconvenient time to go a-rouging. And an old sow is almost uncanny in timing her rooting under the fence. She always picks a rainy, mean-weathered day.

People who declare in favor of toast and coffee—merely that and nothing more for breakfast—haven't pitched hay from sun-up 'til sun-down, milked and fed, both before and after that. It takes a marvel of a man down here in our section to pitch hay from dawn 'til noon on toast and coffee.

So if you're going to follow this farm family through the morning, you'd better put your feet under a real farm breakfast table. Pour plenty of cream into your coffee, and put in two heaping spoons of sugar—then bow your head. I am thankful that my people, "Bible Belt" people, still remember to be thankful three times a day, at least.

Now, help yourself to a slice of ham. Roll up your sleeves and open a steaming fragrant fluffy biscuit, and soak it well with gravy, red-eye gravy, right out of the heart of the ham. Now how about some fried chicken? There's wooly gravy with that. Soak those biscuits well.

Then the farmer's wife will say, apologetically, "I fried a little bacon and a few eggs for them that don't like ham or chicken."

Help yourself to rice, fried corn, or grits or oats, or fried potatoes. Do you like fried apples better? Or apple sauce? Or pear preserves, or jelly?

She passes around the golden pone with ball, cake, or brick of butter, then a jar of honey or a "stand" of good thick, but bright, sorghum molasses. You may like to mix your butter with your honey or molasses, just as the children do—surprising how children know what's best—and lift it gently with spoon or fork from plate to biscuit, and sop it all up together, and cut the biscuits well soaked with butter and syrup into eating sized pieces.

Have another cup of coffee, or try some spring cooled sweet milk, or home-churned buttermilk. There are fruits in season— fresh fruits, grown on the farm.

And now, if you've finished your breakfast, you may sit back and watch the farmer's wife go about her morning's work. If a man, you may push your chair back, reach over and get a toothpick, rise stiffly, and stalk out to the front porch. Or you may draw your chair up behind the kitchen stove, lean back, take out your odorous old pipe, fill 'er up, strike, light and let 'er go.

If a woman is suspected of "toting" a pipe in her pocket (unless she is a mountain Granny, who is permitted special privileges) she would be disgraced for life. That's one of the hamperings of femininity—but I am only saying all this to put off the dishwashing. Who could possibly feel like washing dishes after eating peach pie soaked with thick cream? It has always been hard for me to believe we get energy from food. I don't seem to—not dishwashing energy.

MILK ON HER SHOES

We need to rake those dishes off, stack them up, and feed the dogs and cats. While we think of it, we'd better take some bread out to crumble to the little chickens. It's time to turn them out. So we'll leave the dishes stacked until the morning's milking is done. The farmer's wife likes to get through milking early, because flies pester the cows so bad later in the morning, and because only a steam boiler is hotter to work beside than an old cow's flank on a sultry day.

Milking done, the milk is strained and taken to the spring house. As she comes back to the house she brings the cream for the morning's churning. Often I could get a chance to look over the newspaper or an occasional magazine while I sloshed away at the cream in the old stone jar with the cedar lid and dasher. I always liked the stone jar churn better than the cedar one that Grandma Ussery had passed on down to us because the stone jar didn't have brass bands to be polished, and it didn't leak if left in the sun without water in it. Besides stone was easier to keep clean.

OFF TO SCHOOL

We won't have time to churn now though. There are lunches to fix and children to get off to school. "Mama, where's my cap?" "I can't find my pencil anywhere. Oh, yes, I need a new tablet too this morning." "Have you seen my reader book? I know I left it here on the table last night." "Mama, please sign my report card. You'll have to write my excuse for being absent too." "Hurry up, we'll be late!" "Please, don't put that in my lunch. It's not good cold." "Oh, I don't want any lunch, I'm not hungry." "Mama, do you have another nickel? I've got to pay my class dues." "I need a quarter to pay on the new basketball." "Mother, I just know we're going to be late and you haven't written my 'scuse yet."

They're off! No, they're not. Come back here, Son, and wash your ears. Just look at that rim of dirt around your chin. Why, Sister, you've not even tied your shoes! Would you start off to school that way?

It's a wild scramble, this going to school, and it happens 160 to 180 mornings a year. It's bad enough to have to hustle about and get them ready to go, but the mother who has to get ready herself and take them to school, well, she simply doesn't get the dust out of the corners from September 'til May, and never gets caught up with her patching.

At last we'll have to get back to those dishes, I suppose. But let's get it over as soon as possible, for this farm woman will have to spread up the beds, brush the floors, and rush out to the garden to gather and prepare vegetables for dinner. She'll get dew on her shoes, if she's early enough, and probably dew in her soul. Her shoes will get dry, but let's hope her soul never does.

When she gets back from the garden, she'll stir up and rekindle the fire in the stove, and if she lives south of the Mason-Dixon Line, she'll put the old black-iron dinner-pot down next to the fire, half fill it with water, drop in a fat chunk of salt pork slashed criss-cross (or a piece of hambone) and then start snapping beans. After the meat has boiled awhile, the beans are dropped in; two or three hours more of boiling, then potatoes are peeled and placed on top; then a few pods of okra—they make the beans taste better—an onion, or two, and last some broken roasting ears and some tender young squash are put on the tippy-top to cook in the steam and drip their juices down to blend with those of the other vegetables.

While the beans are boiling, the dessert is made. Perhaps a peach cobbler; a cottage pudding with sauce; apple dumpling, sugary, buttery, and truly very juicy; or it may be gingerbread with whipped cream or cheese, or cherry or berry pie. But it will be good, you can bet!

She may fix up a few extra dishes, too, such as coleslaw, creamed sweet potatoes, candied apples, corn pudding, or some other surprise. And she'll set the bread to bake; corn pone, muffins, biscuits, or rolls. And coffee or tea or both.

And, of course, there's that churning. That's not to be overlooked. She may have to wash out some of the children's school clothes, or press some, or patch some. There may be small children to keep an eye on, too. Or toes to tie up. Or a visiting neighbor who drops in for a minute but stays an hour.

There will still be plenty for the farm wife to do, even when the noon meal is over and those dishes are washed. Supper comes around by and by, but not before the children are in from school—starved, as usual. There are special jobs, too; canning, sewing, sick-nursing, gardening, house cleaning, and flowers to work with—always flowers.

To witness the variableness of farm life one needs only to follow the activities of the farm wife and her husband. Together they make up a team that serves from time to time as butcher, baker, electrician, undertaker, doctor, engineer, nurse-to-man-and-beast, financier, architect, fence-fixer, woodchopper, haymaker, seamster, teamster, plowboy, cook, launderer, gardener, mechanic, toymaker, land-saver, forester, food preserver, shepherd, swine feeder, milkman and maid, chick-raiser, turkey-chaser, butter-maker, thresher-crew, landscape artist, painter, mason, carpenter, cellar-digger, kindergarten specialist, adolescent adviser, a community leader, wise parent and grandparent, general manager, specialist in dozens of vocations and avocations—and just as many other things as you care to mention.

Farm life is as variable as the weather. Sometimes as glorious, sometimes as miserable, and usually less talked about. We take it all in stride. We rarely consider ourselves (even the busy, always efficient farm mother) as classed with "skilled labor." To the census taker we are still "women of no occupation."

⚓

Spring Cleaning

Spring Cleaning is an intangible something that gets into a housekeeping woman on any unexpected occasion between the middle of February and the middle of June.

It upsets the entire household; turns the house itself inside out; moves the bureau where the cedar chest used to be, and replaces the bed with the wardrobe.

It takes the rugs out and tents them on the clothesline and fills the fresh spring air with the winter's dust they held. It takes the pictures down and places them back foremost against the wall on the front porch or face down on the grass in the side yard. It takes the curtains off the poles, soaks and shampoos them, and washes the blankets, the woodwork, and the what-not bric-a-brac.

It is the time of year when good housewives attempt to assert their superiority over the elements, spring mud especially. They try to take Old Man Winter dirt by the horns and give it a thorough shake-down and shake-out.

It is the housewife's way of working the winter "humor" out of her blood. Like the old time dosing of sulphur and molasses, although she hates it, she endures it and she wouldn't miss it for anything.

One strong point against Spring Cleaning is that it always comes at a time of year when a housewife and her family might be enjoying to the fullest that no-account, don't care, let-me-rest sort of feeling which is the very essence of Spring Fever. And when Spring Fever Time clashes with Spring Cleaning Time, what a struggle there is!

My strong complex against Spring Cleaning must have begun very early in life, but it reached a climax, I remember, when I was about ten years old. I was in the fourth grade, and doing Long Division. Arithmetic was then, as it has always been, one of my pet abominations.

Long Division and cube roots were classed in my mind along with castor oil, quinine, and ipecac. Nevertheless, I had worked out my dozen or more difficult problems and had "proved" them. They were that exasperating kind that wouldn't come out even—always a "remainder." I had left the neatly folded arithmetic paper with all its answers and proofs on Mama's room center-table with my books, pencils, and other school paraphernalia, and had gone upstairs to bed.

Next morning, even before I had crawled out of bed, the Powers That Cleaned had decided it was time to begin. They had begun in that very room! By the time I was ready for school, the pictures were off the wall, the curtains were down, the carpet was up, and the center table nowhere to be found. My poor arithmetic paper was never seen again.

I plodded to school with premonition. There was stark fear in my heart and weakness in my knees. Arithmetic was first class to be called and, of course, I was requested to read the answer to the first problem.

I told the teacher honestly that I had lost my paper. Of course, she didn't believe me. She had heard that excuse too many times before. She impatiently sent me to my seat, kept me after school, and gave me a demerit (my first).

Do you wonder that ever after that I hated Spring Cleaning? And demerits?

It is not merely arithmetic papers, well worked and proved, that disappear during that perennial chaos. It is so many of the comfortable handy things we're used to. And those things that don't disappear are moved from their regular places.

Throughout the summer I am looking for things I had before Spring Cleaning. And I no more than get settled comfortably again, and get my belongings all fixed handy so I know where they are, until it's time for cleaning again.

I've never been able to see what housekeepers get out of it. It seems so much ado about so little. If you've ever noticed it, the housewives who are most radical about spring cleaning are the ones who never let dust and litter accumulate in their houses anyway. Houses like that don't need spring cleaning, but women like that need to Spring Clean.

Besides all the worry and hard work and misplacing and inconvenience, there is almost always considerable embarrassment connected with house cleaning time. I've noticed that as soon as the house-cleaner gets all the curtains down and puts them to soak, and as soon as all the family portraits are on the front porch, and the chairs, tables, bed, and bureaus are in the front yard—just as soon as she gets the rugs all h'isted up on the clothesline, and ties up her head and takes her beating stick in hand—in will walk someone, usually the preacher!

And as surely as she moves the guest room furniture into the living room and the kitchen furniture into the dining room so she can have those rooms papered and floors painted—just as surely, in will walk Cousin Matildy for a week's visit, or just to spend the night. The Scriptures might have said: As snow in summer, and as rain in harvest, so is company at spring cleaning time.

It is indeed a terrible time of tearing up, taking down, lifting, shifting, scrubbing, scouring. And it is a season that is dreaded by every respectable housewife for 350-odd days in the year. Yet no respectable housekeeper would miss it.

The house cleaning "bug" bites even me. At any time after January it is likely to strike. Although this perennial fever, this irritating itch-to-clean in its acute form usually strikes most good housekeepers in April, I argue with myself in this way: I can't spring clean in April, because by that time I'll be reveling in garden fever; in March I'll be taken up with little chickens; in May I expect to come down with a light form of turkey poults (not pox, and not quarantinable).

So it just seems I'd better tackle my spring cleaning ogre in February. Then I'll have time to recover and rest up during March, April, and May. Of course, I realize that the ordeal will have to be repeated several times—after Locust Winter, Dogwood Winter, and Blackberry Winter. But I usually choose to begin on some bright day in February, groundhog winter permitting.

☙

Florence-by-the-Day

So, early some Monday morning each February, with step-ladder (borrowed), wall broom (also borrowed), scrub brushes, scouring powder, old rags, elbow grease, and Florence-by-the-day, I started doing my housewifely duty, making an old fashioned house-cleaning campaign, the kind that Mama used to make and the kind to which Grandma Jones was chronically addicted.

I belong to the front-to-back school of thought regarding spring cleaning, meaning I like to begin at the front of the house and work the dirt toward the back door. There is another school of thought, which begins in the kitchen and winds up with everything on the front porch. I can't abide that type of cleaning. I tangled with a cleaner of that kind once. She started with the kitchen sink and worked toward the front of the house; I started with the guest room bed and worked toward the back, and we deadlocked by the divan in the living room.

Fortunately, Florence and I agreed as to procedure, so we began our spring cleaning upstairs in the closets and drawers and boxes where I stored away the things that "might come in use again in seven years." We'd take out all those things that were kept from year to year, and each year there was a general discarding and another general putting away.

During each Spring Cleaning ordeal, I'd pick up from the bottom of a box a little piece of green painted wood. It was part of a toy merry-go-round that Jack loved when he was three, and beside it was the front wheel and handlebar of a worn-out kiddy car. I didn't discard. I just wrapped them up and put them back in the box, knowing as I did so that it wasn't the sensible or practical thing to do. Neither the wheel nor the green splinter of wood would come in use in seven years, or seventeen.

In the stack of books and papers were some of the themes I wrote in sophomore days. One was marked in red: "Unsatisfactory. Twenty-one errors. Recopy." I didn't discard that. Also, on this shelf of papers I'd find letters which some precise young ladies had written to my husband in the years before he became my husband. They are dated. I had no misgivings, and I did not discard those either.

In a shoebox, wrapped in soft paper and a piece of old cloth, I'd find "Boots," Margaret's last doll. Around her were packed the garments that the little mother had sewn so carefully: the plaid apron with its organdy ruffle, the dress of yellow and black checked gingham, complete even to buttonholes. (I remembered Margaret's making that while she convalesced from chickenpox). Then there was a white dress with a black monogram, and a pair of perfectly made pajamas with matching negligee, and a black taffeta evening dress exactly like Margaret's own first one.

When I'd look at Boots, where the paint had worn off her fingertips and cheeks, and think of the nights when her painted head had lain on the pillow beside Margaret's tousled one; when I'd look at all those saved-back scraps intended for doll dresses, it seemed that the dust got into my eyes, or the wind coming in through the open window was giving me a cold. Anyway, I'd tell Florence there really wasn't any need of throwing away any of the stuff in that closet. So we'd just put it back and go on to the rest of the house.

So we'd work from the guest room, through the hall, through Jack's room, another hall, and Margaret's room. Then to the downstairs bedroom, hall, living room, yet another hall, and then dining room and kitchen. The old-time Colonial was built in ell-shape, with plenty of room: plenty of halls, plenty of floor space, window space, and wall space to clean in each room, so don't think that the cleaning was as easy as the mere telling of it.

Finally the Kitchen Stove

One particular Spring Cleaning will always stand out in my mind. Our old house and I had been wrestling together for 26 years, two months, and five days to see which one of us could wear the other out. Now, on the ninth day of the 27th annual spring cleaning it looked as though the old house was about to win.

I was always afraid spring cleaning would be my downing. Each year I try to postpone it as long as possible, and this year I might have put it off until after "blackberry winter" if

Margaret's soldier-husband hadn't gone on bivouac and allowed her a brief visit home. Margaret is such a good house-cleaning help that I couldn't bear to see so much woman-power sitting around knitting, and there was opportunity for spring cleaning.

Fortunately, Margaret and I agree as to procedure, too. So on the second day of her homecoming we began. It took eight days of double hard work for both of us and all the help Dad could spare from his farm work to get us through. But at last, on the morning of the ninth day, we could survey the results of our toil with satisfaction; everything cleaned but the kitchen stove. The china closet had been dusted, piano polished, floors waxed, freshly iron curtains hung, and all fairly well done. Finally came that kitchen stove!

We realized that this year the stove and pipe were unusually logy with soot. During the farm labor shortage we had been forced to burn a bit of coal to save stove wood. And as taking down a stove pipe is usually a messy job anyway, we put newspapers down all over the kitchen floor to catch the flying soot.

Then began the dismantling: Dad put a stool on a table and climbed up; I put a stool on a chair and climbed up; Margaret generalized and directed from the floor. The pipe came down in two parts. Dad carefully handled the heavier horizontal piece. I just as carefully took the perpendicular pipe with the elbow.

Margaret opened he southwest back door which had been bolted against the strong March wind, and we proceeded outward, Dad in front, me trailing.

We had done a neat job. I looked back as we neared the door and remarked: "We've never spilled as little soot on the floor as we have this time."

Dad turned to survey the perfection of our accomplishment. As he did so he tilted that heavily laden stovepipe, which he carried at shoulder level, so that the outside end caught the full impact of that south west wind.

Swoosh!!!

My face, head, shoulders—all the world that I could see—went into immediate blackout!

Later I found that this blackout had included to a certain extent the piano keys, the cups in the china closet, the guest room bed spread, the clothes in the wardrobe, all of our carefully washed and painfully ironed curtains! That soot went everywhere!

Did you ever try to sweep soot? It does itself into such pesky rolls and balls—the kind that have to be gently persuaded, not smeared by sweeping or dusting in the usual manner.

So, on the ninth day of the 27th annual spring cleaning, it really looked like the old house was winning. And it was time for Margaret to go home.

I washed out the dust cloths, shook out the broom, oiled the mop, sat down for a good cry, and started again.

Ode (Owed) to Spring

Another blessed scourge of spring that comes in deluge form is the recurrent onslaught of seed catalogues. We'd no sooner get the Christmas cards put away before those bright, enticing reminders from enterprising seedsmen began to pack the mailbox. We'd try to cast them aside, hide them behind the stack of glass front envelopes, or the mid-winter sales announcements, but the thought kept coming up: "If the catalogues come, can Spring be far behind?"

Then, some lifeless January morning or afternoon (like as not it would be on a Sunday) we'd take pencil and scratchpad in hand, settle down in a comfortable chair before the fire, and stack the seed catalogues beside us.

It's the blood of Old Grandpa Adam, that first gardener, I suppose! At any rate, by the time the fire had died down, we'd have hollyhocks in bloom by the garden fence; a row of Canterbury bells nodding alongside; giant dahlias, rainbow-colored gladioli, "bigger and better" snapdragons, pastel asters, fluted poppies, shy little candytuft, mignonette; and all the others, blooming and blowing in unison on that bare brown spot outside the kitchen door.

The vegetable section of the seed catalogue then would march like a bright colored circus parade before our armchair reviewing stand beside the fire. The parade would be led by asparagus and artichoke, on down through the alphabet. Page after page, they'd pass, row after row, in appetizing array. Even spinach looks good in catalogue pictures and dream gardens.

It is a sort of mania, I suppose, this love for green and growing things, but do not be distressed. There are cures, several of them. A flock of scratching hens can cure almost the "ravingest" patient. And what they can't accomplish cutworms, squash bugs, and beetles can carry on. Late frosts, broiling sun, droughts, and hailstorms are all effective, but scarcely any cure is permanent. The patient is likely to have another attack of arm-chair gardenitis next January when the seed catalogues come again.

I'm so glad that an all-wise Providence decreed that garden-planting time come in the spring. Just as we are all worn out with winter, winter, winter, and it looks as though we'll be completely submerged by weather, there will come one of those gorgeously balmy days which impel us to plant our gardens.

The air seems so new in the spring, and the winds so soft. The rain and sun seem child-like in their gentleness. All that I ask on days like those are more dirt to stir, more seeds to sow, longer days, a stronger back, and the ability to forget that in each row some weeds will come and the mid-summer sun will be hot and sickening.

Not only does the making of a garden put gravel into one's shoes and grime under one's nails. It also puts something intangible and very satisfying into one's soul. It relaxes taut nerves and restores a tired spirit in a way nothing else can. There

MORNING AND EVENING WERE A FULL DAY

is strength in the earth, but one must come close to Earth to get it. One must put knees on the sod and fingers in the clods, or lie down on the soft grass to feel that strength.

One needs, too, to plant seeds, to let those dry little pellets of latent life slip through one's fingers in order to know what living is like. Earth still is Mother of all.

In the spring human notions likely turn to thoughts poetic. The true and would-be poet breaks out in stanzas and sonnets, all hedged in by meters, rhyme, or rhythm. He calls the result of his efforts "An Ode to Spring" or some such title.

But a busy country woman can't be bothered with complicated matters like those three "R's," rhyme, rhythm, or reason; she just has to say what she thinks and let the accents fall where they may. Being a genuine 116-pound, milk-on-my-shoes, hay-in-my-hair country woman, and being better acquainted with "please-remits" and "will-be-dues" than with couplets or quatrains, I'll pay my tribute with an acknowledgement of obligations and name it simply:

Owed to Spring
By Lera Knox

A billion blue violets pushing through Earth's leafy blanket to see what this thing called Spring is all about.

Small, lady-like anemones blowing on a sunny south hillside.

The distinct odor of onions or wild garlic in the old blue cow's milk.

Hens cackling about the barn, in the chicken-yard, and under the house.

A frisky brown wren trilling in the plum tree near the back door.

Lambs dancing on a ditch-bank, daring one another to fall in.

Calves romping like rabbits about the pasture and nuzzling up to their mothers to be fed.

And yes, the swish, swish, double swish of a lamb's tail when its owner is at dinner.

A flush of goldenbells showing beauty near the chimney corner.

Redbud trees coyly putting on spring dresses of fuchsia-tinted chiffon.

Pussywillow catkins trembling in the wind, as though frightened by the budding dogwood twigs nearby.

Hillsides greening; plum buds swelling and peach trees showing pink.

The smell of burning trash as yards are cleaned, the whiff of wood smoke from burning tobacco beds—those beds that look like fiery snakes creeping across the hillside at night.

The rhythm of the sower's stride and the swing of his arm as he scatters seeds to the breeze.

Mr. and Mrs. Redbird's quick darting in the fence row, the bluebird on the gatepost and the mocker high in the hackberry tree.

That host of golden daffodils blowing and swaying in the breeze.

A whiff of trillium in the air, the "bite" of Indian turnip.

Freshening green moss on a rocky ledge.

Helpless baby chicks needing crumbled bread and buttermilk.

A bed of old-fashioned blue and pink Roman Hyacinths; lilac buds daring frost; sudden showers and Easter snow.

Perky bonnets, new shoes, bright coats and dresses.

The feel of crumbly clods of garden soil, the fragrance of the fresh turned earth.

The cuddlesomeness of baby rabbits whose nursery bed has barely escaped the plowshare.

Ribbons of pressed earth across a cloddy field, meaning that corn is planted.

The wobbly jointing of winter grain, giving promise of daily bread.

Sunfishing, grunting, squealing piglets—hope of next year's sausages.

Lettuce, mustard, radishes and onions, all chopped up together and "dressed" with vinegar and hot ham gravy—and hoecake, of course.

Men and boys digging fish bait in damp places, women planting flower beds.

Squirrels cleaning up their winter stores; and the racket of a jaybird orchestra.

Hog jowl and turnip "sallet" topped off with poached eggs and homemade pickles.

Easter lilies, rhubarb pies, fried chicken, strawberries, asparagus tips, house-cleaning, spring fever, apple blossoms, cold winds, rosy dawns, and tulips.

Blue skies and gray; and as Mark Twain said, "One hundred and thirty-six kinds of weather inside of twenty-four hours."

All things made new; the slow growing and cautious coming-out of all those patient things that wait beneath the sod all winter.

Life, Nature, Humanity—all at their best.

For these things and many more I am indebted to Spring. It is a debt that I can never repay. I may not say my thoughts in rhyme, nor even in proper words, but I can enjoy and appreciate Spring's gifts and be her grateful debtor, and Spring never sends a bill.

CHAPTER 12

Spring and June
on Cow Path Lane

On Cowpath Lane

The children grew. (With what joy I cut up the coat of my wedding suit to make Margaret her first little-girl coat). With their little tin cups in hand they would follow their Dad to the barn and would drink warm milk fresh from the cows. They always had a row of carrots in the garden, right next to the fence. Many's the time I have seen Margaret in apron and Jack in overalls plod up and down that row, pulling carrots, rubbing the dirt off with grimy hands, and eating them as though they were candy. "Getting the children to eat" was never a problem in our family. The problem, if anything, was getting something and enough of it prepared for the children to eat.

We lived a rich, full life. Of course, Dad had his troubles wrestling with the mortgage, the crops, the bugs, the weather, and markets. I had my hands full with the house, garden, chickens, sewing, laundry, canning, and such, but in emergency or rush we could always help each other.

I learned to drive four mules to a harrow in planting time and to ride the binder at harvest. Alex would help me on wash-day when the tub was too full or he would peel peaches or snap beans at canning time.

Our life was simple but never dull. On a farm where there are animals and children one learns to live in constant anticipation. It was the children's great joy to follow their Dad to the field. They'd trot along behind him in the furrow when he plowed, and the chief pleasure at end of day was to be permitted to ride home on the mules or horses.

Pat and Will were team mates. Their gray Percheron backs were as broad as our kitchen table and Margaret and Jack were delighted to be hoisted atop one or both horses to ride to the barn. The children seemed so small and their mounts so large that Dad said they looked like a couple of horseflies up there.

One day Margaret came to the house in tears. Her dress was torn! Her dress was torn! That was all I could learn of the reason for her tears. And Jack had done it, had torn her favorite dress. She was inconsolable.

Dad came in chuckling, but nervous nevertheless. He explained that the two children had been riding Old Will, Margaret in front, holding the reins, Jack behind, holding onto Margaret. Clumsy Old Will stumbled; Jack began to slip; he caught Margaret's dress, but that did not keep him from falling to the ground, taking part of Margaret's dress with him. She never forgave him for the loss of that skirt.

Like most children at sometime in their lives, Margaret and Jack yearned for a pony. And after that tumble from Old Will's back we felt that at least from a pony they wouldn't have so far to fall. A neighbor whose children had outgrown their pony, Prince, loaned him to us, and our own two were delighted. They curried, petted, and pampered him all summer.

That autumn when Margaret was eight and Jack was six they begged to ride Prince to school. We doubted that it was wise, and considered long before giving consent. It did seem simpler, though, than taking them and going for them every day in the flivver, but still I was uneasy. Finally we decided that they might try it if Dad went with them a few times to show Prince the way. So with the two children on Prince, and Dad on Old Will, the school year began.

Prince would plod back and forth over the country dirt road with little need of guiding—would plod daily, that is, except on cloudy days! On those days, no matter how far along toward school he might be when a cloud came up, Prince would deliberately turn around and trot back home with the children; or if he was already at school when a cloud appeared, he would slip his bridle and head for home, sans riders.

We suspected that the children offered little argument when Prince decided not to go all the way to school. So when the three of them came back into the yard in the middle of the morning after I thought they were safe in school, I would fasten Prince in the stable, give the children each a dose of castor oil, and put them to bed.

One day, remembering the castor oil, the children succeeded in getting Prince to school, caught him in the act of slipping the bridle, and secured him with a rope to a fence until school was out. It was at about that time that the bottom seemed to drop out of the sky. Knowing of the lack of protection for the children, Dad and I started toward the school in the flivver. It was a soaked trio we found halfway home. Jack with red hair plastered to his forehead, Margaret with silk pongee dress plastered to her skin, and Prince coming as-near-showing disgust as a so-called dumb animal could.

❧

Bobwhite

Not only the family pets were comedians and actors. The farm animals, too, could give us amusement and tragedy.

The clown of our farm at one time was a fat, mischievous little white pig. He and several brothers and sisters arrived one night during zero weather. By the third day, he alone was left to see the sunshine—and he had lost the outer two thirds of his tail. Because of his misfortune and his color, we called him Bobwhite.

He became the pet of the place. He got the choice table scraps that the hens should have had. He got every drop of milk that was left over from family use. He had shelled corn spread out before him until he had to sit down to eat. Of course any pig will lie down and roll over when someone picks up a corn cob and scratches him, but Bobwhite rolled over when he saw anyone start toward him with a cob; he did not wait to be scratched down.

Any pig can find a hole in the fence and go out it, but Bobwhite was so much more intelligent than ordinary pigs he could find the same hole in the fence and come back to the barn through it when Buppo started after him. The two, Buppo and the pig, were great pals when Buppo was not playing policeman. They ate corn together, basked in the sun, and slept side by side. But when the pig went where he shouldn't, Bup did his doggish duty to bring him home again. Of course, we couldn't bear to make bacon of that pig that fall.

☙

Henry the Eight

No story about the farm yard would be complete without the Soothing Saga of Henry the Eight.

Henry was our big, bad, frightened, frightful, pawing, and bellowing bull. Perhaps I should spell that last word with a capital B. We felt that way about him. For Henry had horns! We treated Henry with Respect, for Henry had a Disposition.

Ordinarily I hate to see man or beast with a ring in his nose, but many a time I breathed a prayer of thanksgiving for Henry's. More than once, that ring was a life-saver for either Henry or his handler. Sometimes that wasn't enough, though. He persistently charged every creature in his sight, and jumped every fence in his path.

The important part of this story is a piece of tin, one about eight by twelve or twelve by fourteen inches, or at any rate, a piece of tin just a little larger than Henry's face. This invention of a desperate owner was designed to serve as behavior-modification for Henry—or soothe him, whichever served.

With the ring securely in his nose, and a rope in the ring, and the rope tied to the fence, and Henry on the other side of the fence, we fitted the tin crosswise his forehead, noggin, or whatever you call the space below the horns on an impatient papa cow; then we clipped the lower two corners slightly so he could see his grass, feed and water. Next we punched holes in the tin, top and bottom, and with soft wrapped wire fastened the scrap of tin to the horns above and the halter below. Finally we sprayed Henry's back, chin, nose, and ankles for flies, gave him a pat on the head for the good behavior we expected from him from then on, and turned him loose.

Henry was like a calf again. He "talked" about his troubles, his handicap, his blindfold, or whatever the scrap of tin might be called. He pawed and bellowed. Very likely what he was trying to tell the world was "a woman's to blame for this."

Henry was really and truly a masculine creature. But we thought he would not try to jump a fence or charge a man he could not see. And that is just what proved to be the case.

❦

The Calf that Made a Pig of Himself

Did you ever see a little Ferdinand try to make a pig of himself—literally, I mean? Well, we had one of those, too.

He was Lady's little calf, a well-bred rascal with the blood of famous Jerseys in his veins, but that didn't keep him from wanting at every opportunity to put a pig's dinner in his tummy.

From the time he was three days old he'd had only a tin pail for a mother. But as soon as the old red sow found pigs, things were different.

There were only eleven pigs. But little Pogis Ferdinand decided that the mother needed more, so he stepped in and made it a twelve-some. He took the back teat on the right-hand side if the pigs were present. But when he found the mother out in the pasture alone, he began with that teat and went from left to right until, well, the eleven little pigs had no supper.

They had to take up board and lodging in the plum-thicket until we discovered what it was all about and moved the old sow out of Ferdinand's pasture.

❦

June Rambling

One mid-June Sunday morning, feeling the need of getting closer to Divinity than I could get sitting behind a neighbor's hat in a church pew, I suggested, with selfish intent, that instead of the whole family piling into the old Model T and jogging off to church and Sunday School in the usual fashion, we make it a do-as-you-please Sunday, and let each one spend the morning as he liked or according to his own dictates. The family agreed.

Jack and Daddy went to church. Margaret tucked a book under one arm and her cat under the other, and retired to her own room—a room selected because of its farawayness, upstairs at the back of the house, where she could see no people and hear no telephone. Uncle Fayette chose to sit on the woodpile and smoke his "homemade."

I picked up two books—not to read, but just for company. One was a book of Psalms, the other of poetry. I had a pencil and pad for sketching and note-taking, if I felt inclined, which I probably wouldn't. With Buppo at heel, I wandered off down our semi-private country lane.

It was one of those rare June mornings when one could wear a sweater or leave it at home. There was beauty in everything, even in the seed-balls of wild garlic and in the feathery blooms of Johnson grass—both of which were regarded as nuisances supreme in our neighborhood.

Queen Anne's lace held fairy umbrellas over the gently nodding heads of clover ladies. The Judas tree held a red heart—one which seemed ready to burst—on the tip of every branch. Always before, the Judas tree had been "redbud" and the "hearts" had been merely reddish new leaves, but on this mid-June morning they were hearts. And the coloring of the Judas tree leaves! Do you remember those beautiful "change-able taffetas" that our elders used to wear? Somehow, the colors of the redbud leaves (red and green all beautifully mixed together) reminded me of those taffetas. I always wanted one of those scintillating silks.

It seems too bad that they ever put such a name as Judas tree on our redbud bushes. It seems unfair to give such a beautiful shrub such a stigmatic name. Anyway, it seemed that the Judas tree reached hearts to passers-by and across the road on that June morning, and at any time it favored us with more than the usual run-of-the-mill roadside beauty, whether in twig, or leaf, or bloom.

Look sometime at the leaves of a so-called wild rose. Its unopened buds in their clusters are favorites with Dame Nature and one of the loveliest of all her bright June children.

It is interesting to notice how roadside plants and woods-dwellers seem to help one another. Near the hackberry and wild rose bush, a trumpet vine was entwining itself in a cedar and neither had ever seemed so beautiful before. Underneath them, adolescent blackberries clustered about the mother branch like bees around an apple core.

To enjoy to the fullest a country road on a June morning, one should not motor nor ride horseback. It is better if one merely walks; the best plan is to loiter leisurely—no place to go, no time to get there—but time to stop, look, move a bit, stop again, and perhaps retrace.

Time may be taken on these rambling walks for communion, so I reached for the rich ripe fruit of the vine, the raspberry vine, then later the dewberry vine, and finally I tasted a blackberry that was half-past red. Next I noticed a plum thicket in a fence corner, and took time to fill my hands and pockets with juicy red and yellow fruit.

Then I did just what you would have done: selected the most comfortable looking mossy rock I could find, one close to an inviting tree trunk, sat down, leaned back, and just looked.

Sitting on a rock by a roadside, just looking, is good medicine. It is recommended for blues, for bewilderment, for jitters. In fact, sitting on a rock in a quiet, woodsy place is good for whatever ails you—unless, perhaps, the rock is damp and your complaint be rheumatism.

Sitting there I watched birds carrying dead grass, feathers, and worms, and heard them chirp, chatter, and apparently gossip among themselves. Sometimes one would be so filled and thrilled with that June day and all the world in general, he'd simply have to take a high limb and bubble over with song. I watched an old grandfather squash bug—he must have measured an inch from tail to nose—repose with dignity on a horseweed leaf. A brown and yellow butterfly seemed motionless in the air. A bee buzzed like a fly in a country parlor. "Busy as a bee!" That reminded me that I had left the breakfast dishes unwashed! And the sun, getting high enough to beam down on my rock, reminded me that it was time to put beans on for dinner.

Still with the book of Psalms and the one of more mundane poetry unopened, with no sketching done and no notes made, I rose stiffly from the rock and sauntered back toward home. I wondered as I went how the same sun that puts the pink in the rose, the juice in the plum, the sugar in the berry, the song in the heart of a bird, also puts the squirm in the snake and the urge of the chigger to get under one's skin.

Sitting on a rock, by a woodsy roadside, is definitely conducive to chigger culture, I found. So still with Bup at heel, I rambled toward home, to wash the dishes, to put on the beans—and to dip a small piece of rag in the kerosene-can for chigger medicine.

❧

A Wardrobe of Cats

DUMPLING

During the years the children were growing up the farm had a continuity of cat life. When Margaret was small there came into the household an almost brand new kitten. This small cat was deserted in babyhood by a delinquent mother and left to starve on our barn doorstep.

For a while the kitten was reared with a silver spoon in its mouth. I don't mean that the spoon was kept there constantly, but that it was inserted regularly and often enough to keep the orphan growing and to help her develop into a healthy and well-mannered cat.

This first cat in our family was named Dumpling. She was as black as night, except for one white spot under her chin and one white foot. She looked as though she had one shoe off and reminded us of the jingle:

"Diddle, diddle dumpling, my son John,

One shoe off and one shoe on...."

So Dumpling she was and Dumpling she remained throughout all the years our babies carried and dragged her about unprotestingly by the "handle," otherwise known as tail.

We had resolved to teach our children kindness and sympathy for dumb animals and began with Margaret and Dumpling, but children of her age are more likely to obey impulse and notion than parents and the S.P.C.D.A.

One cold January afternoon, just before supper, I was bringing in wood and water for the night and next day. I had brought in two buckets from the cistern, and had set one on the side table, the other on the floor. Soon I heard a terrible commotion. Margaret was industriously and thoroughly dipping Dumpling up and down, up and down, in that bucket of cold, fresh water. And you know how cats abhor water in any quantity more than a lapping sufficiency.

I rescued the kitten and scolded and shamed the little baptizer. I reminded her of how cold and pitiful the poor shivering cat was. Margaret seemed really penitent. I then went out to bring in more wood and water and returned to start a fire in the cook-stove to prepare supper.

While the fire was getting well started I sat down beside the stove, took the child on my lap, and started to put on her a dry dress. Before long, I noticed noises from nearby that did not seem to come from the roaring fire. I don't know why I opened the oven door, but when I did, out jumped a distressed Dumpling.

"See, Mother, I fix her so she get warm!" explained Margaret.

After Dumpling, there was a whole string of felines in our household—sometimes about as many as our house would hold. The names I recall were Freckles, Laddie, Niddy, Noddy, Boots, Snooks, Swope, Spot, and Snuffles. There were also a Brindle, Priscilla, and Snowball, and a number that were called just "Kitty."

But one season it looked as though our place would be entirely without cats, and the mice and rats would run rampant. We let it be known among friends, neighbors, and relations that we were in need of a cat or two, or perhaps a kitten, and for weeks we were showered—the sky, the mail, the country peddler, and even our own barn loft threatened to rain kittens on us.

The first offer was a genuine Persian, one that would be six weeks old in four more weeks, off-spring of "Haile Selassie" and "Catherine the Great," and related either directly or indirectly to such cattish nobility as "Cleopatra" and "Hezekiah." There were offers of other cats, more Persians, semi-Persians, pseudo Persians, and near Persians. And there were offers of black cats, albinos, and Maltese, tall cats and short cats, long cats and tawny cats, and plenty of kittens.

Cats could be supplied, their potential donors said, by boxful or bagful.

KITTEN BREECHES

We had to turn down most offers though, for we had decided to consider the first offer. At the end of four weeks we gratefully accepted and received the genuine Persian that was then six weeks old.

She came to us a cuddly ball of softness with large quizzical eyes. We enjoyed the kitten; watched her through the sprawling, bouncing, dancing, prancing, and high-stepping stages. We made for her cotton mice and paper boots.

We watched her hide in tall grass and jump out at nothing at all. We fed her with a medicine-dropper, and went through the ordeal of trying to find a name good enough for such a high-spirited little animal.

Friends helped with name suggestions just as they had with offers of cats.

After juggling names from history, geography, and the classics, Margaret resorted to something simpler. She resorted to her nursery rhymes and came out with the decision that the new kitten regardless of pedigree and ancestral dignity should be called Kitten Breeches. That name did seem to suit the young animal then, but we did not consider the future.

As the kitten grew the name shortened, until within a few months we found ourselves in possession of a full grown and very dignified cat answering to the name of Britches. And imagine having to say later, "Mother Britches"—the embarrassment that cat brought us to!

She was rather retiring with her first batch of kittens. The home she made for them seemed secure enough, certainly it was inaccessible to us—between the living room floor and the cellar or basement ceiling! Except for their serenades we would never have known they were there, and certainly we couldn't reach them without tearing the floor up or the ceiling down. We couldn't decide where to begin tearing.

Then all meows ceased together. Living room and basement were quiet except for human noises and the cries of their heartbroken mother. The least we could do, it seemed, was to offer sympathy in the form of milk and extra petting.

Finally she allowed us to assist with the funerals. I was hoeing out a row of touch-me-nots when she brought the first little corpse and laid it at my feet. I buried it at the end of the row. She took the second to Daddy out in the tomato patch. And Margaret presided at the burial of the third. Every member of the family, including the pup, mourned with Britches over her loss.

BRITCHES AND HER WARDROBE

And then one day, sometime later, Margaret came bouncing into the house with the exciting news: "Mother, it's no longer just Britches, it's Britches Plus Four!"

Even Dad the Dignified and Jack the Scoffer condescended to go out to the chimney corner to see the new family. They looked like oversized grubworms squirming over and under Britches-cat, but she purred over them as proudly as though they were a superb variety of dark diamonds.

I say dark, but one was straw-colored. Jack the erstwhile cat-hater immediately adopted that one. There was a certain similarity—the kitten's fur was only slightly less red than the boy's hair.

Then came the matter of naming the kittens. For the group as a whole we kept the name Margaret had first given them, Plus Four. As they began to show their individual "Kittenalities" we chose and applied individual names.

Three resembled their tawny mother so much that we decided they should be named for her, or at least have similar names. One, with a rusty tinge, we called Knickerbocker,

Knickers for short; one dark, rich gray and black, we called Trousers. The third, pencil-striped gray and white, we named just plain Pants—though, as the children said, that name could be stretched to Pantaloons for poetic purposes.

For the fourth cat, Jack's red kitten, only one name would do. That cat was named Red Flannels, called simply Red. Red was an outstanding cat, even from his grubworm days in the chimney-corner box-apartment. He seemed the friendliest, the most cuddlesome, and the playfullest. He was the first to open his eyes, both of cornflower blue; the first to drink from a saucer, the first to climb out of the nursery box, and the biggest explorer of them all. Jack always said that Red excelled in every way—he even had the most fleas.

Then came the problem of deciding the future of the kittens. It couldn't be the creek—not after we had loved them for a month! And it mustn't be the roadside. Chloroforming the kittens presented the same problem as belling the cat—a good idea perhaps, but who would do it? Yet we realized that something must be done with our quadruplets—Knickers, Trousers, Pants, and Red Flannel—else cats would be accumulating and cluttering up our place like old clothes. Besides Britches would likely bring in a new "wardrobe" next season.

Pants and Trousers found good homes. Knickers had to be nursed through attacks of fits. Then he disappeared. Only Red Flannels was left, and he turned out to be not a flannel red but rather a bright orange in color, a beauty—selfish, greedy, but cunning and adorable.

That kitten's first accomplishment was learned at our big old square piano. He learned to follow Margaret's fingers as they rippled through "The Minuet" or "Home on the Range." The cat and girl made an odd duet. Then, as Margaret said, the kitten learned to "solo." By using a pencil or a straw for a baton she could make the little fellow race over the keys, backward, forward, slowly, or "fortissimo." He seemed to know the difference between the black keys and white ones, she said, and would walk or stand only on the white ones, and gently pat down the black ones.

After a few lessons the kitten needed little or no urging to mount the keyboard. Even in the middle of the night sometimes we would be wakened by weird notes, frightening at first, as though from a ghostly hand—then we'd realize it was just that cat again, perhaps searching for the lost chord.

We nursed Mother Britches through flu and pneumonia, or what seemed like such. We left her for dead once or twice, but always she seemed to have just one more life in reserve. I don't know how many of her allotted nine she used during the time she was with us, but one day she disappeared. We never knew where nor why she went.

PEDIGREE OR HANDICAP

After her going, Red Flannels became Cat Supreme of the place and practically cat boss of the entire neighborhood. We didn't know whether it was his pedigree or his prettiness that wielded the most influence—perhaps it took both. He was a handsome critter, exactly the color and almost the size of a red fox. More than once neighbors mistook him for one as he raced across the field, path, or country road.

One day in his youth I noticed him sitting on his cushioned stool behind the stove. A yardstick was nearby, so I picked it up and measured him. He was fifteen inches high and ten inches across his heavily furred back. And sitting there on that stool he looked simply too regal for ratting.

Perhaps that was his trouble. He was just too magnificent to be a mouser. He sat on that stool looking as wise as though he might have been a cross between a who-who owl and a Solomon-come-to-judgment. Almost too high-hat to purr. Certainly too dignified or too lazy to be bothered with the catching of mice and rats. Or maybe he didn't have barn-cat tastes.

Perhaps his pedigree was his handicap. Maybe that was the subject to which he was giving thought on those occasions when he was so quiet and so dignified—looking so wise in the ways of the world, but not demonstrating enough cat-sense to make a living for himself in the corncrib. A pedigree is a burden that plain alley-cats and barnyard cats don't have to bear.

SILENT SKIES

Nevertheless, we noticed that as Red Flannels flourished, the birds around our place rapidly disappeared. We seldom saw the flash of red-birds' wings above our backyard. We missed the proud scarlet beauty that used to sit in a shrub near the backdoor and preen himself before the glass in the kitchen window.

He could no longer be seen in the golden bells bush above my woodsy little rock garden calling, "What's here?" "What's here?"

I used to look up from my digging and tell him that any bonafide bird of the woods ought to know that this new flower was a crocus, a very fine purple one, and that the other flower was a yellow crocus. I'd show him too that the one next to it was a neat little bloodroot plant, and that others were called purple mist, shooting star, and chicken-fighter violet. But the red-bird was a joker. He would continue to sway and chatter, inquiring over and over again.

"What's here? What's here?"

After Red Flannels took up the habit of purring around my feet as I weeded the garden, Sir Cardinal didn't ask about my garden so much. I missed him.

Most of all I missed the wrens. For years Madam Jenny (I believe it was the same one every year) would sit on a trellis in the backyard and call out shrilly, musically, no matter what the weather,

"Oh, this is a beautiful day! This is a beautiful day!"

She seemed as sincere and as enthusiastic as a certain radio announcer who always said, "It's a beautiful day in Chicago."

Then after the cats came, Jenny was seen no more. The cats played in the trellis, but they couldn't sing and they couldn't eat caterpillars so the trellis was soon deleafed.

We noticed too that after the cats came to Knoxdale, Persian though they were, the mockingbird family had deserted us. Years before a pair of them had discovered the honeysuckle vine on our front porch and had rented it for a song. Each summer they would build a house there and rear another family.

Then we would watch the babies grow from egg stage to awkward aerial acrobats, watched Dad and Mother Mocker fly directly over our heads with food when we were sitting on the porch or working among the flowers around the door, watched them cram squirming wiggly worms down first one greedy yellow throat and then another. Indeed we enjoyed our mockingbirds.

They paid their rent-songs in early morning or in dark midnight. They were indeed good neighbors. But after the cats came, the mockers came no more.

Indeed, one grandfatherly old gray-breast would boldly mount the top twig on the hackberry in our front yard occasionally; our mockingbirds always were top-twiggers and front-yarders, they rarely would sit in shrubs and even more rarely would be seen around in the backyard. From his high perch in sun or wind Grandfather Graybreast would throw his scorn at the world in general, the Knox family in particular, and the Knoxes' cats most particularly.

Then with a flash of white he would flit away hoping, evidently, that he had made us feel very badly about being cat-keepers.

The bluebirds, too, gave up their hollow post nest-apartment in the garden fence. Many a time they had pulled out worms from before my hoe, and many a time I counted their eggs day by day and watched their babies grow. But after the cats came we rarely saw a bluebird. We had to depend upon cats for happiness.

Cats, however, wouldn't catch cutworms. And cats wouldn't keep the green worms off our cabbage plants. Nor would they protect the walnut trees and fruit trees and tomato vines.

Well, we considered the cats and we considered the caterpillars. We missed our birds and the cheer they gave. We decided that though we couldn't cuddle them, we could enjoy watching them. We decided that probably the songs that came from high in the hackberry trees were more worthwhile than the purring on the hearth or even the jingling, jangling of a kitten on the piano keys.

And we could get traps for rats and mice.

So with due regret, we allowed His Majesty Red Flannels, the last of his clan, to go to a city apartment where he would be beautiful, would be petted, would get his food from a tin can rather than from the trellis, and probably would be happier and better off all the way around. And for a time, at least, we kept our farm a no-cat-land and worked to induce the birds to come back.

❧

The Young of the Species

ELEVEN LITTLE MAGELLANS

Here is the saga of "The Eleven Little Magellans," barnyard gifts to a countrywoman.

They were the softest, downiest gifts you can imagine. They dropped right out of not the blue sky but the hayloft; and they didn't exactly drop, either; not all of them. But they got down to earth anyhow.

It was this way: one of those bright October afternoons Jack and Dad went back to the barn after midday dinner, and I went along. We noticed something peculiar—springtime noises in October up in one corner of the loft. We went into the stable and found that it was almost raining chickens—wee, soft, little just-hatched chickens. Somewhere over our heads we could hear the crooning of a mother hen.

Jack climbed up, scrambled around among bales and mows until he was in reach of the hen. After becoming a "much henpecked man" as he expressed it, he began to hand them down to me, one at a time. After the chicks came the unhatched eggs, then the old hen herself.

Almost Human In Her Poor Judgment

It was a sort of April thrill in autumn, and I must confess I enjoyed it, but through it all I could see what lay ahead. October is a very poor month for new chicks. The mother hen was dropping her feathers as rapidly as the trees were dropping their leaves, and during the next few weeks I thought I would probably be making eleven pairs of chick-sized outing pajamas.

I guess we excused their enthusiastic ambition to see around the world when we put ourselves in their places, figuratively, and imagined how it must have seemed to get a chick-eye-view of the world. Can you imagine what it must be like to spend three weeks in an egg-shell? And I don't mean a cold storage egg-shell either. Just think what the "Magellans" had to weather while living twenty-one days next to the breast of a chicken running a temperature of 106 in the shade! And besides that the barn had a tin roof! Some shade!

Once out of the shells they began exploring. (To Margaret, their "adopter," they were explorers supreme, hence their historical name). Among the first of their discoveries were the holes in the barn-loft floor. Through those the Magellans went, "raining" on mules and pigs and calves. Finally Daddy decided the old white hen would never be a fit mother, so he picked up a double handful of chicks and took them to the house and to Margaret. They never saw their natural mother again, nor would they see the barn-loft again until they could rise by their own wing power.

Margaret had never been as much of a livestock lover as were other members of the family, but she could not resist twenty-one little bright eyes (one chick was half-blind), eleven little hungry beaks and eleven balls of fluff. She put them on clean papers in a fruit-jar box, with a crumbled-up muffin and a saucer of milk. Well, surprising to say, and this is always a surprise to me, those wee innocents knew just what to do. Nature is marvelous.

For a week they lived in the box with bread and buttermilk. No more of the world could they see than that; then Margaret upturned the box one day and dumped them right out into grass over-their-heads, grasshoppers hopping all about, caterpillars, ants, and all sorts of stuff like that. And out in that big wide ocean of grass, there they were with not so much as a cluck or a compass to guide them. In the grass they ranged for quite some time, and although they never made the history Magellan did, they did a lot of going around their own world.

Bull Headed

I believe that the orneriest, most provoking, most exasperating job on the farm is that of trying to teach a calf to drink milk from a bucket after he has learned to take the natural way. I learned that the hard way. A Jersey breeder gave Jack a little bull calf a few days old.

Talk about persuading a child to drink a quart of milk a day. Young mothers don't know anything. Try to persuade a calf, a bawling, kicking, and surprisingly strong and hungry calf to drink four quarts a day and skimmed milk at that. And remember that the calf doesn't know how to drink. He's born a sucking animal, that and nothing more. Try that sometime, and you may participate in an unscheduled comedy skit.

For economy sake we decided that the cream would be skimmed off the whole milk and sold, and that the calf would be fed skimmed milk, which after all contains vitamins and minerals and other makings of a calf. It all seemed so easy.

So I started to the barn with a bucket of warmed skimmed milk, saying in what I hoped was a persuasive tone, "Come little calfie, nice little calfie. Stick your nose in and drink your milk. It will make you a big fat vealer by and by."

The calf came, stuck his nose around and about, sniffed, butted, bawled, and bucked. He knew his supper was in the vicinity, but he couldn't get his tongue on it.

I held the bucket under his nose, and quickly half the milk left the bucket. But be assured it didn't go into the calf. It splattered over me and the landscape. I wiped my milky face and determined to try again.

With one hand I held the bucket; with the other hand I pushed the calf's head into it—or intended to. Suddenly the calf's forehead (hard with latent horns) met my chin with a vim, and the remainder of the milk showered me and the feedlot. I can smile now, but I didn't then. I did not even remember then that I had heard it said that milky showers are conducive to beauty. And what I said was not, "Nice little calfie."

I went back to the house for more milk. By this time an onlooker advised that I put my finger into the calf's mouth and persuade him to suck that, then gently lower (get that "gently") the finger into the milk, so that the calf's subconscious, or something, would tell him he had found his mother. It was as easy as that—to the onlookers.

So again with one hand holding the bucket I put an arm around the bawling calf's neck. But what about that extra finger? I needed a third hand. At last I managed it somehow. I got astraddle the calf's neck holding his head with my knees; that left the one hand to hold the bucket, and one finger free to slip into his mouth.

I was afraid he would chew my finger, but he didn't. He really didn't bite, not hard anyway. That was one fear out of the way. Instead he began to suck that finger just as the advisor had said he would. Ah! The plan worked. To be sure I was standing in a cramped position, but I would soon have that calf taking his milk. I gently brought the bucket of milk and the sucking tongue together; and I said, not so gently, "Now suck, you sinner."

I cannot tell you at what second it happened, but happen it did. And it came so suddenly! The calf gave a quick jerk. My finger went in one direction, the bucket in the other. The clatter of the falling bucket frightened the calf so he decided to run. I had no time to untangle my legs from around his neck before he started. This was before the days when women wore slacks or jeans, and a skirt simply complicated the situation.

I yelled something to the effect that he was a "bull headed scoundrel," and his poor old mother in the stanchion shifted her cud to the other jaw and gently bawled, "So like his father."

Did I try again? Well, why go further into this? Some words are not intended for print, and those are the only ones that could finish that story. There are some trials of patience that Job didn't have. It is not recorded that he tried to make veal out of skimmed milk from a bucket.

ℛ

Counting Sheep

Our farming operations seemed incomplete one year, for we had no sheep. On the verge of the Depression, we sold our flock and for various reasons did not restock. The farmer who has slept with both ears listening for that pitiful cry of sheep chased by dogs, and the farmer's wife who has gotten up at all hours of the night to give an orphan lamb his bottle both might envy us our sheepless freedom, but we missed the baaing, bawling rascals.

No green field can quite be at its prettiest without a flock of ewes and lambs peacefully grazing about. While the farmer of the household probably missed most the check from the lamb sales, the thing I regretted missing was the jovial capering of the spry young fellows. No circus, even a three-ringer, can put on a funnier performance than can three or four lambs on a grassy bank. If lambs can find a place like that on which to play, and if they think that nobody is watching, they can cut more didos than the funniest clown. The child who has not watched a circus of lambkins has been cheated out of superb entertainment.

But a lamb's life is not always fun. I have been strongly reminded of another side.

One springtime Sunday morning we had just finished breakfast and had walked out on the porch to "view around," when we heard a terrific commotion in a neighboring field. Sheep were stampeding, dogs were barking. That meant one thing—dogs raiding the sheep. Daddy grabbed his gun, which was always loaded (and treated as we thought a loaded gun should be), and sped across a field toward the noise.

I ran to the telephone and called the owner of the sheep. He was there in a hurry. One dog was brought down; the others got away, but not before they had left a path of bloody damage.

Among the injured animals was a tiny lamb that had been bitten through the back of the neck. The wool and flesh had been torn off over a space as large as a man's hand, and the tendons in the neck appeared to be severed. The little fellow could not hold up his head nor move it.

The children were young enough to cry over suffering animals, and I didn't act much older. Jack had chased after his Dad and had reached the field shortly after the men and guns had broken up the raid, so this one of the casualties was of his own discovering. He cried when he found it, and cried even more when the men said that the injured lamb must be killed. No need to prolong its suffering, they said.

No lawyer ever pleaded harder for his client than the small boy pleaded for the life of the dog-bitten lamb. The owner rid himself of the problem by giving the lamb to the boy, and Dad helped him bring it home. Right into the kitchen they brought it, and right into my arms they laid it, bleating, and with its head hanging limp.

What could I do? It was hardly a case for woman's traditional remedy, the hairpin. But a needle and thread might help, I thought. With Jack holding the lamb's body and Margaret holding its head in position, I slipped my fingers through the torn and bloody tissues, sought out the ends of those severed tendons, and with a sharp needle and some stout patching thread—the kind I used for knees in overalls—I patched up muscles and flesh in the lamb's neck. How I ever did it, I don't know now, but when two children and a baby lamb are all crying, a woman can get up a lot of nerve.

In the name of sanitation we poured in a considerable quantity of strong Creolin solution and bound up the patch with clean soft old rags. The children became nurse and doctor. Alex and I were sure the lamb would die. The children were determined it shouldn't. A lot of mulality runs in our family.

It was a long fight, and a hard one. It was early spring when the lamb was hurt; it was late August before the wound was entirely healed. Perhaps you can imagine doctoring a sheep through the hot summer months with a deep open wound and a heavy fleece—but don't try.

We had every complication except gangrene, and perhaps a little of that. But the little fellow was so pitiful we could not neglect him. Dad saw that he had the run of a private pasture, a field next to the house. And as regularly as the hours passed we went out to that field with a bottle of milk in one hand and a bottle of antiseptic solution in the other.

As pitiful as anything else was the fact that in my haste to perform the operation that Sunday morning, and due to the fact that neither Margaret nor I could look at the wound we were treating, Margaret held the lamb's neck crooked and I sewed it in place that way. So as long as we kept the lamb he had a twisted neck. He always looked as though he had a chronic crick.

Icabod

If you have never had a little Icabod on your doorstep, you may not be able to appreciate this Idyll of Icabod, or The Weaning of the One Chick.

Icabod was the frequently-overlooked member of the Old-Hen-With-One-Chick family. He was an important member, however, for without him, Cecilia, his would-be-flapper mother, might never have come to our special attention.

Cecilia was a high-ranking member of the breed which Aunt Ann called "Bleached-out Dominickers," or "White Barred Rocks." We named her Cecilia as a pullet, for then she deserved that pretty name. She was really a beauty in her youth; but after a winter of heavy laying, and a spring of "setting" and more or less solicitous motherhood, she looked somewhat frazzled and middle-aged.

The fact that Cecilia was snowy white and that Icabod was inky black should not be considered a reflection on the mother's morals. A hen can never know what kind of eggs are being put under her at broody time in return for the ones she has contributed to the family egg basket. After all, you know, a hen is a tolerably defenseless being. But this story is not about the hen; it's about the chick.

We had hoped he'd die a natural death, this singleton chick who was certain to cost more in energy than his worth warranted. But he persistently refused. He was hardy, was

Icabod, you can chalk that up for him, and he apparently had enough stamina for an entire brood.

Icky had pipped his thick brown shell during one of those cool, rainy spells, those miniature January's that a Tennessee April seems to borrow from winter. I believe it was the cold spell we called Locust Winter, or maybe it was Dogwood Winter. At any rate Icky cheeped and squeaked through "Dewberry Winter" and "Blackberry Winter," and came into "Little Turkey Winter"—the one that comes after mid-May—still a-cheeping and a-squeaking.

You see, his mother was a somewhat aspiring creature. She might have had a little leghorn blood in those big veins under her wings. Anyway, she seemed to over-flow with nervous energy. She had little time or inclination to be maternal, and she certainly didn't have the patience to settle down and hover one squawking little Barred Rock rooster.

But again this story is about Icabod. He was always underfoot when we went into the chicken yard. He was always just outside the back door when we threw out dishwater. He and his mother got the first ripe strawberry, and several others. He was present when my lettuce bed was riddled. And I believe he had a part in the upheaval of my fine eggplant seedlings. All spring Icabod seemed to be just one chicken too many.

It came about one day that this flapper mother-hen Cecilia decided to abandon family ties, namely Icabod. It was time for her to drop the hum-drumness of motherhood, preen her feathers, rouge her comb, and, you might say, "set out" again. And when a setting hen sets out there is not much chance for the chicks unless some more maternal old matron of the chicken yard will take them under her wide and hospitable wings.

And then, too, when Cecilia decided she'd be a mother no longer, it was a marrow-chilling afternoon. Icabod was out late—out in the garden eating worms, like the unloved child in the song. I don't think, however, that he was particularly despondent at the time; he just thought he'd get the jump on the early bird by getting the worm before dark. But all of a sudden a cold shower struck him. With haste he made for his usual warm place under his mother's wing in the northeast corner of the henhouse. But the wing was not there.

Icky craned his long neck, and squeaked and squawked, but Cecilia, high on the roost pole above, had her mind on other matters.

Icky was ingenious, however, give him credit for that. He thought he saw refuge in the lower feathers of a would-be-setting hen I had just thrown off a nest. She had settled down under the roost poles on the straw-covered floor, too lazy, too broody, or too sulky to move or even stand.

Icky, cold and wet as the proverbial drowned rat and just about as bedraggled, thought he'd find warmth in those soft fluffy feathers, so he crept under from behind.

The would-be sitter, shocked and overwhelmed at this sudden introduction to advanced motherhood, gave one terrific squawk and hit the roost poles. Icky, just as scared and just as shocked, made for the open door and took refuge under a rambler-rose in an iris clump that was just as wet and as cold looking as he.

No human coaxing could bring him out. Just then came rescue in the form and feathers of Abraham. Abraham was one of those rare diadems of the poultry family, a kind and motherly old rooster. Abraham had all the dignity of his breed, plus three years of crowing experience behind him. What can be more dignified than a Plymouth Rock rooster three years old when he chooses to be patriarchal?

Abraham coming into the fray late, especially for the head of a harem, passed the rosebush and the clump of iris and noticed the wet, woe-begone chick, cheeping and shivering. He made a few deep-throated chuckles—or what would you call them? At any rate Icky understood and meekly but still rather timorously, trekked along after the old fellow back to the chicken house.

Abraham took the lowest roost pole and chuckled again to the orphaned Icabod. Finally, by aid of an orange-crate nest box nearby Icky too achieved the lower roost pole. When I left the chicken house for the night, Icky's rain soaked little body was warming itself up next to Abraham's breastbone. I never ceased to marvel at Nature's way of handling things.

Nature vs. Nurture

There was an old hen on the farm that made me feel very inefficient. She was the mother of three little chicks that were hatched about the time another hen came off with a dozen.

The hen with twelve chicks I managed to catch and bring to a good warm box on the back porch. There I could give her babies the best of attention and could make them grow into Thanksgiving broilers, so I thought.

The hen with three chicks was as wild and uncatchable as a deer, so I let her go. She'd soon drag and chill the chicks to death, I thought, but that would be her own bad luck. I hated though to lose those three, for I knew that old hen didn't know a vitamin from a valise.

The twelve chicks on the porch were raised "by the book." I don't say I exactly counted calories or spelled out their vitamins, but they had everything a chick is supposed to need from cod liver oil to buttermilk. The chicks in the barn were dragged about, clucked over, and scratched for.

And in ten days you should have seen the difference. Shadrack, Meshack, and Abednego of Daniel's day didn't have a thing on those three little chicks that the old Dominicker had raised the natural way. They were so much "fairer and fatter in flesh" than the chicks that had been pampered by the book's way. I decided then and there that in the future I was going to let the hens make out the diet-lists for baby chicks on our farm.

Cod liver oil is no substitute for worms or an old hen's clucking and scratching.

⚮

Yellow Cows with Blue Blood

Then there was the October day when our old red cow came out of the thicket with a sprawling-legged autumn baby at her heels. And, would you believe it, that babe was already wrapped in his winter red-flannels, snug enough for a November day and December and January days into the bargain.

Who would ever have thought it? I remembered well how sleek the spring calves were in their silky yellow dresses; how trim their necks and ankles looked. They were truly stream-lined. But this little winter calf, and one that the old blue cow brought out of the thicket a few days later, were positively wooly. Their ankles looked as though they were wearing leggings and their thick little necks seemed to be wrapped in mufflers. Indeed, Nature is a careful and provident mother.

One year, wanting to improve the breed of our herd, we pooled our resources and stretched our credit enough to purchase two royal dowagers of the registered Jersey kingdom, yellow calves with Blue Blood.

One was U. T. Fauvic's Mona Lady and the other U. T. Landseer's Duchess—but in everyday life they were Lady and Duchess, or collectively, "their majesties." High regard probably made us take a little better care of them than of other cows in the herd. We had already learned a few things.

For one, if a cow has a pedigree it doesn't keep her from jumping every fence on the place and taking up regular "office hours" in the middle of a flowerbed. And even if a cow has a placid peaceful look, it doesn't keep her from going down the wrong end of the lane, and going so fast that you cannot head her off. She takes her placid looks from her mother and her bullheadedness from her father, presumably.

Lady was well along in, or past, middle age, and Duchess wasn't what she used to be, else we couldn't have bought them. Lady was so plump she no longer cared about her figure and Duchess frankly limped with rheumatism, arthritis, or something. But we bore with their infirmities because all our hopes were pinned on the "blessed events" the two cows were expecting in late May or early June. We were hoping for heifers, of course, and we'd have liked to have twins. But we had to take what came, and be happy if both mothers and babes did well.

I couldn't help noticing the difference in the manners of these two cows of high breeding and good training, and the common-grade cows we had been milking before. Maybe we were a bit partial to the royalists, but somehow they seemed so much more genteel than the cows we bought from a trader. They had more dignity by a long sight, and more self-respect. Our hope was for their offspring to be daughters and granddaughters, and many of them.

Calves at our farm were always big events. If one seemed a bigger event than another, it was not because he weighed more pounds, but because he had more pride of ancestry.

Take, for example, Old Heff's calf. He was the biggest little bullikin that had been born on our place for many a year, but because his mother was only an ordinary cow and his father only an ordinary sire, the poor little fellow was likely to rise no higher in the world than veal stew or at the most bologna.

But Lady's calf—he was an entirely different matter. In size he was really smaller than Heff's son; his markings were no more striking, his eyes were no brighter, his ears no perkier—but in his veins there was the difference—or there was supposed to be.

In those veins ran the blood of animals bearing such aristocratic names as Landseer, Pogis, Fauvic, Mona, and others in the blue ribbon class. And his pedigree was weighted heavily with the recorded pounds of butterfat his dam and granddam had produced. For this reason Lady's little son would probably never go near a soup-pot. He'd spend his days in paddock, show-ring, and wherever else good bulls are supposed to be.

Then there was Duchess. For several days we had been keeping an eye out for birthing signs in old Duchess, but she finally managed to elude us. In the lane from the barn to the woods-lot I could follow her tracks in the mud, but after she reached the leafy carpet on the hill tracks were indiscernible.

Then I had to call Bup who was trailing rabbits and whatnot up and down the lane. Well, I searched and Bup searched—at least he seemed to, but his mind might still have been on the rabbits. It was he though who finally found her, whether by design or accident.

She gave a soft little warning "moo" from somewhere beyond a big cedar. Bup backed off, but I ventured nearer, and there she, stood—the Madonna of the Cedars. You wouldn't have guessed at first, perhaps, that a baby was near. I had to look hard several times, rub my eyes and look again before I found it, all curled round in a nest of leaves, with two of the biggest eyes and two of the dearest ears. No artists that I've ever known have painted such a picture as I saw there—the Madonna of the Cedars with New Baby in the Oak Leaves. That woodsy hilltop held a thrill that couldn't be put in an art gallery or museum.

That bovine baby gave me a hearty laugh when she got up on those four wobbly legs and tried to follow Mama through the briars and cedar brush to the barn.

Buppo

A PLAIN DOG

And, of course, there were dogs. The best loved of these was Buppo. He was just a plain dog, not far different from other dogs in breeding and background. His mother was an intelligent little shepherd. His father, or sire, or whatever you call a dog's papa, was a clever fox terrier. But Buppo seemed something better than shepherd or terrier. He seemed "individual." He was so regularly at hand when we needed him, so rarely underfoot when we didn't. He was so patient with human foibles, so understanding of human woes. He was petted or scolded, regarded or ignored, according to the family's whims; but he took it all and remained constant in his adoration, steadfast in his loyalty. In other words, he was just like most ordinary dogs.

Undoubtedly we owed much of what Bup was to Uncle Fayette. Buppo spent a large part of his pup-hood under the guiding hand and understanding tutelage of Uncle Fayette, and as much as a dog can be like a man—and a dog can be like a man, don't mistake that—Bup was like Uncle Fayette.

Many's the hour, at dinnertime, after supper or in cold winter weather, when Uncle Fayette would sit on his favorite stool in the shade, or beside the fireplace in the kitchen, and instruct Bup in his "manners." And Bup, standing there with his nose on the old Negro's knee, learned well to "mind" those manners.

Uncle Fayette loved the dog as much as the dog loved the man, and I heard him say many times, "Buppo is a gentleman, if he do have four legs—plenty of dogs walking around on two." And Buppo was indeed a gentleman in manners, if not in appearance. It would take too long to tell of his gentility, even if I were able.

Bup, like many other dogs, was somewhat "allergic" to storms. The only times we would let him come into the house—in flea season—was during a heavy rainstorm. Well, of course, at that time of the year he would get to be quite a weather prophet. Like Elijah of old, he watched the sky for a cloud as big as a man's hand, and used that for an excuse to plead admittance.

Once in and dozing in the dark recesses under my desk, it was surprising how deaf that dog could be. I would say to him when the rain was over: "Bup, it's time to go outside again," but he would not hear me. Nevertheless, let me rattle a cupboard door or pick up a sack that might contain a tidbit or even mention such words as bread or meat, and Bup was all attention.

A GOOD FARM MANAGER

Would you believe that a dog could be considerate? Buppo could. There was no other expression for it. Who says dogs can't reason? Only he who did never knew a dog in close acquaintanceship. Bup was thoughtful. Who says a dog can't think? Bup could remember, even when others of us forgot.

In as far as he was able, Bup would have made a good farm manager. He wanted everything done on time and in order. And times when we seemed to forget, he gently and unobtrusively reminded us.

For one thing, he wanted the mail to be brought to the house on time, and as faithfully as mail time came he would come to the door and softly whine. He seemed finally to learn that the mail didn't come on Sundays, but holidays were something he didn't understand. There were times when I found it easier to walk down to the mailbox with him on a holiday than try to explain to him or see him disappointed.

And he wanted the cows milked on time. He was always ready to bring them up and to help get them to their places too. And, as well as I did, even better at times I thought, somehow he knew which cows were which. He'd never let a dry cow come to the barn. And he knew enough to keep the bulls and heifers and calves in the pasture, cut them back out of the herd when he drove the milk cows in.

You'll find this hard to believe, if you've never owned a dog like Bup, but out of our milking herd of twenty-odd cows, he knew several by name and would cut them out of the herd, or heel them when called on to do so.

Old Duchess, for instance, was always a slow poke with her rheumatism. She required special attention at almost every herding time. But all I had to do was say to Bup, "Get Duchess." And Duchess was "got." Lady, too, was a big old lumbering bovine, with an udder so big she couldn't hurry along. But Bup seemed to understand, and to let Lady make it along as best she could without too much hurrying.

But that sly Louella—the pest and prankster of the herd— always ready to break and run up the lane, into the cornfield, or in any direction she thought she wasn't supposed to go, but Buppo knew Louella's way, and kept an alert eye on her movements, always in position to nip at her heels.

Yes, Bup was a worker when working time came. Bup was a protection when he thought protection was needed. No strange man came nearer than the gate when our own menfolk were away from the house.

For the life of me I don't know how Bup knew so well the different traits of various members of the family and how he managed to fit in so well with our many moods.

If Jack pulled on a sweater after supper, or picked up his lantern or gun, Buppo would be all attention, ears up, tail a-wag, standing tensely by the door ready to go polecatting or 'possum hunting.

When I picked up the milk buckets in early morning or late afternoon, he would gallop away to the pasture to round up the cows. He knew well that I didn't care for polecats or 'possums. So Bup never "struck a trail" when he was with me. How did he know?

When Dad and Jack would ramble around the farm in daytime, Bup slept on the hearth or beside the back door. He paid them no attention. But let me or Margaret step out that door and walk so far as beyond the garden, and he'd be at heel— protector plenipotentiary, a true gallant.

DUMB ANIMAL?

Did you ever argue with an animal? Don't try to! Ten to one the animal will win. And if the animal happens to be an ungentlemanly gentleman-cow, or a fractious and irate four-hundred-pound sow, you'll find yourself up a tree or a fence, or wishing you were.

Lesser animals also know how to carry their point in an argument, especially a dog. All his life I argued with Bup about the matter of burying bread. I maintained that it was a waste of good cornmeal or wheat flour to take a corn pone, a hoecake, or a biscuit out and hide it in the asparagus patch. Bup, however, seemed to believe that burying bread was conservation.

He would come into the kitchen, take his bread, and stand beside the door, ears pricked, tail a-wag, bright eyes dancing, until someone would open said door and let him go a-burying. What chance have words against wags?

Then again, I liked to sleep until six o'clock, or later, if convenient or possible. But Bup thought everyone in the house ought to be up by five. He was not noisy about it, not ugly at all, just quiet, haunting, polite but persistent.

Whether the five o'clock morning whistle, the one over at the phosphate mines several miles away, blew, or whether it didn't; whether the clock stopped or struck, he would take his stand beside my pillow, and would seemingly try mental telepathy or something of that kind on me. He would stand there like a conscience, looking at me as though he knew I knew I ought to be up. If I shut my eyes and tried to ignore him and go back to sleep, he would give a soft little whimper that made me feel more ashamed than if he had howled.

He would stay there, too, until my feet were on the floor. As dumb as an alarm clock, that dog! Even without whining, he would wake us. Dumb animals? If dumb means inarticulate, as the dictionary says, we need to revise our dictionary or get another adjective for our animals.

And you can't teach an old dog new tricks? So what? Whoever started that idea, anyway? Breathes there a dog-owner, young or old, who to himself or anyone else would admit that the old hound, cur, shepherd, or what-not that has tagged at his heel for lo! these many years, needed to learn any more tricks at all?

You know how it is. If your dog is even a little past middle age you know. If that dog has chased your rabbits, sniffed your 'possums, scratched for your rats, shaken your snakes, heeled your cows, barked at your visitors, and begged for your hoecakes over a period of years, you know that if that old dog—Rover, Fido, Bob, or Fiddlesticks—learned any more tricks than he already knows he'd give some human beings an inferiority complex.

Over the years every step I made away from the house or about the farm was guarded by Bup trotting along in front of or beside me, watching for snakes, grasshoppers, or anything else his mistress might need protection from. I remember one day as we started toward the dairy barn he set up a furious barking in the weeds along the path thirty or forty feet ahead of me. I had rarely seen him so excited. The "booger," I thought, must be as big as a bear, but I couldn't see it.

After watching for a while and wondering, I "sikked" him as encouragingly as I could. Bup lunged in and gave the enemy a furious shake, then walked off sheepishly. What he had shaken had been an empty snake-skin that had been left coiled realistically. But it had come off a big snake; I had to admit that.

But then came the sad day when Bup was gone, and as someone said of someone else, nothing in his life became him like his leaving it. He had been ill for a week, eating practically nothing, just lying around in the yard, under the shrubs or beside the porch. He did bark at the telephone men when they came to test out the line one day. And he did try to go to the dairy barn and after the cows for a time or two, but had to be brought back, too weak to stand.

Finally we made him a soft bed, put him in a box, gave him some medicine, and began treating him as we thought a sick dog, a very deserving one, ought to be treated. But Bup seemed to know what was coming. He seemed to want to spare us shock, grief, funeral, and all that. So, sometime during the night he got out of his sick-bed, a super-canine effort it must have been, and wandered away. So, due to that last bit of thoughtfulness we will not say, we cannot say, he is dead. He is just away.

Who says dogs don't think?

Root from a Honeysuckle Bush

It all began years ago when "Mammy" Stone gave me the honeysuckle bush. "Mammy" Stone was just about the dearest, sweetest little old lady that one finds in a lifetime. She was my closest neighbor—half a mile away—and although she was three times my age we were as chummy as schoolgirl pals.

Later, when the children were small, after a hard morning's work I could wag one and drag the other over to "Mammy" Stone's to spend the afternoon. Just to be with her and to hear her tell jolly tales of olden times was refreshing.

She would always give me a bouquet of flowers to take home with me, and one day, it was winter, too, she said, "I am going to give you a bunch of flowers today from my winter-blooming honeysuckle."

We went out to the garden, and sure enough the bush was covered with tiny yellowish blossoms; the bees were humming busily about them. As she broke off some bloom-laden branches, she said, "You ought to have a bush like this; I am going to root you one." She bent down a limb, laid a brick over it, and pulled some loose rich dirt over the limb for several inches of its length.

Several months afterward she came over to my house one day, bringing my rooted honeysuckle bush wrapped in a newspaper—and, as usual, a jar of her peach preserves. "I've just been thinking," said "Mammy" Stone, "you'll have this to remember me by when I am gone. You must put it where it will grow well and bloom every year and where you will see it often; for every time you see this, you will think of me. Its evergreen leaves and its blossoms will be a better monument for me than a block of cold marble out in some lonesome, overgrown, country graveyard."

"Mammy" was right. That honeysuckle bush has been a living, daily reminder of her. I enjoy it all the year, and think of the happy times we had together.

I told someone else of my memory flower, and she said, "Now you must have something to remember me by." She gave me a clump of daffodils, and what gay reminders they are of her. Another friend gave me a dishpan full of violets, and another a mock-orange bush. I was collecting quite a number of "friendship flowers."

The time came when I must decide where to put them. I read in the papers that flower beds set in the middle of the yard were out of style; I couldn't figure any particular place for a flower garden; so I finally decided on a border of shrubs and perennial flowers around the yard. At first a five-foot border on one side seemed too much room, but as the flowers grew, and as more were added to the collection, I needed more room. Soon my friendship flower border spread itself out over a ten or twelve-foot width, stretched all around the yard, and even over into the garden. And how we all enjoy it!

There are Mrs. Morgan's pink roses on the fence; Mr. Walker's hardy sweet peas growing up among them; Mother

Knox's lilac and bridal wreath side by side, with a flowering almond in front of them. A red rose nearby makes me think every spring of Mrs. Fitzgerald, and "Mammy" Stone's honeysuckle stands close beside it. Mrs. Howell's crêpe myrtle blooms afresh after every summer rain, and the white violets beneath remind me of someone else.

There are golden bells that make me think of a visit to Knoxville when I brought home those bushes as little cuttings in my suitcase. There is a white peony that Mrs. Parks gave me one February just as a little sprig. Neither of us thought it could live, but it did, and has put forth an abundance of bloom every year since.

There is a wall-flower from Mrs. Collier's garden, and a wild snapdragon from Mrs. Lamb's; these iris came from Mrs. Frierson and those from Mrs. McLemore. All that mass of iris around the border—Mr. Ridley called me one morning and asked if I would like some iris. Of course, I would, and he left two bags full at a store in town for me. Now those iris have stretched all around the yard, doubled back, and have gone down the lane to the mail box and back on the other side. If you don't think they are lovely, you should see them in bloom.

Aunt Mollie's buttercups (I know they are jonquils, but I like to call them buttercups) and Mrs. Dodson's short-cup narcissi have done the same thing. They are scattered helter-skelter all among the iris all the way to the road and back. It's no task to go to the mailbox when those flowers are in bloom. There'll be poppies among them, too, this year when the iris blooms are gone; at least I scattered poppy seeds that Mary Harris gave me all among the flags and buttercups; and later there will be hollyhocks—they, too, come from "Mammy" Stone's garden or rather from around her back door.

❧

Old Kate

TRAGEDY

Tragedy stalked in Knoxdale fields last week and did more than stalk—came in and gloomily sat down. To make us feel even worse, she brought with her hundreds of those black pall-bearers of the air, turkey buzzards.

Yes, tragedy came. And Old Kate is gone.

Perhaps I've never told you much about Old Kate; perhaps we never appreciated her enough 'til now. Kate was a wiry little bay mule, 28 years old this spring. She's been in just about every furrow that has been plowed on our farm from the time the farm was bought, when she was five years old, until Oscar came (he's a tractor).

Kate has made every garden, stirred the soil around every tender young corn plant; given each crop of tobacco its first and last plowing; stepped daintily close, but not too close to the young orchard trees since they were merely switches—you see, we've always reserved Kate for the finer pieces of work about the farm. And we've used her, too, where steady dependable pulling was desired.

Other mules have come and gone. There have been Black, and Tobe, and Brownie; Gray, and Dick, and Will. Last, there have been Red and Jane and Neil; all have served as team-mates, but Kate was the one who set the pace. Kate was the one whose neck stuck out first and farthest when a big load began to move up hill.

Kate was our lead mule. She was an institution on the farm that like the barn, the garden, the pond, the flower beds, and Buppo, we never figured we could do without. But Kate is gone.

And it all came about so suddenly. We had recently acquired Ranger Boy, a blue-blooded, black and white, Spotted Poland China papa hog, and all his harem of spotted sows and his family of darling little spotted pigs. Hogs have been cheap, so we thought it a good time to stock up on a really good strain of good breed, and, like everybody else, get ready for the times when hogs may go up.

So Ranger Boy was one of them, head of the sty, you might say. And he and his brood, or broods, were hunting grubworms down in the lower pasture that afternoon, when Dad turned the team loose to go to the pond for water before supper.

Ranger Boy raised his head—and what a head that is! You can imagine when I tell you that although we call him Boy, he's about four feet high and seven feet long—or he looks that big when he starts toward you.

SHE WAS JUST SURPRISED

He must have caught a whiff from Europe in that east wind, for like a Stalin or a Hitler, or a cross between the two, he lumbered out at his fastest, and before anyone could realize what had happened he had begun his slaughter of the innocents; he had torn the heart out of poor Old Kate. And she looked surprised— surprised as the Finns must have looked.

I say tore her heart out. Perhaps it wasn't her heart at first, but so many other vital organs that it was evident she must die. Dad called Jack, and together they looked at the Tragedy. Meanwhile Ranger Boy was making war on the other mules, and Nell the mare. Then he started toward the men. Only stout locust poles with seasoned muscles to wield them prevented Tragedy from coming to the house.

They got him in the stable, and wired the door securely, and he'll be there, they say, until he can have his belligerent front teeth removed. And we'll all watch him until he goes to head another herd.

Meanwhile, something had to be done for Kate. And on the farm there is just one remedy for livestock injured as badly as she was. I think they didn't even discuss it. But Jack knew how Daddy felt about Old Kate. He had raised her from a colt. Kate had been here years before Jack came; and when he was just a toddler he'd go to the barn and poke shucks through the stable door.

But Jack knew how Dad felt, so he came to the house for the rifle. It took five shots before she fell. Kate was a mule of marvelous vitality, native Bedford Countian, by the way. So it took five sharp heart-jerking trigger-pulls to make her easy at last.

The thing Dad asked when Jack came into the house was: "Did she struggle?"

"No," Jack answered, "she just looked surprised."

Miles of Them

Consider the fence rows how they grow. They are plowed not, neither are they trimmed; yet hardly a field on the farm, not even the garden, grows such a number of plants to the square foot, or such a wide variety of plants as do the fence rows.

When they named Texas, "Lone Star State," Ohio, "Buckeye State," and Kansas, "Sunflower State," I don't see how they missed calling Tennessee, "Fence Row State." Surely it has more miles of forgotten fence rows than any other state in the Union.

There is something about a fence row—in fact there is a great deal about a fence row. I stood before one of ours once and noted the following flora and fauna:

Persimmon, redbud, dogwood, wild cherry, hackberry, walnut, cedar, buckbushes, blackberry, raspberry, hickory, hedge orange, wild plum, saw briars, golden rod, wild rose, grapevine, iron weed, white top, wild violet, wild strawberries, cross-vine, wild fern, oak, ash, and numerous others—all interwoven and as close together as they could stand and climb. I should say there is something about a fence row!

One can surmise from this list of plants that grow neglected in spots that are not cleared, that Tennessee soil would grow a wealth of vegetation if protected by negligence.

It is probable that man in his ambition to clear land and make crops, sell crops, buy more land to clear, and make more crops to sell, and so on, might entirely eliminate some forms of plant life if it weren't for fence rows. They are Nature's way of preserving our environment.

So fence rows serve as archives, we might say, or preserves, or nurseries, or depositories, or asylums for plants that man may think he doesn't want and will not need. Fence rows, however, protect these plants, save them, and turn them loose again to multiply and replenish the earth at any time man rests on his job of crop-making, or at any time he puts his grubbing hoe, plow, and mower aside.

Fence rows make resting places, nesting places, feeding places, and protection for birds and for other creatures of the wild. Of course, they harbor bean beetles, grasshoppers, other insects, good and bad, and even fungi and diseases. But perhaps all those things have their places in the general scheme of things and life.

The beauty of sight and sound that comes from fence rows—the blooms. In spring and summer, the color in autumn, the flash of bluebird's and red bird's wings, the song of the thrush—those things in themselves pay good rent for the space that the fence row occupies. And remember that fence rows have their own methods of insect control. The birds take care of a number of most nuisances, both in the row and in the fields adjacent. So I reckon it all balances up.

Another credit that might be chalked up for overgrown fence rows is that they hold up fences. And when a fence is no longer a fence—just a rusty strand or two of wire clinging here and there to a toppling post, the fence row turns the cows. Perhaps, if it is neglected enough it may stop even sheep and hogs. Some of our Tennessee fence rows would almost turn an army. Perhaps that is one reason we let them grow, for another form of protection.

One of the most obvious purposes that some fence rows serve is that of hiding poor crops from the passerby, or a neighbor in an adjoining field. A farmer who wishes may have this very effective resort to fall back on. If his corn is poor or weedy, if his hay is short and straggly, if his wheat has rust or cockle, the neighbors need never know, for such a farmer usually has the tallest and broadest, and thickest and thriftiest fence rows in the entire community.

What's going to be done about fence rows? I'm sure I don't know. It would take an enormous amount of chopping and sawing, pruning and digging, to clean out these rows and make the fences stand on their own and face the world and the cows and sheep and hogs. But perhaps it would be worthwhile. Perhaps we could grow more crops and pasture in the space they occupy. Perhaps, on the other hand, we might lose more than we'd gain. I couldn't say. I refuse to advise.

Perhaps I'm just so broadminded I can see both sides of the fence row, even the widest, tallest, and thickest one. Perhaps I'm just too unambitious. I don't want the grass and crops that would grow where persimmons, dogwoods, berry vines, and sumac grew, and where the red bird and bluebird date, and the thrushes sing.

I'll let nature follow her interesting trend of survival-of-the-fittest.

CHAPTER 13

October Days, November Nights

A Christian Gentle Man

UNCLE FAYETTE

The relationship between Southern whites and Southern blacks is as hard to explain and describe as are the brightness and haze of the Southern sunset. There are relationships that are bright with mutual appreciation and understanding and there are relationships that are gray with the blur of misunderstanding. Happily, most of my friendships with the "colored" people and the Negroes have been of the bright variety.

From as far back as I can remember, starting with Aunt Ann, we had colored friends and helpers. Most faithful and best loved of all our old family-helpers was Uncle Fayette. During all the long years I knew Uncle Fayette, he was always "'bout forty" years old. From the time I was a very small child until my own children were almost grown up, Uncle Fayette, according to his own calculations, was never a year older—despite the fact that he had one or more birthdays every year. It was not until the talk came up about old age pensions that he remembered he was born in June 1861, or as he counted, "the year the War broke out."

We had heard the old man boast many times that he was "born a slave," and when he finally figured out the exact date I said to him, "Well, Uncle Fayette, if you were born in 1861, you just did get here in time to be a slave."

"Yes'm," he replied, "Jes' did git borned in time! Specks if I had to do it all over again, feeling like I does now, I specks I'd be late."

According to his "rickoleckshuns" Fayette Thornton had a variety of birthplaces. Sometimes he mentioned Lawrenceburg, Tennessee, sometimes Pulaski, Tennessee. But most of the time it was Florence, Alabama—I think that was because he thought Florence a prettier name, and because Alabama sounded more like a "foreign country." He had a great yearning toward "foreign countries"—until World War I came along. After that he was strictly a native Tennessean.

It was always a source of great concern to Uncle Fayette whether his father was "dead yet." It seems that when he was a year and a half old, as his mother told him many times, his father "got on a big black horse with a mean old nigger woman, and rode away to the North, leaving his wife and three little children in a cold world torn by a hot war."

Uncle Fayette said that from the time he got to be twenty-one he had been hoping to find his father and tell him what he thought of him. As long as he lived he still had hopes. Frequently, when he was a really old man, we'd hear him mumbling to himself out in the garden, and saying over and over again the things he was "gonna tell dem two niggers" if he ever found them.

Going on with his life's story, he said that his mother and her small impoverished family moved to Pulaski, right up within half a block of the courthouse, and that they were living there when the Ku Klux Klan was organized there on the court square.

Many's the sleepless night, he said, when he and his brother and sister, with their mother, would huddle in a corner of their upstairs room and listen to the tramp, tramp, gallop, gallop of the big horses, and the weird whistles of the Klansmen.

"What'd they do?" we'd ask him.

"Well, they'd go out to some old, no-'count nigger's house and call him out, an' if they was a rain barrel handy, they'd turn hit over, an' turn him down across hit—and then—they'd shore wait on dat nigger!"

From the time Papa died in 1906 until Mama married again many years later, our small family of Mama, Elsie, Clarence, and I were Uncle Fayette's special charges. It was his religion, he said, to look after widows and orphans, and we can testify that during these years he practiced his religion thoroughly.

There was never a cold zero morning that he didn't come trudging across town that long mile between his house and ours, each foot wrapped in a gunny sack, his head wrapped in a red wool scarf under his hat, two coats and a sweater under his big greenish-brown black overcoat (no telling how old that coat was, but it was always well-brushed) and his hands wrapped in sox and thrust deep in his pockets.

He thought he'd better come over, he'd say, and see about his widow and his orphans. He'd thaw out by the kitchen stove and eat a small hot breakfast; then he'd go out to the wood house and begin loading up our house with wood, coal, and kindling. He'd do any other odd jobs that needed doing, such as thawing pipes, feeding the chickens, and shoveling snow. He'd eat a bowl of hot soup at noon, take the little package of supper that Mama had fixed up for him and plod back across town, his "religion" 'tended to for that spell of weather.

HIS RELIGION

When Mama was no longer a widow, when Elsie and Clarence had married and moved away, and when I found a husband and settled down on the farm, Uncle Fayette looked us all over and decided, I suppose, who was the neediest one of the four. I was the lucky choice, so when "Aunt" Fanny died and his son went to "Dee-troit," Uncle Fayette, after much persuasion, did the thing we all knew he wanted to do—came to the farm to "take care" of us.

And what priceless years those were! There are few people I have known whose influence I'd exchange for that which that stooped and hoary old colored gentleman had on our family, especially on our growing boy and girl. They adored him, as did we all.

Uncle Fayette was genteel and quiet. He was humility itself, beautifully so—and not of the Uriah Heap kind! But somehow he always managed subtly to make up about three-fifths of any group he happened to be in. The same was true in our family circle. In his quiet, unassuming way he had a part in most of the farm and family activities, in the house or out-of-doors.

There were mornings when I'd oversleep (greatest of all luxuries) and when I'd get up so late I'd be ashamed to look the clock in the face. But, just as I'd expected, Uncle Fayette would be up and "a-lookin' after his white folks." He would have the wood-box filled, the water drawn, the fire made, and the coffee water boiling.

Uncle Fayette had at one time been cook in a hotel, in the Old Maxwell House in Nashville, he said, and we never had cause to doubt that for he was an excellent cook. The Maxwell House was lucky. For years, we knew, he had also been chief cook, and part of the time the only cook, for a crew of men on the railroad "boarding cars," men engaged in roadwork and bridge building, so he wasn't lost in the kitchen. And he was a model dishwasher—that was another thing I appreciated about him.

He was just as much at home in the flower garden, too. As long as he could see well he could tell weeds from flowers, but sometimes a new variety would fool him.

I had a bed of Newport Pink Sweet Williams that I had coddled for a whole year in hopes of blooms next spring. The next spring had come and the clumps had survived the winter and were looking as sturdy as vermifuge. That, I suppose, was their undoing.

One afternoon while I was away from home, Uncle Fayette figured out a nice surprise for me. He'd get that bed ready for me to plant. When I came home every Sweet William plant had been carefully pulled, had the dirt shaken from its roots, piled up and hauled off. Uncle Fayette had then turned the bed upside down with his spading fork and had it all ready for "Mis' to plant flowers in." He was never told that the "vermifuge" would have been a bed of gorgeous beauty in two more weeks.

Uncle Fayette fairly reveled in garden work. A well-prepared bit of soil, a row of sprouting beans or fruiting tomatoes was a supreme joy and source of pride. He would often say, as he hoed along, "I gener'ly notices dat when I pleases myself wid my work, I always pleases ever'body else. So I jes' works to please myself, but I keeps myself mighty hard to please. Dat's de way I gits along."

There was one morning when the old man put a new term into our family vocabulary without ever knowing he'd done so. We planned to have some fun by asking him, point-blank, while all were present, just which member of the family he would do the most for. Jack? Dad? Margaret? Me? Buppo or Kitty

Boots? Or fish or canary? Margaret added a note of warning, "Be careful how you answer, Uncle Fayette, we're all here."

The old fellow grinned wisely and answered, "I guess I'd better keep out of that trap. I's always been taught to shine de ver' 'pearance of evil." From then on in our household the expression "polishing sins" meant "shining de ver' 'pearance of evil."

Uncle Fayette made a practice of allowing Buppo to stand beside him at mealtime with the dog's nose on the old man's knee. Each time the man divided a biscuit, the dog got half of it.

"Why do you do that way, Uncle Fayette?" I asked. "Why don't you wait until you finish eating and then feed him?"

"Now Mis', don' you mind him. He ain't a-hurtin' nuthin'. It ain't no harm for him to jes' stan' dere peacable-like, a-waiting fer de pass-over."

And pass over it was. I knew the old man well enough to realize that he would have passed over all his food to the pup if there had not been enough for both.

There is no doubt that Uncle Fayette, in some matters, had more endurance and patience and consideration than did other members of the family, but one morning we saw him "stumped!"

That was the morning Buppo came to the house holding all records for body odors. He must have treed two polecats before breakfast, but he was so naive he couldn't understand why we pinched our noses and shut the door when he came up, tail wagging, to tell us about it.

Uncle Fayette didn't invite him in to breakfast with him that morning, nor for several mornings thereafter. But I did hear the old fellow say in his soft, easy voice to the friendless, mystified, odorous, and despondent dog, "Anybody as sociable as you likes to be ought never to fool wid no skunk."

ANOTHER CO-PILOT WILL COME

There was one week when Buppo, Jack, and Uncle Fayette had a considerable bout with snake-killing. Bup would "tree" them, Jack would shoot them with his 22 rifle, and Uncle Fayette would aid and abet—especially abet, and at a distance. He didn't like snakes except when they were at a great distance and very dead. But he did like to tell stories about the big ones and the odd ones he had seen and heard of.

One day Jack yelled from the sweet-potato patch, "Sister, bring the gun quick! Here's a rattlesnake!"

Margaret lost no time getting the gun, but when the snake was dead enough for examination, the rattlers were not found. It had all the markings of a diamond-back, Jack said, except that important noise box, so he began to inquire of Uncle Fayette what manner of snake it might be.

From his vast fund of information and experience the old man brought forth the fact that the monster was a "co-pilot"—I know not what the word may be; I spell as 'twas pronounced to me.

"And three days after you kills a co-pilot," said Uncle Fayette, "a rattler will come to take his place." So for three days the snake-hunters were on the alert.

Sure enough, on the third day, Bup's shrill bark told the farm that another snake was on the premises, this time in the cotton patch that Uncle Fayette was so carefully tending. He and Jack rushed to the scene of the commotion with stick and gun. The snake was so coiled that one shot punctured him in three places. But to the great surprise of the party it was another "co-pilot." Uncle Fayette couldn't offer any explanation except that it really was a dry summer and that all signs fail in dry weather.

The incidents, however, reminded him of the time he saw a copperhead twice bite a boy as big as Jack.

"We wuz working on the road," he said, "and one of de old hounds hangin' 'round chased a young rabbit into a rotten log. The boy was sorter fast, anyhow, so he ran ahead of de others and stuck his hand in de log to get de rabbit 'fo de others got there.

"Mr. Copperhead wuz hidin' in de log, so he nabbed dat boy right on de end ob his finger. De boy snatched his hand out, looked at it, and stuck hit in agin. He got another slash and when he took his finger out, hit looked like somebody done cut hit wid a knife. Next thing, he stooped down and looked into de log and dere lay dat snake. De men all took hold ob dat log an' turn hit over, and out come de snake. Dey killed it, and found out what kind it wuz and den dey got scared.

"De boy's pa, he had on a pair ob ol' yarn galluses, an' he took 'em off an' tied 'em right tight around de boy's arm to keep de blood from goin' up to his heart, you know. And den he sent me after a "mad stone."

"De woman dat had de mad stone lived about a mile and a half away, an' when I got dar she wasn't at home. But I got de stone, and got back to whar I started in less'n 45 minutes.

"While I was gone, dey had took a black chicken and had split it open down de back, and had stuck dat boy's finger in de chicken while hit was still alive. Dey jes' tied dat chicken to de boy's finger, and made the young'un drink about a quart of whiskey. After dat he wuz so drunk you couldn't tell how sick he really wuz.

"Den we got some cockleburs, and made some tea outen dem, and made him drink cocklebur tea wid sweet milk, and dat brung him 'round all right, but I tell you right now, Jack, snakes ain't good things to fool with, 'specially in August when dey're blind."

And that very day Uncle Fayette decided it was time to lay by his cotton crop.

Some of the neighbors laughed at the old man staying out of the cotton patch because a snake had been found there. But when he heard some of their kidding he remarked: "Wal, now, it's always been my belief dat my time ought to be divided into two halves. I ought to spend one-half 'tending to my own business, and de other half a-lettin' de other fellow's business alone. Them snakes is de other fellow's business, an' if dey waited fer me to come out dere an' kill 'em, dey could stay out dere 'til dey's old enough to vote."

So for years and years the old colored man, gentleman that he was, was Our Man "Friday," and Our Man "Saturday," "Monday," "Tuesday," and all the other days of the week. There was a strange affinity always among the boy, the dog, and himself: where you saw one you saw the others. Uncle Fayette taught both boy and dog, to some extent, to "mind their manners," after the fashion in which he himself had been taught.

A RECOMMENDATION

One summer after the old fellow had been "'bout forty" for well along toward 35 years, he said to me in the garden one day: "Lil Mis', I been thinking, looking backward over de years an' lookin' forward over de years to come, dat I ought to set down some day an' write myself a recommendation.

"Now you's out here in de garden wid yor li'l book whats you writes down where you plants yore flowers, an' you got yo' pencil wid you. S'pose you set down dere on de zinnia bed and write out my recommendation jes' like I tells it to you."

Nobody could refuse Uncle Fayette anything he asked, and always he asked so little. So I was glad to write on the order blank in the back of my seed catalog these words just as he dictated.

"Been working hard ever since I was big enough. Never mistreated anybody. Always tried to pay my just and honest debts. Never been arrested in my life. Never been on a witness stand. Never had trouble wid my neighbors anywhere I ever lived. Never got drunk but once. Always asked for what I wanted and paid for what I got.

"Was born in Florence, Alabama, June 22, 1861. Named after de ol' General Lafayette. Mother and I left Florence in 1863. Went to Pulaski. Raised up in Pulaski until I was 20 years old. Then went to Lawrence County. Have been a citizen of Maury County for 33 years.

"To the readers of this: receive my thanks for the time you have consumed in reading this notice.

"Younger generation might take pattern from de old heads. Be sure to cultivate de masses of ol' people. You'll be better off by hit. Very well satisfied wid life as I have lived it. Always tried to live obedient, have manners, and respect, and be trustworthy.

"Things I couldn't buy hones' I let alone—I have bought things on credit but I always got 'em paid for somehow.

"I don' bother other folks an' dey don' bother me.

"I always try to tell de truth an' I been honest.

"Anybody that wants to know more about my record can jus' write to Alabama, or Giles County, or Lawrence County, or Maury County.

"An' if anybody want to dispute dis record an' prove otherwise I will give him 25 cents or they can give me 25 cents."

Thus, in his 75th year Uncle Fayette summed up his "recommendation," his record, his "yardstick" for living, and his philosophy. And may I say that I don't think any 25-cent pieces ever changed hands. His "recommendation" was accepted by those who knew him.

The following Christmas, 1935, he went to Louisville to spend the holidays with his brother. He became ill and never returned to Tennessee. In the spring of the year he went to that "Far Country" and entered the service of Old Master himself.

If there was a stronger term in our language than Christian Gentleman, I'd use it for him. If there were words in my vocabulary to eulogize him I would do that. But there aren't, nor do I feel he would wish it.

I can just tell about these little aspects of him I knew, and let you know where he is, so that when you knock at the Gate you will know the identity of the Precious Black Angel sitting at the right of "Ol Marsa, De Lawd," at the foot of the Great White Throne, or sitting on the Heavenly Woodpile, whittling thoughtfully and puffing on a corncob pipe.

October Days

Let those who will, sing of September—September in the Rain. My song, if I could sing, would be of October—October in the

Sun—that honey-colored, autumn-flavored, Indian-summer sun!

Of all months, October is to me most satisfying. April indeed is beautiful, thrilling; April is a month of promise. But October is a month of fulfillment, of completion, of maturity.

April's buds are October's fruit. April's tender mossy grass is October's cured hay. And the timid green shoots that spring from grains of corn planted in April are tall, husky stalks, heavily laden in October. Walking through a cornfield at this time of year one can hear the stalks and leaves whispering, chuckling over the secrets that summer has put in their ears.

In April the earth seems like a bride—with showers for her veil and plum blossoms for her coronet. And "the sun is as a bridegroom coming out of his chamber rejoicing as a strong man to run a race."

In October the earth is a matron, a happy, smiling mother. She and the sun are parents of a large family—buxom harvests, stalwart crops.

Not least among the joys of being a country woman is the privilege of living neighbor to Earth and Sun with their large varied and supremely interesting family.

Anyone who has walked in Tennessee woods and fields in October knows well that—

> To him who, in the love of Nature, holds
> Communion with her visible forms, she speaks
> A various language:...[1]

---

[1] "Thanatopsis," by William Cullen Bryant

Purposely to hold communion with her visible forms, and to learn their various language, our family took frequent walks in the woods and fields in October.

We weren't sentimental about those walks. We didn't talk a great deal about them; didn't plan them; didn't make picnics of them; and didn't go dutifully or from habit. We just went walking—sometimes singly, sometimes by twos, sometimes by threes, or all together; sometimes the family, sometimes with guests or neighbors.

We didn't philosophize orally about those walks, but deep down within us there was always an unspoken understanding. We knew well that walks in woods and fields, these close associations with the children of Earth and Sun, put something into the souls of human beings that can be had from nowhere else we know. Nature does much for man, if man permits.

It is not just tall trees and tanglefoot; nor goldenrod framing a field; not the bright red of sumac, nor dogwood berries making faded leaves look greener; not haws hanging high; nor wild grapes in heavy handfuls, nor pink smart weed nor white ageratum—it's not just the showier things, nor the more fragrant or flavorful. Nor is it the live things, birds, bugs, beasts, although every ant or grasshopper has a lesson if we'll only look and heed, and so has every bug and butterfly, every blade of grass, and even the lowly morning glory that tangles itself with the corn. There are lessons of faith, hope, good cheer in them all.

The trees in early October remind me of men and women in middle age. They hold their growth at a standstill for several days and seem to glance back at summer and peer forward at winter. Then, finally, their decision is made. Almost overnight they plunge into their last riot of beauty—sing their swan song of color before taking on their slim black and lacy garments of winter.

To me the morning glory seems the greatest hope of them all. Right up to the day before frost we can see morning glory seedlings putting up tender shoots of green, each holding up its two little hands as though imploring for a few more days in which to make blooms and seeds.

Meanwhile the older morning-glory plants, those climbing over fences and twining around cornstalks are not losing time. They don't speculate on when frost will come; they keep right on opening new blooms every morning, and trying to make as many seeds as possible while the sun does shine.

Has man ever painted a picture that can compare with the sight of dew-touched morning glory vines decking brown cornfields with pink, blue, and white blossoms? Not only does nature "paint" this picture, she frames it then with goldenrod and adds touches of autumn leaves and autumn weeds as highlights. Nature is indeed a lavish artist.

I remember one autumn particularly, it seems we had been unusually busy. We had stayed out of them as long as we could, those October woods, so on the last Saturday of the month we shut our eyes and turned deaf ears to the fact that there was so much to do, had an early mid-day dinner, gathered up bags and buckets, and hiked off to the woods.

There was a large hill near our house, which (although we have never paid a nickel's worth of taxes, insurance, interest, or rent on it) gave us each year and each season more pleasure than it ever gave its non-resident owner. We could see it from our farm-kitchen window, watch it change from month to month—white and black in winter; pale green, white, and reddish lavender in spring; dark green in summer; and red, dark green, and gold in autumn. Always when we felt a special need for exercise or inspiration we climbed to the top of Stone's hill, mounted an old charred stump, on the very tippy-top of the hill, and there surveyed the horizon from all sides. We always felt that from the top of Stone's Hill we could see over the top of every other hill in sight. It gives one's morale a boost to be able to look over the tops of all the other neighboring hills.

In the spring when we made this special pilgrimage we'd watch for rare wild flowers for our wild flower garden—I found a dog-tooth violet blooming against an ash tree one season. It was so snug and secure among the tree's roots I couldn't and wouldn't disturb it; I merely marked the tree and went back each season after to hunt for it again, but we never could even find that same tree. We weren't very good woodsmen, but we had the joy of the hunt.

But this is about one particular afternoon—which was typical of others. In going to the hill we crossed a cut-over tobacco field. Talk about courage, those tobacco plants had had their heads cut off weeks before, but even after that they were trying to carry on and were trying to put on a party appearance. The fresh young leaves of the second growth were just that delicate, beautiful shade of green that only burley tobacco knows how to make in its "second childhood." The few plants which had escaped the cutters' knives were blooming with that shade of pink that only burley tobacco knows how to make in its maturity. The rich brown color of the dirt between the ribbon-like rows helped the interesting color scheme. As we crossed the field we observed that a tobacco field looks better when the year's work is done and the crop is all in the barn—or better still when the crops have gone to market all in the baskets.

We crossed through a cornfield where the leaves seemed to be whispering among themselves. Now and then we thought we could hear a giggle, and then a small cackle of laughter. Corn leaves are not rude; they were not talking about us; I know, for I've heard them whisper and giggle that way when they didn't know anyone was about. That's just their way—or perhaps it's just the wind's way.

We climbed the squeaky old wire fence into the lane and followed the wagon road up and around the hill. The old road had been abandoned for years; the soil was all washed off and only the rocks were left—rocks of a million shapes and sizes, weather-worn, gray, yellow, dingy white—they were all huddled together, bracing themselves as best they could to withstand the torrents of muddy water that rushed down the old road bed when it rained.

ROCKS AND RILLS

Walking up that old road bed I could sincerely say:

> I love thy rocks and rills,
> Thy woods and templed hills.[2]

"Rocks and rills"—beautiful words in themselves. They are brief and simple, but how full they are of meaning only God and nature lovers know.

There is something about a rock, something substantial, everlasting, that surpasses living things. Men may come and go. For all their sanitation, their progress, their brains, their gland experiments; their stay on earth is short and most uncertain.

Trees grow up and flourish for perhaps a century or two; then they go back to woods dirt. But there stands the rock. It doesn't grow. It doesn't experiment. It has neither brains nor glands. But it has something that men and trees have not—enough security to laugh at centuries, storms, progress, at wars and financial depressions. Indeed rocks do have something superior.

---

[2] "America," by Samuel F. Smith

I love rocks in their natural settings, hugged tight by mosses, half buried in soil, nestled closely among the plant life that loves them best. Certainly that must be the way that rocks are happiest. The meanest things we mortals do to rocks, I think, is the way we have of digging them out of their sturdy beds, blasting or chiseling them into odd, regular, unnatural shapes, standing them on edge or on end, or sticking them together with mortar into ugly, regular formations—in short, trying to "civilize" them. Yes, man and dynamite are rock's worst enemies, but it will be a long time, I think, before these enemies will conquer all our rocks.

Somehow I don't believe that rocks like to be civilized any more than do rills. And a civilized rill, if you'll agree with me, is almost a synonym for sewer.

But on up the hill we went. A young maple tree was spreading her gold and scarlet shawl over the brush of on abandoned fence row. A prim little cedar tree stood beside her, and on the other side of the cedar flared the rich crimson of a "frying size" dogwood tree. The three—maple, cedar, dogwood—seemed to be holding hands there dancing in the October breeze on the edge of the old road-bed turned stream-bed.

A tiny little cedar tree was trying to grow out of what was apparently a solid rock—she had "made her bed hard" but she was bravely staying with it, and thriving. Only a stout hearted little cedar could thrive among the hardships that surrounded that little tree. But we decided that afternoon that if she continues with that same steady courage, if man, bugs, or disease don't interfere, she will finally break the heart of even that hard hearted solid rock.

Jack, walking on ahead, called us to see his discovery, a really beautiful bed of ripe prickly pears. The big flat leaves were spread out like innocent little cushions—but they didn't fool us. Those with pears on them looked like fat hands stuffed into green gloves with pink fingers sticking out and turning blue with cold.

Jack declared that he had heard that the pears were good to eat, and boy-like, he dared us to taste them. At first we refused, but Margaret declared that although she couldn't claim to be as brave as the man who ate the first oyster, she would try one if he would promise to pick all the briars off first.

Jack responded with pioneerish ingenuity—he pulled the pear off its prickly parent with two sticks, rolled it in the dirt, and then between two stones until it was well-polished of briars. So Margaret then had to keep her part of the bargain.

As Grandpa Adam once told, "She did eat and gave to me and I eat." In fact we tasted all around. We liked the sweet-sour first taste, but not the sticky after taste.

Jack always scouted on ahead of the rest of us like a frisky hunting dog. And he made numerous discoveries that we might have missed. Once he called us off to the side of the rocky path to see a groundhog den, then a place "where foxes go under the fence", "a natural rock garden," and a "good place for a spring."

It always amused him that we didn't recognize trees with their summer clothes off. The one we thought was an ash was really a linn, he said, and "anybody ought to tell an elm from a walnut."

AIR THICK AS HONEY

Has it ever occurred to you that sunshine seems thicker in the fall than it does in the spring? On that October afternoon it seemed as thick as honey, and as rich in color. It even seemed to have what we might term a "rich, full-bodied flavor," or maybe the air carried the flavor in the form of autumn woods fragrance. How we did enjoy it; and how we missed it as we moved on into the shadows on the north side of the hill; but there we found moss, lots of it, growing over the rocks and banks and tree roots and the fallen tree trunks. And how we enjoyed the crackle and crunch of dry leaves under our feet. The woods sounds that afternoon seemed to make almost a symphony—or what we understood as a symphony.

Margaret had just stopped to shake the dirt out of her tennis shoes; I was gathering up some abandoned snail-shell houses; Jack had climbed an old rotten snag to see if it had a squirrel den in it; and Dad came wending on up the hill. As we started on up to join him and came just over the rise, we all saw it at once—a flash of green and red and blue as beautiful and as colorful as a picture. We all cried out in chorus, "Haws! Haws! Haws! Black Haws!"

I don't know why they call them "black" haws for they are really blue. And the leaves that day were green in the middle and red all around. We supposed they were haws, at any rate we tasted them, and we didn't get sick, so I supposed they were non-poisonous anyway. Dad really knew more woodscraft than any of the rest of us, and he said they looked like haws to him.

As though that were not enough we next discovered a whole colony of wild grapes growing in the top of a weak little sapling. I feared we would never be able to get them down, but Jack, with the thoughtlessness of youth, began shinning up the sapling, and Margaret yelled, "Ride him down, cowboy." Dad grinned. I let him go, thinking that if he did fall he wouldn't fall far, and the ground was soft with leaves to catch him. And the grapes did look good.

He didn't have to ride the sapling down after all. It was a strong little tree, and he managed to get all he thought we would eat without going too far up. We left plenty for the 'possums to climb for and the foxes to wish for. But even then as we started off from the tree with our large bunches of grapes Margaret said we reminded her of the spies who were sent by Israel to spy out the land of Canaan when they came back with the fruit of the land. Jack said she and I would be CALEB and JOSHUA and he and Dad would be the other ten spies, that they were doing most of the scouting anyway.

We had hardly finished this bantering when, like a little Indian, Jack gave a sort of whoop, drew his knife, and galloped off through the bushes at the left.

"Now we'll have some chewing gum!" he yelled back.

Margaret explained: "It must be slippery elm." (No, we didn't say "ellum," even if we were real country "hicks.")

PASSION FLOWER

But the joke was on Jack—he who knew his trees so well—it was just plain non-slip elm. To change the subject quickly and to keep us from laughing at him, he cut us all some sassafras bark and twigs to chew. That lasted until we came to a bed of apricots; you may not call them apricots, and neither would the fruit-store man. The poet calls the plant passion flower, and I understand that another name for it is okole or something like that—the fruit sometimes called passion fruit.

For a long time the passion flower was Tennessee's State Flower. When I was a school girl in town I couldn't understand why it was selected. At that time I would have understood well why the state flower was changed from okole to iris. But now and ever since I've been on the farm, and since I know the good old apricot vine first hand, I doubt if we could have had a more admirable plant for our emblem.

For one thing it seems really native. It comes in the most unexpected places, and stands any amount of abuse, but continues to grow and spread, although not making too much of a nuisance of itself.

This plant we country people call the apricot is beautiful in leaf, strong in tendril, gorgeous in blossom, and delicious in fruit. To me it seems actually clever. Take its method of distributing seeds for example. Of course, it attracts insects to its blossom by both beauty and nectar, and thus accomplishes cross-pollination.

But why, you ask, does it produce such shriveled, ugly fruit?

Did you ever notice that there is a degree of ugliness that is attractive? Have you not known people who were so ugly that they fascinated you? The wild apricot figured that all out, probably without benefit of psychology. It probably said to itself:

"If I make myself very ugly, people will be curious as to what such an ugly ball could have inside and will open it just to see."

Then on the inside she put an enticing odor so that one could not resist tasting the contents. She coated each seed with a delicious sweetness, then as a joker she put underneath the sweetness a tang of sourness, even to the point of bitterness.

The result is this, and just as she probably expected: you and I walk along and see that shriveled, brown, little ball hanging on the vine, we take, we taste, we walk along. As we get thirty or forty steps from the mother plant we begin to taste the bitterness, then we spit out the seed—and the old apricot vine laughs in her leaves. We are doing just what she wanted us to do, leave that seed to come up next year far enough away from the mother plant that she can still watch it grow, but not close enough that it will be too crowded by the rest of the family. I nominate the Passion Flower as an emblem of shrewdness and wisdom.

We had just started to fill our buckets with apricots when Jack discovered a hickory tree; but the squirrels had found that first, so only faulty nuts were left. It mystified us to notice that they could know without looking inside which nuts had bad hearts. But they certainly knew, and bad nuts were the only ones they had left.

On up the hill we moved, as Margaret said, partly by "shank's mares" (our feet) and "marrow-bone stages" (our knees); we crossed the bed that wild fern feathered so beautifully each spring; the little clearing where we gathered "chicken-fighter" violets in late winter; the rocky ledge where we found little blue-purple flowers we called wild delphinium; and the brush pile that protects the deep-set bulbs of scillia, which will send up spikes of lavender glory again next spring; and another rocky bed that will give us larkspur next summer—the seeds were sprouting and small plants were starting even then.

Nearby was another patch that promised fire-pinks, and not far away a place that would be a veritable garden of timid little wild anemones putting forth dainty blossoms to sway and nod in spring breezes. We remembered as we passed the spot where we first found fairy lilies, as we called them, and nobody else has told us a better name. Farther up the hill we watched for signs of wild geraniums that would also be a glory of pink next spring. But those, together with the myriads and hoards of trillium and Jack-in-the-pulpits, were taking their late autumn naps.

DEVIL'S RIDING HORSE

Just then a gun boomed from the other side of the hill and I was tempted to start preaching about people who couldn't enjoy woods without a gun in hand, when Margaret discovered a "Devil's Riding Horse," as she called him, and I proudly introduced him as a "praying mantis."

As we watched him, the pious-looking old fellow started performing. He lifted his awkward, twig-like torso, turned his head about to look all around to see if everybody was watching, then apparently folded his hands to pray for us, or perhaps for the fellow on the other side of the hill who had fired the gun. Just then smarty Mr. Jack, as Margaret called him, rushed up and ground the pharisaical old insect into the ground with his heel.

"Don't you know," he said, pitying our ignorance, "that those things are poisonous. He'll kill you if he bites you, and he's bad luck to look at. Mrs. So-and-so's little boy told me."

Then I told my son some things that Mrs. So-and-so's little boy had perhaps never heard, and I told Jack he must "look up" the insect when we got home, and learn that the praying mantis is really the friend of man, and not a poisonous enemy to anything except other insects. I supposed I was correct in this, but at any rate I did not want my boy to learn cruelty and superstition.

We were looking off across the beautiful valley below us when our dog flushed a covey of partridges right at our feet—hardly 3 yards from where we were standing. They certainly make you jump when they fly up that way so near.

I trusted my weight to a grape-vine swing, had my confidence betrayed, and tumbled to the ground. The children laughed, but I didn't mind. It wasn't far to fall and the ground was soft, so I rolled over and rested awhile.

We discovered a cornfield on the top of the hill, but too many wasps were apartment-hunting in that cornfield for us to be much interested in staying there long. We did each steal a pumpkin though—small ones for we were a long way from home. Margaret's was about the size, shape, and color of a bald-headed Chinese baby's head, Jack's would, he thought, make a horrible pumpkin face, and mine was destined for a pie or two. We told our consciences that we would take our neighbor a piece of the pie.

All the way up the hill and all the way down and still we never did find what we greatly wanted—a persimmon tree; but we planned to make another foraging trip to find that, for

Jack always knows where to find one—that is almost always, he says.

We found a spring that was whispering, chuckling, and singing to the mossy rocks all around it, and there we rested before starting on our homeward trek.

At last we reached home, pumpkins, grapes and all, tired and happy, but not quite satisfied—we never get enough of scouting around in autumn woods.

Washday Rainbows

Have we other joys of October?

Then, if ever, come perfect washdays!

I didn't really have to wash that day. The laundry bag was not more than three-fourths full. Usually I waited until it was packed down and overflowing before I took my board in hand, put its ridges under my knuckles, and bent my back to rubbing. But that day was such a perfect washday. Not too hot, nor too cold. Sun shining lazily down, and promising to shine all day. Tank full of soft rain water; plenty of home-made lye soap in the cellar—soap made in the dark of the moon in March and been aging ever since. Tubs just sitting around in the way, and old black kettle already perched up on three wagon wheel thimbles just ready for the fire to be started. Who could resist a washday like that? Not me, I'm sure.

By the time I had soaked, scrubbed, boiled, then rubbed the white clothes "out of boil," and had run them through three rinse waters, one bluing and one extra, just because the day was so perfect, I decided that still I hadn't enough clothes in wash to enjoy the day to the fullest; so I went into the house and brought out two blankets and an old quilt, and put them through. Believe it or not—mostly not, maybe.

Then came pants. I do despise washing pants, as a rule, but on a golden October day, with white and silver suds, crystal clear iridescent bubbles splashing up around my wrists and elbows, curling wood smoke smelling like incense that no cathedral ever knew, and the sun shining all day in a manner that sent soft thrills clean through (I know that may sound mushy, but you know sunshine does do that sometimes)—well, under circumstances like that I could almost enjoy washing pants.

I had set my tubs, as I always did when the weather was fit, so I could look right out on the garden, facing the corner where pink cosmos were waving like Cleopatra's fans (in pictures—I never saw them in reality, of course), and where a bed of Michaelmas daisy spread itself out looking like a lavender cloud come to earth. A yellow blooming plant—I don't know what it was, but it must have belonged to the pea or lupine family, it's a weed in some places, but it's pretty in our garden— well it was standing near enough to the lavender Michaelmas blooms to make them look all the more lavender.

At one edge of the garden was a row of asparagus flaunting green plumes and red berries to and fro in the gentle breezy breeze. Down across the valley I could see a herd of red white-faced cows congregated in one corner of a browning field. They made a perfect picture. The corn shocks in another field made another picture, and a field being sown to wheat was certainly a study in green and brown. In another direction I could see brown shocks of lespedeza dotting a dark tan stubble field, and beyond that the trees just turning—do you wonder I wouldn't give a snap for washing machines that take all the exercise out of washday, or indoor tubs that fit against the cellar walls and give no outlook on washday except the blank cellar walls. No sir, I like scenery and exercise and sweat with my laundering.

All day, or most of it, I rubbed and rinsed and rubbed and rinsed. I splashed suds to my heart's content in luxury of rainwater and lye soap. Then I spread the snowy whites, the blues and pinks and yellows all out in the sun to dry.

Yes, I guess cleanliness does come next to Godliness. That's why God put Monday next to Sunday. And that's why he gives us days when we can revel among the suds and see rainbows above them—or do you? I admit I don't always. It's just on certain days. October days for instance. When there's plenty of rain water and lye soap—made in the dark of the moon in March.

November Night

I was coming back from the mailbox one morning when I saw Jack making "seven-league" strides toward the barn with a hunk of bread in each hand.

"Where are you going with that bread?" I asked in a tone that any cook might use.

He didn't slow down or shorten his stride but he called back over his shoulder, "Gonna feed my dog."

"What do you mean 'your' dog? Here's our dog with me."

"I know, Mother, but this other one is a very special dog. He's a stray and I just know he's a huntin' dog."

"How do you know he's a huntin' dog if he's a stray?"

"Well, he's a houn' and houn's usually are huntin' dogs."

I heard strange noises from around the barn several times that afternoon, and I noticed strange maneuverings about the farm. But I didn't, somehow, connect them with the stray dog.

That night during supper Neighbor-boy Joedy came in. And after he came it seemed that Jack had little appetite for supper. He and Joedy made some mysterious trips up and down stairs to Jack's room. Then our dog began to get excited. He, too, had no appetite for supper.

Soon the gun was brought out, then the lantern, and the old hunting coats and caps. By that time I knew what we were in for. The stray dog was going to have a chance to show his "houn'ism."

Dad had just settled himself down in an easy chair with a pan full of hickory nuts, a few after-supper apples, a newspaper, and a magazine. But I noticed as the boys were oiling the gun, he got up and stretched, zipped up his leather jacket and 'lowed' that if I didn't mind staying by myself he'd "walk a piece with the boys."

I didn't mind at all, but why should I? I 'lowed I might as well walk a piece, too. And so it was that the "spirit of the hunting hound" permeated every member of the family except Margaret, who was away in school, and the cats who were on a hunting expedition of their own in the store room.

November nights are just made for hunting—at least some of them are, and this was one of the best. It had rained that morning and then had brushed up a soft wind, not too strong nor too cold. Just right was everything.

We'd no sooner got into hunting togs and gathered up our lanterns, flashlights, and guns, and started out the back door, than we heard a soft whistling coming across the barley field. Our dog didn't even bark, so we knew it must be a friend. It was. His name was Claude. He's a Negro boy from a neighboring farm, and he'd brought his own gun and dog—not by accident. He'd heard by grapevine of the stray hound that must be a huntin' dog.

It was decided we'd take a try up in Mr. Younger's hollow, and as it was a "far piece for a woman to walk," we thought we'd better go in the car as far as we could.

STRANGE THINGS WERE HAPPENING

Into the old bus we packed; Jack and Dad and I on the front seat, Joedy, Claude, our dog, the hound, and Claude's dog, Pretty Boy, on the back seat. You'd have thought it would take a Secretary of State and a Nine-Power Conference to keep three strange dogs on one back seat from fighting; but one white "diplomat" and one black "diplomat" managed to keep the peace.

Strange things were happening that night. We'd no sooner turned into the lane by the mailbox than the car lights picked up two waiting figures. Folks don't do much walking or waiting in our lane at night, so we paused. The figures proved to be two more Negro boys, Roy and Willie B, who had also heard of "the stray houn' that must be a huntin' dog."

There wasn't room for the latest recruits inside the car, so they hung on the sides; anyone meeting our car in the lane that night could have thought we were wearing "ears"—that's what the extra passengers must have looked like in the car's silhouette.

When we got out of the car and started trekking out across a newly-plowed-and-planted rye field facing a night wind I was glad to be wearing heavy shoes and a wool sweater, but I didn't need to put my hands in my pockets—it was that kind of a night.

It was decided that as there was a woman in the party, some concession ought to be made—boys of 17 or thereabouts like to concede to the feminine—so they made it up that Dad and I would walk along the easier path up through the hollow, while they climbed the big rough hill to the east and scared the 'coons and 'possums down. The dogs, of course, went with the boys, and Dad and I slowly picked our way up the hollow over the soft irregular clods.

The one word that describes that night better than any other word or string of words is that word "soft." The ground was soft. The night wind was soft—the air so clean and newly-washed it seemed soft—the noises of the night were soft; near us crickets (or something) chirped and buzzed and whirred softly in the blackberry briars along the fence. The rustle of the leaves was soft as we stirred them with our feet. The voices of the boys talking, chuckling on the hillside, were soft as they came down across a weed patch to us—I never noticed before how beautiful adolescent voices could be until I heard those carefree black and white boys on a November night.

The fact is I almost felt poetic:

"Soft in the stilly night - - -"

But that's as far as I got with my poem; our dog interrupted it with a sharp yelp from somewhere to the northeast of us. The boys yelled. Dad did too—he's that kind of a grown-up boy—and we all hastened toward the noisy dog. The hound did come down the path to meet us once and let me stroke his long silky ears—I thought at the time if we can't make silk purses out of sows' ears we might be able sometime to use hound ears.

But the man, boys, and dogs were not thinking of silk purses. By the time Dad and I had huffed and puffed up the hill to the tall twin beeches, the boys were already there trying to "pick up his eyes" with a lantern. Our dog sat proudly under the tree—as self-important as the ringmaster in a three-ring circus. The boys circled the tree with their lights, and Dad joined them—he knew he could shine his eyes if anyone could. So 'round they went and up shot the gleams of light. I found a soft spot on a rotten log, spread the game bag on it, sat down, hugged my knees, and played doubting Thomas for the party. Somebody has to do that, and it's one thing I do very well on a hunting party.

I sat on the log, our dog sat under the tree, and the man and boys and lights went round and round—all of us looking up, seeing nothing, just hoping.

THE SCOFFER

Once we heard, or thought we heard, a noise in the tree. Leaves rustled, bark was scratched. "He's coming down!" someone yelled, then all sounds ceased together—all sounds except the rustle of leaves on the ground, the "tree-bark" of the dog, and the "Hoo-oo-o-o! Hoo-oo-o-o!" of an owl on a far hill. Still no eyes could be "shined" in the tree. Once we thought we saw him looking down from the forks, but it must have been dew on leaves or a belated firefly roosting in the beech.

Finally we decided, or rather they did (I was the scoffer), that he must have crossed from the large beech to the smaller one. The lights were turned on that, but still no eyes. Then it was suggested that someone must go up. Jack came out of his boots—it took two boys to separate boots and boy—and then out of his coat, and up the tree he skinned. The lights were shined again to see if he could discover the varmint's outline against the trunk, in the forks, or on a high limb. Jack "thought" he saw him a time or two. Then he "thought" that he had discovered a solution to the whole mystery—he saw what looked like a hole in the tree—the varmint must be in the hollow.

That brought Dad's young blood into action. He'd climb the big tree. He came out of coat and shoes and in doing so he thought he stripped off a score of years—but I laughed at him—I was the scoffer, you know. Dad was determined to go up that tree. At least he was determined until he put his arms around the big trunk. They reached hardly halfway around, so Dad admitted that the tree was bigger than he was and calmed his determination, put on his coat and shoes again.

The masculine part of the party did hate to go away without bringing down the first coon that had been treed. I hated it, too, but I couldn't say anything, considering my role.

Finally we did give up, and we began to turn our eyes and ears about for the hound "that must be a hunting dog." He still hadn't done anything to bark about. He'd been rustling around in the leaves and weeds but had made very little vocal noise. The third dog, Pretty Boy, had been sitting on the log with me most of the time. I'm afraid that all told we weren't a very cooperative party.

We left the twin beeches and moved on through the bushes and undergrowth in some indiscernible direction. The only direction I could be sure of was up. The sky was beautiful—and yet, if you've ever seen a November sky through beech limbs you know that beautiful is not the word I need.

Looking up, it seemed that the sky was wearing a soft pearly gray "evening dress" with trimmings of black lace in intricate and irregular pattern. Close around us the young beech bushes tried to hold us back by stretching their slim, pointed, graceful fingers out across the path in the shimmering light of our lanterns—it was a night!

We tramped a while farther into the woods, stopped, and waited for the dogs to "speak."

"That old hound will open up before long," Dad promised. At last he did. I know now what men mean when they say a hound's voice is "opening up." That hound sounded like hollering down a rain-barrel—even worse, it sounded like hollering down a whole big cistern. It made the woods ring, echo, and almost shake. Even the hoot owl hushed when the hound opened up.

But he wasn't a "hunting dog" for long. He soon "signed off" and gave the air to the owls again and to the rustle of leaves and the buzzing of bugs, and to our small chatter. It was an evening full of waiting and listening. We'd find a clearing, spread out our sacks and coats to sit on. Wait a while and listen, then move on and wait and listen again.

At last Dad and I decided we might as well go home. The boys decided to go on. They rambled over two more hills and through two or three more hollows, but the biggest "game" they found that night was a truck stuck in the mud—they helped push it out, and came home.

It was a night, a great night. The hound that "ought to be a hunting dog" is still hunting, I suppose, unless he has found his master. His ears might make silk purses, but I don't think he'd be useful for anything else. Dad admitted that he can't climb like he "used to could." Our dog admitted that he might have been mistaken about the coon. Jack promised to let Joedy and the Negro boys know by "grapevine telegraph" next time a stray hunting dog turned up. But the only good thing the game sack did that night was to soften the seat of the scoffer.

The Turning of the Lane

One morning, with the farm's newest pup at heel, I started to the mailbox. Going there was always a highlight of the day's adventures for both the pup and me. I don't know what he thought he'd find on the way there and back. I never knew what the mail carrier would bring me when he came over the hill and around the bend, and so the mailbox trip was high adventure.

We were early; we sat for a while and waited. We walked up the road a piece, then down the road a piece, then we sat down again and waited. Suddenly I heard a shout. The pup's ears pricked up and I suppose mine did, too. It was a man's gruff voice and the sound was short, just one word. It wasn't "Help!" I was sure of that, but beyond that certainty I was puzzled.

The sound came from one of the Stone family's fields, just across the high fence row and not too far from the road. What could men be doing over there? The Stones had all moved away, and the place was vacant.

Wondering what was on the other side of that fence I thought of "Mammy" Stone, how she hated that overgrown row. She never could see what went on down the road, who passed by, or when the mailman came. But again I wondered: what could a strange man be doing over in the Stones' fields? Mammy would say often: "If I had the strength of fifty men I'd clean up that fence row." But she didn't.

The pup and I went on up to the gate, really just a gap in the row, and peered into the field. Sure enough, there was a strange man, and furthermore he was doing a strange thing.

Dressed in khaki, with a terrapin-top hat, he was leaning slightly over a tripod, holding his hands outstretched. As the hands moved slowly up and down, I glanced across the field to the far fence row and there was another man. He was holding up a red and white striped pole.

There could be no doubt about it; they were surveyors! What on earth could it mean? Had the heirs decided to sell the old Stone place? Impossible! Were we at last going to get a new road across the hill, giving us easier access to the highway? Maybe a railroad would be coming our way.

Curiosity got the better of me. I walked up to the near man and said, "I don't mean to be meddling, but what on earth are you doing?"

"Prospecting for phosphate," was the answer.

Then I said, lightly, "Well, when you get through here come on over to our place," and he answered seriously.

"Thank you, we will."

And they did.

Of course, there was the matter of signing some papers, drawing up an option and things I like that. I had my fingers crossed and my doubts working throughout the whole deal.

Following the surveyors came the real prospectors, whole gangs of men with joints of pipe and 4-inch augers. The surveyors had measured the land, "chained" it, and put stakes every 100 feet each way. All the "real" prospectors had to do was to bore a hole by the side of the stake, bore down, and take a sample of the soil, put the sample into a bag and write the number of the stake on a card. Other men came around and picked up the samples to have them tested.

Alex and I had the fidgets. We'd prowl about from one hole to another, questioning the men. "What are you finding? Does it look pretty good? How deep is that hole? Is this sample as good as the last?"

Then came the day at the lawyer's office, where he sat back in his chair and read pages and pages of whereases and wherefores. Finally we were handed one small piece of paper, a check that meant we could pay off the mortgage. We could buy a new farm over on the highway and build just exactly the house we wanted—not thirteen barn-like rooms "lovely to look at but the dickens to live in," but a few small rooms and a bath and electricity and there would be hollyhocks by the door next summer. Our love might get to a cottage after all.

Somehow I had never thought that those pesky phosphate pebbles I had chopped among when I planted the first cabbage patch might ever come in so handy one day.

CHAPTER 14

Chimneyside

The Fireplace Talks

> 'Twas the week before Christmas
> And all through my mind
> Not an idea was stirring
> Not a thought could I find—

It was December and I'd lingered late by the old fireplace at Knoxdale. By this time I was writing a regular feature column for a local newspaper and I had to find inspiration tonight, but not a thought could I find. Everybody else had gone to bed except me, and the coal-oil lamp, and my pecky old typewriter, and the fireplace. I was sleepy. The lamp, I could tell by its weakened light, was tired; the typewriter was patiently waiting with me for an idea; but the fireplace was softly humming and whispering to itself.

As I searched my mind for Christmas ideas and stories, I thought to myself: "If I could browse round a busy shopping district, I could find something to write about. If I could have a hand at a great library, I would perhaps find an idea in some musty old volume. If I even had one person to talk with, an idea might come," but nobody at my house wanted to talk that night, unless perhaps it was the fireplace.

As I thought of old and well-loved stories, the legend of "The Other Wise Man" came into my mind. Could I find an idea in that? I did not.

Then the story of "Acres of Diamonds" popped into my head, and kept popping. You remember that old legend, I am sure. It tells how a man searched the whole wide world for diamonds and failed to find them; but when he came back home, worn and tired, he learned that right on his own farm, the place he had deserted, there were acres and acres of diamonds.

Then the idea came. It struck me like a flash. My fireplace— the only thing that wanted to talk that night—was my "acres of diamonds." That would be my library, my source of a story. Why the humble, smoke-blackened, warm-hearted fireplace had seen generations of happy children take down Christmas stockings and explore the depths of heel and toe for surprise packages. Why not, I thought, turn the lamp low, draw my chair and typewriter a little nearer, and catch the stories that the fireplace was whispering of a hundred Christmas eves.

"You won't care for what I could tell you about Christmas," mumbled the fireplace. "In these days of steam-heated Yuletides and jazz bands, radiators and radios get all the attention; my nose is broken, as they say. The simple, homely stories I could tell would be far too tame for the lively, thrill-seeking crowds of today."

"Oh, come on, Fireplace, do your stuff, I must have a story, and you are my only hope."

ALFRED

"Well, did you ever hear about little Alfred's red-topped, brass-toed boots?" asked the fireplace. "He was happier over that little pair of boots and his little homemade chair than modern children ever seem over expensive toys that wind-up and perform. On Christmas morning he put them on and admired his feet all day. He even wanted to sleep in his boots that night, but parental authority persuaded him differently. But next morning. Oh, Tragedy! Just as he might have expected, somebody had stepped on a beautiful brass toe and mashed it flat. Alfred was enraged. Summoning all the temper that he had inherited from the "other side of the house," he shouted.

"Who doned my boot 'is way? Whoever doned it had better doned it back again, I can tell you." So angry was Alfred on that occasion that only a threatened dose of "peach tree tea" would quiet his temper."

STELLA

"Speaking of boots," said the fireplace, "reminds me, too, of Stella. Boots and shoes meant a great deal to children in her time. Each child got a new pair for Christmas, and if that pair did not last until the next Christmas, somebody's toes got frosted."

"One Christmas—times had been rather hard, but Stella was expecting a big time just the same—her father awakened her saying, 'Get up, Daughter, come quickly, and see what Santa Claus has brought you.' Stella climbed sleepily out of the old trundle bed and followed him to where her mother lay. 'See,' he said as he drew back the covers, 'it's a baby sister.'

"Stella gave one look, turned quickly, and came and dropped to her little stool beside me," continued the fireplace. "Then with her face in her hands she burst into tears. 'To think,' she sobbed, 'that old Santa Claus would bring another squalling baby here, as bad as I wanted new shoes.'

"But Fireplace," I asked, "didn't children get anything else except shoes in those days? Weren't there toys, and nuts, and candies, and things like that? Didn't the little girls get dolls and didn't the boys get wagons and guns?"

"Oh, surely," chuckled the fireplace in throaty tones which I could hardly understand. "There was striped stick candy sometimes, but molasses candy more often. There were dolls, not the kind that children have nowadays, but they brought happiness to their little mothers despite the fact that they were made of rags, shucks, cobs, wax or china, and sawdust.

MARY JANE AND NORA

"I can hardly remember seeing a happier face than that of Mary Jane, when she clasped to her small bosom a smiling rag dolly wrapped in a scrap of turkey-red calico, which Mary Jane could sew into dresses for her cotton-stuffed darling.

"Little Nora was so happy over her first waxen-headed baby and the little red rocking chair, which Santa Claus brought her one Christmas, that she would not even go to the breakfast table on Christmas morning; instead she drew the little chair up near the hearth, and taking her baby in her arms, sat rocking and singing, ecstatically happy.

"Then came," said the fireplace, "an occurrence of which I shall always be ashamed and regretful. I scarcely know whose fault it was, perhaps father had laid on too much wood, perhaps Mary Jane was sitting too close to me, anyway, the doll's beautiful waxen curls and complexion were so disfigured by the heat that ever thereafter she looked as though she had had smallpox on one side of her face. But Mary Jane forgave all, and loved her baby more for its affliction."

MATTIE

"Little girls in those days were as eager to give their dollies the best of everything as mothers are today or have always been, for that matter," the fireplace went on. "Take little Mattie, for example. Her father was a Baptist preacher, and many times she had seen him take people to the creek for the baptismal ceremony. Mattie took her first China doll to the creek likewise and plunged it beneath the waters just as she had seen her father do his people. But alas, however much religion that poor, poor dolly got from the experience, she surely 'lost her head,' for when the waters of the old creek came up about her neck, the glue was softened and off went her head.

"And wagons. Of course, the boys had wagons. What would Christmas be without wagons for boys? They were crude perhaps and homemade sometimes, but they had wheels that would roll and tongues that would pull. But even the wagons were not quite so important in some cases as the red-topped, brass-toed boots."

FAYETTE

"At least that was the opinion of little black Fayette. In addition to the 'Christmas gif's from the big house,' one Christmas there was a little red store-bought wagon and a pair of red-topped boots. Mammy had made him a white suit out of brown-domestic, too, that Christmas, and he was so happy in that new suit and his shiny new shoes, as he pulled the red wagon down the road to show it off, that he really forgot the color of his skin.

"But clouds must pass into every life, as I've heard them say," whispered the fireplace, "and this is the way I heard the results of that walk as it was told around me and the hearth that night. Fayette was happily sauntering down the road, stepping high in his new boots, and drawing his little wagon, when two boys from a family of 'po' whites' who got no boots, no suit, and no wagon that Christmas, came out into the road to see the resplendent 'nigger.' Fayette marched merrily along until the boys began to spit on his new boots, then he grabbed up handfuls of dust—the nearest weapons at hand—and threw them on the white boys.

Whether it was a 'race war' or an 'interracial war,' it was a dirty affair, as the 'white brown-domestic suit' showed very plainly when Fayette came in to face his indignant Mammy while she was baking salt-risin' bread for dinner in the old oven before my face," and the fireplace chuckled at the memory of the scene.

"I could tell you many tales," he continued, "of hidden gifts and family secrets. I could tell tales that would break hearts that are happy and others that would mend hearts that are broken, but those secrets are sacred to me. I'll just keep them up my chimney, I guess. But I will say that there would be more good than bad in the stories I could tell if I would.

"How happy I used to be when the children would sit around and write letters for me to take up the chimney to Santa Claus. How I did my part in popping boxes of popcorn to be left on the hearth for Santa. How I used to laugh with the children over the socks full of ashes and switches that father always got, and one Christmas morning there was a rolling pin for mother.

"It always amused me that on Christmas morning the first things the little girls would do was to dress and undress the new doll, set the tiny table with tiny dishes, and enjoy a quiet little tea party with the dolls on the rug near the hearth.

"But the boys, now they were different. No quiet for them. They wanted to make a lot of noise. Before the time of fire crackers, they were always glad if hog-killing time came before Christmas, then there would be hog-bladder 'pop guns,' blown up tight and dried, to burst with a big noise on Christmas morning."

PARTIES & DINNERS

"But I must tell you about the parties, too, and the dances—not the kind of dances that have come into modern times with those disgusting, spitting, rumbling steam radiators, but clean, wholesome, graceful, beautiful square dances, games, jigs, and reels. Now those were the days," said the fireplace. "Or perhaps I should say the nights. Dances then didn't begin at 11 and last until 2, they began at dusk and lasted 'til dawn, and the whole family went, not in a limousine but in a wagon.

"And I can never, forget the dinners, they were given every day 'during Christmas,' at first one neighbor's and then another's, and everybody went and everybody had a good time.

"When my family all went off I had a rather lonely time, I'll confess, but the cat and dog stayed with me and they were rather poor company; but on the day that all the kin and neighbors gathered around my hearth, well, now that was some time. They told stories, and laughed and joked, and discussed important questions of the day. Any fireplace that kept its eyes and ears open in those times could know something about everything that was going on.

"In my lifetime," he went on, "I have seen Christmases that were merry, hilarious, and rolicsome; and those that were cheery, happy, and joyful. But there have also been Christmases that would almost break the heart of me; there have been empty stockings many times, but there have also been empty chairs, and once an empty cradle—sometimes hearts that were empty. I have seen many sides of life and of people.

"I am glad that Christmas comes in midwinter, for then the folks come nearer me with their happiness and with their sorrow. And I can give them warmth of my sympathy, my pleasure or displeasure, as no modern radiator can do. People are beginning to realize that, too. They are coming back to me— but that is enough story for one night. You should have been asleep long before now, Story-loving Lady, and so should I.

"If you will just take a few shovelfuls of ashes and throw over my embers, I think I can quiet down now, and wish a good and happy Christmas to you, and to faithful old Pecky Typewriter and all."

ॐ

Around the Fire

Winter evenings around that old fireplace. How we had enjoyed them. Our fireplace was not one of those white-throated beauties of the modern, newly built house. It was more practical than fancy, wide and high, if not handsome. The smoke of a hundred winters had blackened its throat—but that black background only made the flames look brighter. We loved it; we were always thrilled by the beauty of the flames, even though we knew that there would be ashes to take out in the morning.

We had a definite line-up for our family circle as we gathered around the old fireplace when the evenings began to get cold. Close up, in the chimney corner on the right hand side, sat Uncle Fayette. His business was to smoke his "home-made" in an old corncob pipe—that was our incense. Next to Uncle Fayette, and as close to him as he could get, was Jack on a little stool. He lighted the old man's pipe and shelled the popcorn for Uncle Fayette to pop. The swish of the shaking popper and the odor of popping corn was an integral part of the fireside's atmosphere.

Jack, we knew, should be studying, but he never could bear to have lessons clutter up his mind when Uncle Fayette was available for company: Uncle Fayette and the mail order catalogue! Boy and man took turns holding the big book on their knees, turning pages, and discussing guns, traps, fish-hooks, and baseballs in undertones. There were sixty-odd years of difference in their ages, but they had many tastes in common.

In the center of the fireside semi-circle was a little table holding the coal-oil lamp. Dad sat on the right of the table, reading aloud. Margaret and I sat on the left, I patching or sewing, Margaret studying. The remarkable thing about her was that she could listen, talk, and study all at the same time. She could sit there absorbed in lessons and never miss any conversation or a word of the story being read.

POPCORN AND PEANUTS

As each fresh batch of corn was popped, it was passed around, and then we passed the pan of peanuts that had been parched in the oven while supper baked. There were usually cookies, and sometimes fruit. If, as often happened on winter afternoons, we had dinner in the early afternoon, we would have supper cooked slowly on the fireplace: potatoes roasted in the ashes or a pot of oatmeal cooked over the fire. A skillet full of corn-pone baked in Dutch-oven fashion, and perhaps ham or bacon broiled over the coals. When all was ready we'd bring out a cake of hard, country butter to serve with the potatoes or corn-pone; home grown cream for the oatmeal; and sweet milk with apple pie to finish off the meal. We did not like winter, but we did love the winter evenings around the fire.

There was humor, too, of a homemade type. Old Uncle Fayette was full of wit. We all had our wisecracks. It was when fun came unexpectedly that we appreciated it more. Here's an example:

Margaret (studying English): "In this sentence, 'The horned toad resembles a lizard.' Is that a direct object or a subjective complement?"

Jack (looking up from the toy department of his catalog: "I don't think it's much of a compliment."

Such guests we had at our fireside those winter evenings. We'd bring them in by armfuls, all we could buy, beg, or borrow—old and new books, magazines, and papers. With our feet on our own hearthstone, and with Uncle Fayette popping and passing the popcorn and the odors of home-grown tobacco and roasting peanuts and sweet potatoes between courses of snow cream and apple pie, we accompanied the Swiss Family Robinson throughout their adventuring; we walked the streets of Philadelphia with Benjamin Franklin in his autobiography. We wept and quaked over *Kidnapped*, laughed at "Miss Minerva and William Green Hill," admired Pollyanna and sympathized deeply with *Little Women*.

We flew the Atlantic with Lindbergh; shivered in Antarctica with Commander Byrd. We traveled the royal road to romance with Richard Halliburton and shuddered at the ghost of Hamlet's father; chanted at the dance of the witches in *Macbeth*.

Lonesome in the country? Not us! Wanting much? Well, certainly not very much. Jack might possibly have liked a few items of the newer types of fishing paraphernalia shown in the catalogue. Margaret's chief want might have been an "A" on tomorrow's lesson. Uncle Fayette seemed completely at peace with himself and the world.

Alex and I could have wished for no more than merely a stay of time. We'd have liked (or we felt then that we would have liked) to spend the rest of the ages just one long winter's evening by that quiet, comfortable, pleasant fireplace. But as time moved on, we would not roll it back, not even for one more winter's evening to enjoy life's comforts by the fire.

OUT DRIVING WITH THE SAME YOUNG MAN

www.ingramcontent.com/pod-product-compliance
Lightning Source LLC
Chambersburg PA
CBHW020602270326
41927CB00005B/131